Jane Austen's 'Outlandish Cousin'

Portrait miniature of Eliza de Feuillide,
by an unknown French artist, 1780.
'It is reckoned here like what I am at present.
The dress is quite the present fashion
& what I usually wear.'
Courtesy of the late Joan Austen-Leigh

Jane Austen's 'Outlandish Cousin'

THE LIFE AND LETTERS OF

ELIZA DE FEUILLIDE

Deirdre Le Faye

The British Library
London
2002

First published in 2002 by
The British Library
96 Euston Road
London NW1 2DB

British Library Cataloguing in Publication Data
A catalogue record for this book is available from
The British Library

ISBN 0 7123 4762 3

Designed and typeset by Peter and Alison Guy
Printed in Great Britain by St Edmundsbury Press

Contents

✡

Introduction

✡

ELIZA DE FEUILLIDE, to give her the name by which she is best known to posterity, in recent years has acquired a little niche in literary history by virtue of being a first cousin of Jane Austen the novelist. This relationship means that Eliza's letters provide unique information on Jane's girlhood and the lives of other members of the Austen family – information all the more valuable because it is contemporary and impartial, being written long before Jane became an authoress and never intended to be read by anyone except the recipients of the letters – and for this reason Eliza's name has appeared in modern biographies of Jane Austen with ever-increasing frequency.

However, quite apart from the accident of fate which related her to Jane, Eliza's letters are vivid and amusing and well worthy of full publication in their own right. To these letters of hers can be added others, written by friends and relatives – including in turn Jane Austen, in later life – which, with some further miscellaneous documentary references, enable a short biography to be constructed, almost in the form of one of the epistolary novels that were then so popular, that gives Eliza her own place in late eighteenth-century society as well as showing how her adventurous life engaged with that of Jane Austen's family in their quiet country parsonage at Steventon in Hampshire.

Notes on the provenance of the surviving letters will be found at the end of the main text, together with simplified family pedigrees showing how Eliza was connected to the various cousins whom she mentions from time to time. Her handwriting was remarkably fine and delicate and she filled her paper very closely, with hardly any punctuation except commas; for present ease of reading, paragraphs have been created, but it has not always proved possible to divide some parts of the text where Eliza's thoughts flowed on freely from the tip of her quill. Her spelling and capitalisation have been left unaltered. A few words are missing here and there where the letters have been damaged by the breaking open of the seal, and where the sense is obvious the words have been replaced within square brackets [ ]. Square brackets have also been used occasionally to enclose a word of explanation.

I am most grateful to the Austen-Leigh heirs, the Impey family, for their kind permission to study and publish Eliza's letters and other family correspondence of the period, and to Joan Austen-Leigh for the use of the miniature of Eliza. Grateful acknowledgement is also given to the Jane Austen Memorial Trust, the British Library Board and Messrs. C. Hoare & Company, for the publication of material in their collections, and to Oxford University Press for permission to use extracts from Jane Austen's letters; personal thanks are due to Abbé Michel Devert, Mrs. J. E. Downham and Mrs. Sarah Markham, for information supplied in the course of correspondence over a number of years.

Deirdre Le Faye

Jane Austen's 'Outlandish Cousin'

CHAPTER I

My Dear Betsy

1760–77

✡

ELIZA DE FEUILLIDE is an unexpected brightly-flowering offshoot from the solid yeoman rootstock of Austens, mainly prosperous sheep-farmers and woollen clothmakers, whose families had lived for many generations in the villages and small towns of West Kent. This divergence has its origins early in the eighteenth century, when Eliza's mother, Philadelphia Austen, had the misfortune to be born into one of the junior and poorer branches of the family, whose landless sons had to strive to make their own ways in the world in the medical, legal and clerical professions.

William Austen, who was a not very successful surgeon in the town of Tonbridge, died young in 1737, and his children Philadelphia and George were left penniless orphans at seven and six years of age respectively. George grew up in Tonbridge, living in the family of his aunt Mrs. Hooper and under the guardianship of his uncle Francis Austen, who had become a rich solicitor in the nearby town of Sevenoaks. George was a clever and hardworking boy who attended Tonbridge School and won scholarships which enabled him to study at St. John's College, Oxford, and so go on to take Holy Orders in 1755. He was presented to the living of the little parish of Steventon in Hampshire by a distant cousin, and on the strength of this assured income married Miss Cassandra Leigh, the daughter of an Oxfordshire parson, in April 1764. The young couple went straight off to Hampshire, and George stayed there as rector of Steventon until his retirement in 1801; they had eight children, of whom Jane, the future novelist, was their seventh child and second daughter.

No precise information is available as to Philadelphia's childhood; she may have been sent to live with some maternal cousins in Hertfordshire, the Freeman family, but in any event it seems she did not grow up in isolation from her Kentish relations and was able to maintain contact with her brother George. On her fifteenth birthday, 9th May 1745, she was apprenticed to a Mrs. Cole, a milliner in Russell Street, Covent Garden, London, the £45 premium for the apprenticeship presumably being paid by her uncle Francis Austen. The allied trades of dressmaking and millinery were known to be very unhealthy, as the girls sat crouched over their work-tables for excessively long hours in cramped airless back rooms; but at that date and for decades to come there was little choice of employment for respectable but penniless young women: 'accomplished girls, portionless and homeless, were made into governesses, and for the less instructed there was nothing dreamed of but the dressmaking, a trade never over-stocked, its victims dying off quite as quickly as the vacant places were demanded.'

However, Philadelphia survived the five years of her apprenticeship, and then – probably at the instigation of her uncle Francis – sailed to India on 18th January 1752 aboard the *Bombay Castle*, one of the fleet of fast-sailing merchantmen owned by the Honourable East India Company. The *Bombay Castle* arrived at Madras on 4th August 1752 – six months was considered a quite good time for the voyage from England – and on 22nd February 1753 Philadelphia was married at Fort St. David, the Company's military post near Madras, to Tysoe Saul Hancock, the official surgeon at the Fort. Hancock was also of Kentish stock, having been born in Sittingbourne in December 1723, the son of the Revd. Thomas Saul Hancock, vicar of the nearby village of Hollingbourne. He had served his medical apprenticeship in London and went to India in 1745, where he soon found employment with the HEIC. As Philadelphia's uncle Francis Austen was Hancock's English 'trustee' or 'attorney' [in modern terms, funds manager or business agent], it would seem quite possible that the match had been suggested to her by her uncle, or perhaps even pre-arranged by him direct with Hancock – lonely expatriates were prepared to accept girls who came unprovided with the dowry that was an essential part of a marriage contract in England. Very little else is known about Hancock, save that he had a brother, Colbron, who was in business in London as a cut-glass manufacturer, and a sister, Olivia, who lived in Canterbury, Kent. He himself seems to have been a melancholy man – unhappy in his medical profession, frequently ill and given to harping upon his fast-approaching decrepitude, even though he was barely seven years Philadelphia's senior. His letters show that he was nevertheless a devoted husband and father, kind-hearted and with strict moral principles, and it may have been his constant ill-health which led to his gloomy outlook upon life and the frequent failures of the business ventures which he attempted. His wife for her part seems to have been quite genuinely fond of him, and sincerely grieved when he died in early middle-age.

Philadelphia must have written home to her uncle in Sevenoaks and her brother in Steventon with the welcome news of her safe arrival in India and subsequent marriage, and with continuing information as to her life thereafter, but unfortunately no such letters have survived. Other English travellers have recorded their relief at catching sight of the harbour of Madras after many weary months at sea – the white buildings among green trees, the surf breaking upon the wide sweep of sand and the walls of the square fortress, the blue hills in the distance – followed as they landed by amazement at the burning heat of the sand underfoot, which made them hurry towards the cool shade of the long palm-lined avenues of the city. For a girl who had been a penniless seamstress, it must have seemed to Philadelphia an Aladdin's-lamp transformation to find herself dressed in the beautiful Indian muslins and silks which in past years she had painstakingly cut and stitched for other women to wear, and to be the mistress of a household containing perhaps thirty or forty Indian or Portuguese servants. She had four personal maidservants alone, whose names are mentioned in her husband's letters in later years – Diana, Silima, Dido and Clarinda.

The couple lived in Madras for six years, but apparently remained childless. As the Austens seem to have been a fertile race, it is perhaps possible that Philadelphia had miscarriages or stillbirths during these early years of marriage – her daughter Eliza, in due course, had at least two miscarriages, which may point to an inherited weakness – but there are very few surviving official records of the eighteenth-century English communities in the HEIC's trading posts, and in any case it is unlikely that stillborn children, or those who died at birth, would have been noted in registers.

Early in 1759 Hancock was appointed surgeon at Fort William, Calcutta, at the request of his friend Robert Clive, then Governor of Bengal. Here he and his wife met a small, thin, prematurely

Warren Hastings (1732-1818),
by Sir Joshua Reynolds, 1766-68.
National Portrait Gallery, London

bald young man, noted for his abstemious habits and scholarly interest in Asiatic languages; this was Warren Hastings, not yet the renowned Governor General of India, but merely a hard-working junior employee of the Company. In 1757 he had married Mary Buchanan, an old London friend of Philadelphia's; she was the widow of a Lieut. Buchanan who had died in the Black Hole of Calcutta in June 1756, leaving her with two little girls, and Hastings also had two children by her – George, born in December 1757, and Elizabeth, who lived for just three weeks in October 1758. Philadelphia had only a few months in which to renew her friendship with Mary before the latter died in July 1759 while Hastings was away on a business trip; an Indian writing desk, rosewood inlaid with ivory, is preserved in one branch of Austen descendants, with the family tradition that it was given to Philadelphia by Hastings for taking care of his children, presumably while Mary Hastings was ailing and dying. As well as carrying out his medical duties at the Fort, Hancock now partnered Hastings in various private trading ventures, dealing in salt, timber, carpets, Bihar opium, and rice for the Madras market.

William Hodges. *A view of Calcutta taken from Fort William, 1781.*
Line engraving with etching by W. Byrne, from *Hodges' Travels in India.* London, 1793.
British Library w3836

Calcutta was then a raw, untidy European settlement stretching along the east bank of the Hooghly river, having grown up only since 1690, when Job Charnock, the HEIC's Chief Agent in Bengal, had finally obtained permission from the Mughal government to set up a trading station there; it subsequently developed to become the greatest and gayest of Anglo-Indian cities. A contemporary visitor to India described the settlement and the life of the European residents during the 1760s:

About the middle of the town, on the river's edge, stands the old fort, memorable for the catastrophe of the Black Hole, so much talked of in England; it was in one of the apartments in it that the wretched sufferers were confined. The fort is now made a very different use of; the only apology for a church is in some of the rooms in it, where divine service is sometimes performed.

In a distinct part of the town reside the Armenians, and the people called Portuguese; each of these have their own churches; and the Portuguese keep up the processions and pageantry of the Romish church, as far as they are permitted; but are obliged to perform it all within their own walls. The chief connexion we have with these people is, employing some of the women as servants, or the men as writers, or sometimes cooks.

The new fort, an immense place, is on the river side about a mile below the town. If all the buildings which are intended within its walls, are finished, it will be a town within itself; for besides houses for the engineers and other officers who reside at Calcutta, there are apartments for the company's writers, barracks for soldiers, magazines for stores, &c.

The town of Calcutta is likewise daily increasing in size, notwithstanding which, the English inhabitants multiply so fast, that houses are extremely scarce ... in all the good houses the apartments are up stairs, and all on one floor; the rooms are large and very lofty; most of the houses are built with a *varendar*, which is a terrace on a level with the rooms in the front, and sometimes in the back part of the house, supported by pillars below, and a roof above supported likewise by pillars, with rails round to lean on. The *varendars* give a handsome appearance to the houses on the out-side, and are of great use, keeping out the sun by day, and in the evenings are cool and pleasant to sit in. Paper, or wainscot, are improper, both on account of the heat, the vermin, and the difficulty of getting it done; the rooms are therefore all whited walls, but plastered in pannels, which has a pretty effect; and are generally ornamented with prints, looking-glasses, or whatever else can be procured from Europe; the floors are likewise plaster, covered all over with fine matt, which is nailed down; for although carpets are manufactured in some parts of the country, they are such an addition to the heat, that they are seldom made use of; the rooms are few, but mostly very large and lofty; many of the new-built houses have glass-windows, which are pleasant to the eye, but not so well calculated for the climate as the old ones, which are made of cane.

In the country round the town, at different distances, are a number of very pretty houses, which are called garden-houses, belonging to English gentlemen: for Calcutta, besides its being a large town, is not esteemed a healthy spot; so that in the hot season all those who can, are much at these garden-houses, both because it is cooler and more healthy.

As the morning and evening is cooler than the day, it is usual to rise early, and sit up rather late; for after the morning the heat is so intense, that it is difficult to attend to any business, and hardly possible to take any amusement. Ladies mostly retire to their own apartments, where the slightest covering is scarcely supportable. The most active disposition must be indolent in this climate. After dinner every one retires to sleep; it is a second night; every servant is gone to his own habitation; all is silence; and this custom is so universal, that it would be as unseasonable to call on any person at three or four o'clock in the afternoon, as at the same time in the morning.

This custom of sleeping away the hottest hours in the day is necessary, even to the strongest constitution. After this repose people dress for the evening, and enjoy the air about sun-set in their carriages, &c. The rest of the evening is for society. Living is very expensive, on account of the great rents of houses, the number of servants, the excessive price of all European commodities, such as wines, clothes, &c. The perspiration requires perpetual changes of clothes and linen; not to mention the expences of palenqueens, carriages, and horses. Many of these things, which perhaps appear luxuries, are, in this climate, real necessaries of life. It is remarkable that those Europeans who have health enjoy a greater flow of spirits than in cooler climates. Except when parties are violent, which is sometimes the case, the society and hospitality is general; and there is no other part of the world where people part with their money to assist each other so freely as the English in India.

The Hancocks' one and only child, Eliza, or as she was called in her infancy, Betsy, was born in Calcutta on 22nd December 1761, and at her baptism the following month Warren Hastings became her godfather and gave her the name of his own dead baby daughter. The first glimpses of the Hancock family in their Calcutta setting appear in 1762 in the gossipy letters of the Revd. Samuel Staveley (nicknamed 'Old Rattle' by his friends, as he cheerfully confesses) to Warren Hastings, who was then away at Murshidabad. Mr. Staveley's correspondence gives a pleasant picture of the 'family party' life of the small English community: there were Governor and Mrs. Henry Vansittart with their two little boys George and Bob, Col. Ironside and his amiable musical sister, a good Mr. and Mrs. Bowers, the latter always ready to do or get anything for anybody, and other young officers and East India Company employees coming and going on military and mercantile business. After the heat of the day the favourite meeting-place for supper-parties was Holwell's Gardens. Festivities were held at the baptism of the latest Vansittart baby, and the English children were evidently the playthings of the whole group, news of their health being anxiously sought and transmitted whenever any member of the community was away. Little Betsy could never resist pulling the nose of a certain Mr. Stuart, as her parents still remembered years later. Hancock attended devotedly to the health of his friends, who had great faith in his skill as a physician – though of course at that date medical knowledge was too limited to be of any great success in saving lives, and indeed Hancock was unable to cure himself of the malaria and kidney-stones referred to in his letters. It was a fact of life in Calcutta that today's guest at dinner could easily be tomorrow's interment in the Great Burying-Ground at Chowringhee.

During April 1762 Mr. Staveley wrote several times from Calcutta:

Greet Ironside. Tell him his amiable Sister & my Dear Friend our Dear Friend Mrs. Hancock sup'd last night at ye Gardens & sup with Us again to Night there all snug. ... Our Friends are all well – Mrs. Hancock & Miss Ironside sup at the Gardens to Night. ... George and Bob [Vansittart] are both very well & Miss Betsy Hancock.... Little Betsy is very fond of Miss Ironside & her Guitar, she is a sweet little Girl. .... I know nothing worth writing to You, but that George & Bob & Miss Hancock (I beg her Ladyships Pardon she should have been first mention'd) are well. ... I was last Night at tete a tete with Mrs. Hancock at the Garden 'tis a fine little Girl, they are very well.

In the following month there is a tribute to Hancock:

Lyon, thank God, is so well that by the Skill of our excellent Friend & Physician Hancock & as good a Woman as I wish to meet with Mrs. Bowers he is able to get off his Cot, be dressed & set in a great Chair. Hancock is gone for the first Time to Holwell's Garden, & with all his Airs I leave You to guess what he must have suffered by being so long absent from his Wife & Child. He has been Night and Day with Lyon. Mrs. & Miss Hancock are both well.

Randall Marriott, another old friend of Hastings, wrote to him from Benares:

I shall now Conclude my Friend, with requesting You kindly to remember me to Mr. & Mrs. Hancock, Mr. Van, Mr. Hurst, the Commodore & all my old Friends – Greet little, Great I believe I should say, Betsey Hancock with many Kisses & my Salaams & George give a good hearty shake by ye hand; I suppose if I was to go to kiss him he would give me a Box on ye Ear. Write me particularly how these little ones do.

In January 1765 the Hancocks set sail for England, in the expectation that the money they had saved, when invested, would provide a sufficient income for a comfortable lifestyle at home. Hastings returned with them on the same ship, which arrived in June 1765, and they took lodgings in London close by each other. The Hancocks now became acquainted with Mr. and Mrs. John Woodman, Hastings's brother-in-law and sister, who lived in Cleveland Row, St. James's, and the friendship between them was so warm that in later years Hastings used to say he regarded the two families as united, and wrote joint letters to them. The Woodmans had a son, Tommy, very much of an age with Betsy Hancock, and it seems that for a time they hoped the children might grow up to marry each other.

Once Hastings and the Hancocks were safely out of the way on the voyage back to England, another member of the English community in Calcutta, Jenny Strachey, whose husband was secretary to Clive and perhaps jealous of the favour he had shown to Hancock in getting him the appointment at Fort William, slandered the trio to her husband's employer with tales of adultery. Her slander was successful in as much as Clive wrote to his wife in England in the late summer of 1765:

In no circumstances whatever keep company with Mrs. Hancock for it is beyond a doubt that she abandoned herself to Mr. Hastings, indeed,

I would rather you had no acquaintance with the ladies who have been in India, they stand in such little esteem in England that their company cannot be of credit to Lady Clive.

Some time later Philadelphia did try to contact Lady Clive, whom she had known since their voyage out to India as girls together on the *Bombay Castle* twenty years before, and was amazed to be rebuffed by her; while, in turn, Jenny Strachey now found it expedient to approach Philadelphia with a request for assistance. Hancock wrote to his wife in November 1773:

You ought not I think have hesitated to tell Mrs. Strachey that her Behaviour to you while in India, which plainly proved her contempt of you, gave her no Right to expect any favor from you. I am much mistaken if Lady Clive's most extraordinary Coolness be not owing to the Pride of that Woman. Surely I did enough for her when I saved her Life; her return for which was the basest Ingratitude to you.

On the strength of this one letter from Clive to his wife, some modern biographers of Jane Austen have claimed as a fact that Eliza was the daughter of Warren Hastings rather than of Tysoe Saul Hancock, and that was why he became her godfather and subsequently set up a trust fund for her. There is however not the slightest hint in Hastings's diaries and other private papers that would corroborate such a claim; while on the other hand his close friends affectionately reproached him with having a 'blameable generosity' which would swallow up his fortune as fast as he made it – 'I never knew you keep even half a crown, if a poor man wanted it'. Hastings's letters and account books show that he constantly provided financial assistance and pensions to his step-children, boyhood friends, old servants, and indeed to anyone in need who sought his help. He was a kind-hearted man and very fond of children, and it was always a grief to him that none of his own had survived. Over the years he and his second wife Marian (whom he married in 1777) acquired many god-children in the families of their old friends from Indian days, upon whom they bestowed both favours and monetary gifts; and for the rest of his life Hastings supported Marian's sons and nieces as if they had been his own flesh and blood, paying far more attention to them than he ever did to Eliza.

The friendship between Hastings and Hancock continued when lack of money had driven them both back to India, after a stay of about three years in England. Hancock's financial troubles were in part due, like those of his friend, to the failure of his Indian investments, and in part to the fact that he had come home ill and left many of his affairs outstanding. He had also underestimated the sum necessary to secure a satisfactory lifestyle in England; in one of his later letters to his wife he pointed out that their expenses at home had amounted to more than £1,500 a year, which meant an invested capital of £44,000 would be required to provide this income. The return to India was itself a matter of difficulty, as there was no system of official leave for either the military or the civil service. A civilian who went out to India remained there until he died or retired with a fortune, and an officer who was invalided home was compelled to resign his commission unless he was entrusted with despatches as a reason for making the journey back. The man who 'found himself under the disagreeable necessity of a second residence in Bengal', as the phrase went, was obliged to return at his own expense and to pester some old acquaintance who happened to be in power into appointing him to any post of profit, however incongruous might be its nature. Hastings had the good fortune to be appointed Second-in-Council at Madras, and Hancock pinned his hopes on obtaining a *dustuck*, or licence to trade privately under the East India Company's protection with exemption from payment of tolls or customs to the native government. Upon his arrival, however, he found that *dustucks* were now only granted to men with at least the rank of factor in the Company, so that he was obliged to take up the position of Surgeon-Extraordinary to the Calcutta garrison; this was intended to be a sinecure, but in fact involved Hancock in far more work than he had anticipated, and unwelcome work into the bargain, as he admitted to his wife that he hated 'the Practice of Physick'.

It was now impossible for the husband and wife to keep in close touch with each other – letters usually took at least six months to make the sea-journey between India and England, many were even longer in transit, and some never arrived at all. Philadelphia and Hancock had to live their lives in parallel and take independent decisions, each able only to report to the other news that would be stale by the time it arrived and might already have been overtaken by events. The only thing Hancock could take with him as a reminder of home was a portrait miniature of his wife, painted by John Smart, which shows Philadelphia as a dark-eyed auburn-haired woman, slender and elegant in a blue silk dress and with a pearl choker round her neck; but even this small

'I give & bequeath unto my beloved Daughter Elizabeth Hancock a Miniature Picture of her Mother ... which I request she will never part with as I intend it to remind her of her Mother's Virtues as well as of her person.'

Jane Austen Memorial Trust

comfort was denied him, for he soon found that the damp Indian climate was in danger of spoiling the miniature, and it had to be sent back to England. Hancock kept file copies of his letters, and from these it can be seen how he gave his wife news of her old Calcutta friends, told her of his efforts to make money, sent her phials of the famous and expensive scent attar of roses, jars of the hot Indian spices and pickles which she had learnt to like, lengths of fine fabrics, and constantly gave her instructions regarding the upbringing of their daughter.

Hastings left England by a later ship than that on which Hancock travelled, and upon his arrival in India immediately wrote an encouraging letter to his old friend:

Fort St. George, 13th September 1769 – With this I send you 4 Letters which I recd. from Mrs. Hancock, whom I left with her Daughter both in good Health. I was sorry to hear upon my Arrival that you continued still ailing, but hope it was not owing to any constitutional Weakness, but only temporary, & that ye Air of Bengal, & the hearty Welcome of your Friends there have sett you to rights again.

On the long voyage out to India Hancock had evidently been revolving plans for Betsy's education, bearing in mind her possible future social status if he could not afford to give her a good dowry. He now put these worries to Hastings, who replied with encouragement:

Fort St. George, 5th November 1769 – Make no Change in the Plan you have already laid down. Neither French nor Dancing will disqualify a Woman for filling the Duties of any Sphere in Life. Her own Natural Understanding & gentle Disposition improved by the Precepts of such a Mother as few Children are blest with will fit her Mind to be satisfied with any Lot that she may meet with & to become it. But God forbid she should be disqualified for a better Way of Life because it is Possible she may not have a Fortune equal to it. A frugal Style of, & an early Practice in Economy will be a sufficient Precaution. – I cannot say all I will upon this Subject. My own Prospects and my Life are precarious, and it will require some years for me to get much above the world, but if I live & meet with the success which I have a Right to hope for, she shall not be under the Necessity of marrying a Tradesman, or any Man for her Support. I would not say thus much, but that I wish in every respect to dispell your Apprehensions.

The first letter to his wife which Hancock copied into his file is from Calcutta, on 23rd November 1769 –

It affords me Comfort that Betsy remembers me, Poor Child! She will find many three Years pass before she will see me again, if ever She may. ... Your Sentiments of Betsy's going to France are exactly the same with mine, & I most heartily wish that you may have received so much encouragement as to be now in France & Situated to your Mind. By the latter Ships I shall write fully about the Child's Education.

17th January 1770 – If it shall please God that I live, I hope soon to amend our Situation so much that you shall not have Occasion to deny yourself anything which may be agreeable to you. It is true this in a great measure Depends on the Existence of a very infirm Old Man: but the Care I take & the Reliance I have on Providence make me hope that I may live long enough to provide for you & my Dear Betsy. ... In a former Letter I mentioned that I would write about Betsy's Education; at that Time it occurred to me that there was very little Chance of her having a Fortune which might entitle Her to a Station in Life Suitable to the Education We give her, and that therefore it might conduce to her happiness to be Educated in such a Manner that She might enjoy a more humble Lot should she be Obliged to Submit to it. After long revolving every thing I could possibly recollect on a Subject of such Importance, I am resolved that the same Plan of Education as We formerly agreed on shall be pursued. In this Resolution I am confirmed by Mr. Hastings to whom I wrote on the Subject. Many Reasons might be given why Betsy's Studies should not be interrupted, but I shall only Mention two. It is very certain that neither Languages nor Exercises can be attained to any Degree of Perfection but in the earlier Years of Life, therefore Time now lost will be hereafter [lost]. Secondly, there is at present a much better Prospect of our Success than there was when I wrote to you before. ... Mrs. Mills has requested to let her Daughter carry a Letter to Betsy. I could not refuse Her tho' I think the Child is not the better for having been in Bengal. It will not be amiss to observe her well before any Intimacy is fixed between the two Young Ladies.

14th February 1770 – I send directed to Mr. Bromfield one Shawl and four Pieces of Muslin. I beg that Betsy may have some Vestment made of one of them and be acquainted that it is sent by [me] with my Love & Blessing.

Left alone in England in semi-widowhood, Philadelphia devoted all her time to Betsy's upbringing. She rented a house in Bolton Street, Mayfair, and later one in Hertford Street, and spent the winters in London in order to engage the best possible tutors for her daughter; during the summers she visited George Austen and his young family in Hampshire, and also travelled to Kent to keep in touch with their elder half-brother, William Hampson Walter (1721–98, son of their mother's first marriage), who lived near Sevenoaks with his large family. Sometimes she attempted to take holidays on her own by renting country cottages, but seems to have been too impulsive to plan such ventures carefully, as Mrs. Austen told Mrs. Walter:

Steventon, 26th August 1770 – Sister Hancock staid with us only a few days, she had more Courage than you had and set out in a Post Chaise with only her little Bessy, for she brought neither Clarinda or Peter [servants] with her, but believe she sincerely repented, before she got to her Journey's end, for in the middle of Bagshot Heath the Postilion discover'd She had dropped the Trunk from off the Chaise. She immediately sent him back with the Horses to find it, intending to sit in the Chaise till he return'd, but was soon out of patience and began to be pretty much frighted, so began her Walk to the Golden Farmer about two miles off, where she arrived half dead with fatigue, it being in the middle of a very hot day. When she was a little recover'd she recollected she had left all the rest of her things (amongst which were a large parcel of India Letters, which she had received the night before, and some of them she had not read) in the Chaise with the Door wide open, She sent a man directly after them and got them all safe and after some considerable time the Driver came with the Trunk, and without any more misfortune got to Bolton Street about Nine o'clock – She is now settled in her Cottage, her direction is at Byfleet, near Cobham, Surrey – The Letters brought good accounts both of My Brother Hancock and Mr. Hastings.

The lonely Bagshot Heath in Surrey was renowned as a haunt of highwaymen, who took advantage of the fact that the little town of Bagshot itself was an important staging-post on one of the main coach-roads out of London, and at one time had no less than fourteen inns to cater for travellers. The inn referred to by Mrs. Austen as the 'Golden Farmer' commemorates one of these highwaymen, who was notorious for robbing his victims of nothing but gold coin – while at nearby Frimley lived a farmer who paid his bills in nothing but gold coin. Eventually the two were recognised as one, and the inn was close to the spot where the robber was hanged. In later years the inn was re-named the 'Jolly Farmer', and still exists.

Unfortunately, the Byfleet cottage evidently lay too close to the River Wey for comfort, as Mrs. Austen later wrote to Mrs. Walter:

Steventon, 9th December 1770 – I find my Sister Hancock has been much incommoded by the Waters, so fancy she won't be sorry when the time comes for her going to Town, which I think she says is to be next Month. I have a great notion she will soon be tired of Byfleet, as it seems to be a very bad Winter place.

At this date most of Betsy's biography comes from Hancock's letters to Philadelphia, as he responds to her long-delayed news with his advice for the education of their daughter, and does his best to keep his memory alive in the child's mind by sending her little notes which he tries hard to make amusing.

Calcutta, 7th September 1770 – Your Letter No. 6 mentions how little encouragement Mrs. Mitchel gives you in your intention of going to France; I am sorry for it, as Betsy will soon be too old to risque her picking up the Levity or Follies of the French. I am certain you will do what is right in this Point as well as in all others. ... Necessity has reconciled me to my Lot and I draw my only Comfort from the Hopes of rendering you and my dear Child independent, by my perpetual Banishment. ... Your letter No. 21 gives an account of Betsy's still having some Symptoms of the Worms remaining. They cannot be watched with too much Caution, as they may be greatly detrimental to her Constitution. Let no thought of Œconomy induce you to Neglect either your own or the Child's Health.

Calcutta, 20th December 1770 – My dear Betsy, I received your Letter of the 12th December with very great Joy to know of your being in good Health. My Pleasure is greatly increased by the improvement, I understand, you make under your Masters. Your Mama writes me of your diligence and that she is well pleased with you. I am convinced that you will continue to do every thing your Mama desires, which will make me very happy indeed.

You forget to tell me your Fox Dog's Name. I desire you will give Him a good Piece of Beef or Mutton, whichever He likes best, and tell him I have a great Regard for him because you are fond of Him, and that if I return to England I hope to be better acquainted with Him. Remember me kindly to Clarinda, tell her that Mrs. Bowers always inquires after her; I told Her Clarinda's Dream on which she laughed very heartily. In your next Letter pray let me know how you spend your Time; at what Hours your Masters attend you and if you make any Progress in Musick; every Accomplishment you attain adds to the

Happiness of, My dear Betsy, Your most affectionate Father.

Calcutta, 26th December 1770 – I have so much Partiality to Betsy that I firmly believe all you say of Her, tho' others might think the Colouring in your Picture of Her heightened by the fondness of the Mother. May she by her future conduct prove that she deserved the attention of so good a Mother. I once fondly hoped to have pleasingly spent my latter Days in assisting you to form her Mind; Providence has decreed otherwise and I must be content to hear only of her Improvement. God grant to you both Health and true Happiness & to me Abilities to gain what may conduce to the latter.

13th March 1771 – I have received Betsy's Picture – Why should I, who hitherto never have hid my Sentiments from you, hide them now? On looking at it I was greatly disappointed indeed. I will tell You its faults – the Drawing is so very bad that the Face is broader than the Breast and the Head bigger than the upper part of the Body; the Face is also very full, and the Features are those of a Child not more than four Years old. I am sure that Betsy was remarkably well-proportioned when I left England. Another great defect is owing I believe to the Materials of which the Picture is Composed. For being made of small Clippings of Hair stuck on by Gum, it is impossible there can be any shading & Consequently the Face must want Expression, without which there can not be a good Picture or a good Likeness. I am not Singular in my Opinion, for every one to whom I have shewn it dislikes the Picture, tho' ignorant of what are the Faults. I intend sending it to Mr. Hastings for his Opinion. Do not imagine from what I have said that I am the less obliged to You for your kind intention in sending the Picture; I esteem it a Mark of your Attention to every thing which may give me Pleasure.

... I cannot help thinking that Mr. Breadmore was premature in drawing those two Teeth from Betsy tho' make not the least doubt of their Place being supplyed with others; give my Love to her & thanks for her little Scrawl. ... I am glad that you have pitched upon a Place to your Mind. I do not know Byfleet but I have searched the Map and thereby made myself acquainted with its Situation. What effect your Removal from London may have on Betsy's Education you are the best Judge, as she will probably (unless I should live long) have but very little more to depend on, it is of very great Consequence; I am certain you will readily give up the Pleasures of the Country for a Month or two more than you propose in the Year, should you find it Necessary to the Child's better Instruction. You do not mention her having begun to learn Musick. ... Let your own & Betsy's Health be your first and great care; in the Second Place Betsy's Education. I have a right to insist upon this as it is so material to my happiness and the only reward I can hope for my Labours.

Calcutta, 8th April 1771 – My Dear Betsy, To convince you how pleased I am with Your Letter of the 25 May 1770 I now send you four Gold Mohars, quite new from the Mint as I suppose you will at the Time you have received this have learned some part of Arithmetick, I send you their Value in figures: They are worth Six Pounds Eighteen Shillings (£6.18s) now do you in your Answer to my Letter, let me know how much each Gold Mohar is worth, and what you lose or gain by exchanging them.

I should have been very Happy to have been at the lying-in of your Cat, could I have been transported thither and back again in one day; but I do not wish it for the sake of the Caudle, tho' I believe it was very good, but for the happiness of seeing you and your Mama in Health and good Spirits.

You have great Courage not to roar till you feel Pain; most people are apt to roar with the Apprehension of it.

Why do not you tell me how Clarinda is? I am sure if she could write, she would tell me how you are; Give my best Wishes to her. I am, My dear Betsy, Your most affectionate Father.

'Caudle' was a warm nourishing drink, a kind of gruel made with oatmeal cooked in spiced and sweetened ale or wine, which was traditionally given to the sick and especially to women in childbed; so Philadelphia and Betsy had treated themselves to this on behalf of their cat and her newly-born kittens.

Meanwhile, in Hampshire, Mrs. Austen passed on family news to Mrs. Walter:

Steventon, 21st July 1771 – Sister Hancock sends us word she has had Letters by these last Ships both from Mr. Hancock & Mr. Hastings, with good accounts of their Health and Welfare; you rejoyce I am certain that the latter is appointed Governor of Bengal. What a comfort as well as of what real Consequence will he be to our good Brother Hancock.

In India, Hancock continued to worry about the importance of Betsy learning to speak French:

Calcutta, 28th August 1771 – I received also your Letters No. 23 & 24 I am convinced that you have taken a right Method in making Betsy speak French, for if she be not well accustomed to speak the Language now, she will never Attain it in more Advanced Years. ... The Improvement of Betsy gives me great Pleasure, as I am on the Subject, I must request you would get for Her the best Writing Master to be procured by Money and that she as soon as possible may begin to learn Arithmetick her other Accomplishments will be Ornaments to her, but these are most absolutely necessary. Happy I am that she has so good a Disposition & not less so that you know so well how to cultivate it.

Calcutta, 21st November 1771 – My Dear Betsy, Your Letter of the 17th September 1770 was more than one Year old when I received it, for it did not arrive till the 23d of September 1771. I am so very well pleased with the Praises Your Mama gives you for your Attention to and Diligence in your Improvements, that I am very willing to indulge you in your request, you may therefore give my Love to your Mama and beg she will purchase for you the best little Horse she can buy. As a further Encouragement for you to do every Thing which may Please your Mama I have sent you some Gold and Silver Coins, which I would have you keep as Curiosities.

Pray give my Compliments to the Miss Paynes; I hope You are in Strict Friendship with them. Tell Clarinda that I always remember her and have the greatest Regard for her. I am My Dear Betsy, Your most Affectionate Father.

The Payne family, who lived at Brooklands, near Weybridge in Surrey, were maternal cousins of the Austens but much wealthier, Mr. George Payne being a successful barrister and also, in modern terms, a high-ranking Civil Servant. His daughters were roughly the contemporaries of Betsy, so it is not surprising, therefore, that Hancock urged his little girl to keep in close contact with these rich relations.

Upon Betsy's tenth birthday, at the end of December 1771, Philadelphia tried to plan ahead by suggesting to Hancock that it would be a good idea if she brought Betsy back to India in two years' time, when she would be as sufficiently well educated as any other girl in her teens; she could not, of course, hope to have an answer to this letter for at least twelve months. In the meantime, she received a letter from Warren Hastings, who was on the point of leaving Madras for Calcutta and so would soon see Hancock again and discover for himself how their joint business ventures were progressing:

Fort St. George, 31st January 1772 – My Dear Madam, I reserve to myself the Pleasure of replying at large to your Letters during the Time of my Voyage, which will afford me both Leisure & Composure of Mind. I am obliged to borrow from the Hours of Sleep this Opportunity of telling you that I shall leave this Place in Health, & in Confidence of future Success. ... I have the Satisfaction to inform you that my Fortune is not worse than it was when I came here; I am not certain that it is better. The best part of it is gone to Bengal, where I hope it has been employed to a good Account. My going there shall be attended with One useful Effect, for I am determined on bringing our Concerns to some sort of a Conclusion. – I shall not have the Difficulties which Mr. Hancock had to encounter, nor he neither perhaps now. I hear he is thoroughly well, though he sometimes talks of his Old Fever, the Gout; & My Health has held out amazingly tho' I seldom stir from Town. I attribute much to the dry Air of Madras, but more to Temperance, which Necessity has now rendered almost habitual to me.

Kiss my dear Bessy for me, and assure her of my tenderest Affection. May the God of Goodness bless you both.

Before I close my Letter let me gratify my present feeling by telling you that great as my Obligations have been to you, you have increased them by a recent & disinterested Instance of your Friendship for me in your Last Letter. My next shall remind you of ye Subject. Till then, adieu, my dear & ever-valued Friend. Remember me & make my Bessy remember & love her Godfather & her Mother's sincere & faithful Friend.

Although the index files kept by Warren Hastings's secretaries show that at this period he wrote about once a month to the Woodmans and Philadelphia, this letter to her seems to be the only one that has survived.

On the same day, in Calcutta, Hancock was happy to tell his wife of the verbal message he had just received:

Miss Yorke is Arrived and tells me that she has seen you and Betsy, she thinks the Child will be short, your Letter seems to say the Contrary. I am pleased to hear that she likes Musick. When you buy an Harpsichord, let it be the best, mind not the Price. Kirkman is the best

Maker. ... Pray endeavor to keep Betsy's Recollection of me alive I fear she will only remember me by the Name of a Father.

Calcutta, 4th April 1772 – My Dear Betsy, I have received your two Letters one dated April 18, 1770 (which I suppose should have been 1771) and the other dated May 1st 1771. I am glad to hear that you was so well received at Canterbury and make no doubt but you will be received everywhere in the same Manner, as I believe you will always take care to deserve the good Opinion of your Friends.

Pray acquaint me with what Success attended Peter's case of the Wild Ducks' Eggs. I shall likewise be glad to know whether You have gotten a little Horse and how you Ride. I hope that you have a Writing Master and that You improve Daily. I am My Dear Child Your most Affectionate Father.

Philadelphia's letter of December 1771 probably reached Hancock in the late summer of 1772, and he hastened to discourage her suggestion of a return to India:

Calcutta, 23rd September 1772 – I will now give you my Opinion concerning Betsy's coming to India. You say She will be so well accomplished at twelve as many are at fifteen Years of age; I believe she will; but let me ask you if it be possible she should have any Degree of Judgement at that Tender Age. Her Arrival Here would be at that Period of Life when she will naturally form to Herself false Notions of Happiness, most probably very Romantick, the Disappointment of which may greatly embitter the rest of her Days. You know very well that no Girl, tho' but fourteen Years Old, can arrive in India without attracting the Notice of every Coxcomb in the Place, of whom there is very great Plenty at Calcutta, with very good Persons & no other Recommendation. You yourself know how impossible it is for a young Girl to avoid being attached to a Young Handsome Man whose address is agreeable to Her. Debauchery under the polite name of Gallantry is the Reigning Vice of the Settlement. I scarcely know to whom I would wish my Daughter Married were she of a proper age; which she will not be for some Years, as I am certain nothing Shortens a Woman's days so much as her being Married when too Young. The Danger and Inconvenience of a Voyage to India are very great, but there is still much greater Objection, I mean the Possibility of your Dying in the Passage. If such an unhappy Accident should happen, is it possible to reflect on the Situation of the Child without Horror? It is very probable from my many Dangerous Ailments, to which the Climate is most unfriendly, that I may not live to receive you. Paint to Yourself the distresses You must suffer in a Place where you are now a Perfect Stranger. Do not imagine there is the least of that friendly Hospitality which was formerly so Remarkable here; its Place is supplyed by self Interest, which is Natural enough when few can afford to live decently but those who are at the Head of Affairs. I have many more Reasons to Urge against your Voyage to India, but I think these are Sufficient to make you of my Opinion, that such a Step would be Highly improper. I am certain no Argument can ever induce me to give my consent to the Introduction of my Daughter to so lewd a Place as Bengal now is, were all other Objections removed.

... I am glad to hear that Betsy has a good Ear to Musick; if she attempts the Guitar at all I beg she may have the best Masters, otherwise she will get a Wrong method of Fingering which can never after be rectified. As I hold myself to be a perfect Judge of this Matter, I shall not Submit to have my Opinion Controverted but insist on your Compliance with my Request. ... Betsy's late Pain from her Teeth will be amply rewarded by their being made to look the better, as I suppose she already begins to View them in a Looking Glass. Let me repeat a former request, that you will put her under the Tuition of the best Writing Master and Accomptant you can procure; if you have any regard to me, Value not the Expense. ... I know no more than you do what will be acceptable to Mrs. Bowers, but pray send her something; I think a Miniature Picture of Betsy in a Shagreen Pocket case will be best, but let it be done by a good hand.

Calcutta, 7th November 1772 – My Dear Betsy, Three of your Letters are now before me, one dated July 11th, another December 6th 1771, the third March 10th 1772. I am glad to hear that your Gold Mohars were delivered to you safely and that they gave you pleasure. Your Mama has told me that you acted your part in the Play pretty well; I congratulate you on your Success. I wish you could perswade your Mama to Ride often; have you gotten the little Horse I desired your Mama to buy for You? I was sorry to hear that you had not begun to learn Arithmetick when your last Letter was written; I request you will apply to it with as much diligence as you do to your other Studies and you will make me very happy. I am, Dear Betsy, Your affectionate Father.

Upon his arrival in Calcutta, Hastings must soon have realised that Hancock, although he did not always admit as much to his wife, was frequently ill and unable to attend to business, and consequently failing to make any profits that could be remitted back to England. Hastings himself, in his senior position in the Company, had been growing richer, and so was in a position charitably to offer support.

Calcutta, 11th December 1772 – What I am going to tell you will, I am sure, make you very Happy: A few days ago Mr. Hastings, under the polite Term of making his God daughter a present, made over to me a Respondentia Bond for forty thousand Rupees to be paid in China; I have given directions for the Amount, which will be about five thousand Pounds, to be immediately remitted home to my Attorneys. Let me caution you not to acquaint even the Dearest Friend you have with this Circumstance; tell Betsy only that her Godfather has made her a great Present, but not the particulars; let Her write a proper Letter on the Occasion.

In the New Year of 1772–73 Philadelphia visited Steventon, to help run the household while Mrs. Austen gave birth to her fifth child and first daughter, Cassandra-Elizabeth, on 9th January 1773. She wrote to her husband the next day to tell him of this latest addition to the Austen family, but before this letter could reach India Hancock was wearily scrawling:

Calcutta, 29th March 1773 – The only comfort I have is, that I endure pain of both Body and Mind for those who deserve much more from me than human Nature can bear. ... Betsy has written me but one Letter this Year; she must have forgotten me further than that by your reminding Her of me, she may have some small Notion of a Father who went to India. I should be glad to receive yearly a Letter from Her, to know what Improvement she may make in her Writing. Give her my Love and Blessing.

Calcutta, 22nd June 1773 .... I am glad that Betsy is happy with her Horse, my Intention in giving it to Her is more on Account of her Health than to please Her. I am convinced that Riding is the most wholesome Exercise in the World, and tho' I think Fox hunting not only dangerous but in some degree an indecent Amusement for a Lady, yet I wish my Daughter to sit gracefully on a Horse and to Ride without fear; both which are Necessary to make Her sufficiently fond of the Exercise to promote her Health by Constantly using it. It has never been in my power to know what Mr. Berg's Temper is, I chose him for his Skill in the Fundamentals of Musick. I am not surprized at his never praising the Child; He sees her not with either a Mother's or a Father's Eye. If you or the Child disapprove his Manner, pray let her have another Master. ...

Calcutta, 9th August 1773 – The *Houghton* has this day brought me your favor of January 10th 1773. I must own myself sorry to hear of your going to Steventon, & for the Occasion of it [Cassandra's birth]; I fear George will find it easier to get a family than to provide for them, pray give my Love to them. It gives me pleasure that you are resolved on your return from Steventon to put Betsy under the Tuition of a good Writing-Master and a good Accomptant; it is high time, for her Hand is not the least mended since I left England; at her age she ought to write better than she does.

On the same day Hancock wrote to his daughter:

Calcutta, 9th August 1773 – Dear Betsy, Your Letters of September 29th 1772 and of January 10th 1773 I have received with great Pleasure, as they give me the good News that you are in Health. I am glad that Clarinda did not jump quite out of her skin and that she was only like to do it, for I am afraid she would not have easily got into her skin again. Remember me kindly to her.

Poor Dido [another of the Portuguese maidservants] has been sick more than a Year &, I believe, will never be well; but her Disorder is not that of her Namesake's – I am very glad that your Horse pleases you so much, and I desire you will ride as often as you can, that is, as often as your Mama thinks it proper.

It will give me great Pleasure to see that you have improved in Writing under a good Master; I know you will be glad to please Your most affectionate Father.

Once again Hancock's ailments overwhelmed his spirit, and in November 1773 he told his wife: 'I am now too Old and too infirm to Struggle with the World again, and can only hope to spend the Dregs of Life in saving what may enable my Family to subsist comfortably.'

In London, the Woodman family always held parties at Christmas-time – one to commemorate Warren Hastings's birthday on 17th December, and another to mark Betsy's on the 22nd, such parties often being held at the home of their old Aunt Hastings in Kensington. This year Mr. Woodman wrote to Hastings, on 10th December: 'Next Thursday Tom breaks up for the Holidays, the next day we keep your Birth day & on the Tuesday following we go to Mrs. Hancock to Celebrate Miss's Birth day. Tommy & She are as fond of each others Company as when you was in England.' A few weeks later he added: 'Mrs. & Miss Hancock, I need not mention, only that Miss grows a fine Girl, very accomplished, & perfectly agreable in her behaviour. Pray remember us to Mr. Hancock.'

It seems that Philadelphia was still hopeful that Hancock might return from India with his finances improved, but he himself now knew that this was impossible:

Calcutta, 16th January 1774 – To your further Enquiries I can only Answer, that what I can leave you, should I dye soon, tho' my all, will not do more than purchase a tolerable Annuity for your Life: this ought to be your Resolution, as Betsy is provided for: I am not certain, but that I may direct it to be so disposed of in my Will. My present Expences including Yours (tho' I never see Company) are twice the Amount of my present Gains; from this judge the probability of my returning to England: perhaps I have said too much, but Matters of Fact cannot well be ascribed to a gloomy Disposition. ... Give my Love & Blessing (of which I suppose she cannot have an Idea) to Betsy; remember me to Clarinda.

Calcutta, 26th August 1774 – Undoubtedly your Method of teaching Betsy French by giving Her a French Companion is the Shortest, I can have no Objections to it till the Child may be old enough to imbibe the Spirit of Intrigue, without which no French Woman ever yet existed. ... Betsy's Picture is Spoilt, the Crayons having mouldered into Dust & fallen from the Back-ground & Hair over the Cheek it is unnecessary to say this is a great Disappointment to me. I am much chagrined that you have given away the Horse, pray buy another, the best You can get: and keep it as long as there shall be livery Stables open in London. I am highly pleased with your Scheme of a Carriage; but some of your Œconomical Expressions hurt me much; they teach me that I ought in future to be silent on the Subject of my Health & Circumstances.

Early in 1775 Mr. Woodman told Hastings of the usual Christmas parties: 'Mrs. & Miss Hancock are very well, whom we have often the pleasure of seeing; we were all very happy there on Miss Hancocks Birthday, & in particular Tommy there being a Ball for the Young Folks.' Later this year Hastings made another kind gesture to relieve the anxieties of his old friend and partner, who obviously had not much longer to live, by giving him the lump sum of £10,000; this was to be invested in a trust fund, with the interest paid to Hancock and Philadelphia, and the principal sum to go to Betsy herself after her parents' death. Hancock could at last have the peace of mind of knowing that the livelihood of his wife and daughter was secured, and be able to admit to them that he was now chronically ill:

Calcutta, 25th March 1775 – The enclosed Paper will sufficiently shew the Intentions of it, but I think it proper to explain to you that it is in Lieu of what the Donor gave to me in the Name of Betsy. I thought no Persons could be more proper for Trustees than Your Brother & Mr. Woodman, but as the latter is best acquainted with Business and in Compliment to Mr. Hastings, He is named first in the Trust. You must get your Brother to come to Town & with Mr. Woodman to sign the Deed taking Care that the proper Seals be affixed at or before Signing. It ought not to occasion any Expence to your Brother, therefore You must repay what his Journey to London may cost.

The Interest of this Money will produce to you while you shall live nearly four hundred Pounds p. Annum, and the whole, should She Marry, be a large Fortune to Betsy after your Death.

As you and the Child are now provided for I may venture to tell you that I am not well enough to write a long Letter ... Give my Love & Blessing to Betsy & remember me to Clarinda.

Hancock's last letter to his daughter was written the following day:

My Dear Child, I have received your two little Letters, greatly pleased that you seem to be at the Time of writing them in good Health & Spirits. Your Writing is so much amended that I have Hopes you will daily improve; You can not please me more than by giving the greatest Attention to Writing and Arithmetick, as they will be most useful to you hereafter.

As your Horse did not suit You I have desired your Mama to buy you another, not only to please You but for the sake of your Health & because I think your good Behavior deserves Encouragement.

The Governor, your Godfather, desired me to send a very fine white Persian Cat of mine to you as a present from Him, which I would have done with Pleasure, but your Cousin Stanhope having quarrelled with a Gentleman who lived at an House next to mine & the Cat having straied into His House, this Gentleman or some of his People shot Her; I suppose to be revenged on Mr. Stanhope. If I should be so fortunate as to procure another I will send it next Year.

May God bless you & make you good! when You will be happy & make happy, My Dear Betsy, Your most affectionate Father.

The cousin Stanhope referred to here was another connection of Philadelphia's on the Hampson side – a wild, quarrelsome young man, who had been sent out to India by his despairing mother and there inflicted his company upon the unfortunate Hancock. He subsequently went into the army, but after some years probably fled to France to escape his creditors, and may have ended his life in exile there.

Hancock's last full letter to his wife was written on 22nd May 1775 –

.... Mrs. Bowers has just called on me & requested that I would acquaint You of her having sent to Betsy, by Mrs. Geary, four Strings of Pearls and a Philagree Bottle sewed in a Bag. The Pearls are exceedingly even. This Mrs. Geary kept an House of Entertainment at Madras (I do not mean an house of ill Fame) what she was in England I know not; but I thought it necessary that You should know so much. ... Give my Love to Betsy, remember me to Clarinda.

After this, only one more brief note to his wife, in August 1775, is recorded in Hancock's letter-book; if he did write a final message of farewell, he was presumably too ill to make a file copy of it, or perhaps felt there was no longer any need to do so. He died three months later, at the age of 52, and was buried by his friends the next day; they provided a brief and mis-spelt inscription for his gravestone: 'Here Lieth the Body of Tyso Saul Handcock, Esq, who died 5th of November 1775 Aged 64 years' – the incorrect age must have been a guess on their part, judging by Hancock's haggard looks after years of ill-health.

There was the usual long delay before the news reached Philadelphia in London, and Mr. Woodman told Hastings of its receipt in his letter of 11th June 1776 –

I thank God we all continue well, but amidst this Joy of your success, have it damp'd by the unwelcome News of Poor Mr. Hancocks Death, by a Letter from Mrs. Bowers, which Mrs. Hancock received on Friday last, we feel much for her, and endeavor to support her under the Affliction. Her Brother & Sister Austen were there when she received the Letter, which has helped to Comfort her, as it adds much to her distress that she has not yet recd. any other Letter from India ...

and on 20th June –

Since my Letter of ye 11th Instant Mrs. Hancock has recd. your Letter confirming to her the Death of Mr. Hancock ... I am sorry to find Mr. Hancocks affairs are in so bad a situation, all his Effects will not more than clear his Debts here.

The executors of Hancock's Will, dated 8th December 1774, were Warren Hastings, 'my generous Patron', and another old Indian friend, Edward Baber of Kassimbazaar. The Will itself was brief, covering only three paragraphs: if, after settlement of his debts, his estate amounted to £11,000 or over, his executors were to arrange an annuity of £30 for his sister Olivia Hancock of Canterbury; but if his estate were less than £11,000 no annuity should be purchased and Olivia would have to ask Philadelphia for whatever financial help she could spare her; all his estate was left to Philadelphia, with one specific small exception:

Item I give & bequeath unto my beloved Daughter Elizabeth Hancock a Miniature Picture of her Mother painted by Sharp [*sic*, actually John Smart] and set in a Ring with Diamonds round it which I request she will never part with as I intend it to remind her of her Mother's Virtues as well as of her person.

This miniature was indeed cherished by Betsy, and after her death passed down in the Austen family, finally coming to rest, in the twentieth century, in the possession of the Jane Austen Memorial Trust. Perhaps Smart had done a companion portrait of Hancock, for Philadelphia to keep beside her; but if so, it is not known to exist. Hancock's gravestone disappeared in the nineteenth century, and the cemetery itself was swept away as Calcutta expanded, so his letter-book now preserved amongst the Hastings Papers in the British Library is the only surviving trace of this sad unsuccessful exile, devoted to the daughter he knew he would never see again, and who could hardly have remembered him.

The last few glimpses of Philadelphia and Betsy this year are given by Mr. Woodman as postscripts in his letters to Hastings:

London, 29th October 1776 – Mrs. Hancock being at her Brothers, we have not seen her since the arrival of the *Talbot*, the letter I have sent you of hers was wrote several days since. ...

26th November 1776 – The important event of your resignation, having occasioned an Express to be sent to India over Land, I cannot omit the opportunity of acquainting you, that we are all well, as likewise are Mrs. & Miss Hancock, who probably would have wrote if she had known of this sudden dispatch. I lately recd. a Letter from Mrs. Forde who seems anxious about Miss Louisa's Fortune, which was in Mr. Hancocks hands, I hope you will have it in your power to make it secure to her, I told her that I would write to you about it.

Mrs. Forde was the widow of a Colonel Forde who had sailed on the *Aurora* for India in 1769, together with other members of the East India Company; but after reaching the Cape of Good Hope in December of that year, the ship and all aboard her were never heard of again. Her daughter Louisa was Philadelphia's goddaughter, a relationship which unluckily had encouraged Mrs. Forde to allow Hancock to manage Louisa's funds for her.

George Vansittart, uncle of the little George who had been Betsy's playmate in Calcutta, also wrote to Hastings on 17th December 1776 –

I called upon Mrs. Hancock in London, & saw her & her daughter. They are both well, but I did not think Mrs. Hancock looked very stout [healthy]. The letter & little parcel you sent by me have been safely delivered to her.

CHAPTER II

Paris has been very gay

1777–86

✡

IT WAS A YEAR OR MORE before Hancock's affairs began to be clarified and Philadelphia learnt that her annual income would in future be about £600, the bulk of this sum being the interest from Warren Hastings's trust fund. She already knew that such an income would be inadequate for life in London, and so decided to move to the Continent, where the cost of living was much cheaper; this would also fulfil her husband's wish that Betsy should acquire some French culture. Philadelphia and her daughter, the latter now nearly sixteen and preferring to be called by the far more fashionable diminutive of 'Eliza', therefore set off for Europe probably late in 1777, accompanied by their faithful maidservant Clarinda. They went first to Germany and Belgium, and by the summer of 1778 had reached Brussels. Philadelphia kept her account at Hoare's Bank in London; and as in those days banks were very much family businesses, their correspondence still had the personal touch, as is shown by the letter Mr. Henry Hoare junior wrote to her on 2nd June 1778:

> I am very sorry I was not at home when your Letter came, as it has occasion'd a Delay, in the answering, which I hope however will not be attended with any Inconvenience to you, as you do not propose to leave Brusselles till the End of this Month. As Sir Robt. Herries's notes are very convenient to Travellers who are moving about, I have sent you four of them to the amount of Two hundred Pounds, & I have likewise sent you a Letter of Credit on Sir John Lambert at Paris for Two hundred Pounds more, which I hope you will approve of.

Sir Robert Herries, who came of a Scottish family grown wealthy by their mercantile interests on the Continent, lived in Paris, and has his claim to fame in banking history by being the first person to invent a universal letter of credit in the form of promissory-notes, which were payable at all the principal towns in Europe where British travellers were likely to find themselves, such notes eventually being encashed back in London – in other words, an early form of travellers' cheques. Sir John Lambert, too, was another private banker, an Anglo-French baronet who lived in Paris and handled all the English business in that city.

Philadelphia kept her London friends advised of her travels, and Mr. Woodman wrote to Warren Hastings on 12th June 1778: 'As this dispatch goes through Brussells it gave Mrs. Woodman an opportunity of writing to Mrs. Hancock, who is yet there. ... Miss Hinchliffes drank Tea with us yesterday, said they had a Letter from Brussells this week and that Mrs & Miss Hancock were both well.'

The Misses Hinchliffe were sisters of the Revd. Dr. Hinchliffe, Master of Trinity College Cambridge 1768–88, and Bishop of Peterborough 1769–94, but it is not known how and where Philadelphia came to be acquainted with these virtuous spinsters. As well as writing to these friends, Philadelphia must of course have told the Austens and the Walters of her journeyings in Europe, but unfortunately none of these letters has survived. Mother and daughter probably reached Paris in the summer of 1779 and Sir John Lambert, who is known to have acted as a contact point for English travellers as well as providing them with banking facilities, was no doubt responsible for finding them accommodation and introducing them into French society. Although Britain had officially declared war on France in February 1778, as a consequence of the latter country aiding the Americans in their War of Independence, this state of hostilities seems to have made little difference to the ease with which English travellers could enter the country.

English visitors of the time were usually most unfavourably impressed by the dirt and dangers of the French capital. The Revd William Cole, rector of Bletchley, was particularly voluble on this subject when he wrote an account of his visit in 1765:

The Water of the River Seine is as thick & muddy as the Channel of the Severne which comes up to Bristol; so that to drink such Water is not practicable ... The Buildings at Paris, in my Eye, are very mean & Contemptible; all built of Stone, & mostly very lofty: but all the lower

Story being for the most Part Warehouses, & ordinary Shops, & the windows of no Symmetry or just Proportion, with bad Glass, altogether have a very mean Appearance. Hotels of the Nobility [are] cheifly situated in good & spatious Court Yards ... Streets in general are very narrow, & no Place for Foot Passengers, except in a very few, so that they are also very dangerous to walk in ... one of the most dreary & gloomy Cities I have been in ... a City of no real Beauty to recommend it, except some few artificial Perfections, in a few public Buildings, situated on a dirty nasty Ditch of a River ... The Shops at Paris are the poorest gloomy Dungeons you can possibly conceive, however rich their Contents may be ...

He was further disgusted to find that the foodshops contained

.. so much Carrion, hung up in their Shops, as eatable Victuals. It has been as much as I could do to forbear putting my Head out at the Coach Window many a Time in the Streets, the principal Streets of this Glory of the World, to bring up the Contents of my Stomach, when I have passed by so much Liver, Lights & other Offal, cut out in Slices & sold on small Tables in almost every Street: whether it is for Dogs, Cats or themselves, it is equally offensive; the monstrous black Sausages in great Guts, or Bladders, hanging by many of their Shop Windows; Quantities of Sheep's Heads boiled & partly dried, in Heaps on Stalls, are all such odious & indelicate sights, as would turn any other Stomach but that of a Frenchman.

A few months after their arrival in Paris, Philadelphia wrote to Warren Hastings on 3rd March 1780:

After a silence of so many years on your part nothing shd. have prevailed on me to have troubled you with another Letter but my earnest desire to have some information concerning Mr. Hancock's affairs, and to whom can I apply but you? Let me therefore conjure you by your Friendship for his memory and by those uncommon marks you have given of it to his Family not to refuse me this request the last perhaps I shall ever make you. – By the very first opportunity let me know how far Mr. Hancock's Affairs have been collected in and how far his Creditors are satisfied or likely to be so. Mrs. Forde continues to write me and distresses me beyond measure on account of Louisa's Fortune wch. was in Mr. Hancock's Hands. I know not what Answer to make her & have vainly waited to receive some Account from you. I shall be happy to hear it will not be all lost. Mrs. Davis is returned from America a Widdow wth. two Children in great Distress. Is there anything for her? Has my Uncle given you any Account of the Money left in his Hands? About two thousand pounds I imagine besides my Brother Hancock's Bond wch. I fear we shall see but little of. I have met with many mortifying & disagreeable Events in my Life, but none that has given such lasting Affliction as the reflection that many worthy Persons may be sufferers by the confidence they have unfortunately placed in the person whose name I bear, not from any fault of his I will be bold to say for never was there a Man of better principles than Mr. Hancock but from a concurrence of unlucky events – I know not what – some people are born to be unfortunate –

I wish also much to know if anything is secured for Clarinda, whose demand I enclosed to you, be that as it may I take it on myself that She shall not be a sufferer in her little Fortune. Alas! She has but too severely suffered in her Health and perhaps may not live to want it – it is now more than five Months that She has been quite helpless and that from so small a beginning as a whitlow on her left thumb which notwithstanding all possible assistance and after six operations performed threatened the loss of her Hand & even her life & before those wounds were healed the humour conveyed itself to her right Shoulder where She has already had three severe operations performed & threatened with a fourth without some extraordinary change in her favor. She has been attended by three Surgeons one of them the first in Paris and a Physician; the latter still attends her and one of the Surgeons dresses her Arm twice a Day – God knows how it will end, though I am assured her life & the use of her Hands are at present in no danger. – This has been a most unfortunate affair on all accounts & has cost me more anxiety than I can describe – the expence too has been and is still very heavy, it could not have happened at a worse time, but of that I shan't complain if the poor faithful creature can be restored to me. –

I once thought to have confined this Letter to Business but knowing your Heart as I know it and being convinced that in spite of appearances it is not changed for your Friends, I cannot refuse you the satisfaction of knowing my Daughter, the only thing I take Comfort in, is in perfect Health & joins me in every good Wish for your Happiness – you may be surrounded by those who are happy in frequent opportunities of shewing their attachment to you, but I will venture to say not one among them who can boast a more disinterested steady &

unshaken Friendship for you than that wch. for so many years has animated and will ever continue to animate the Breast of, Dear Sir, your Obliged Friend, Phila: Hancock.

18th March. It is with pleasure I can add here that Clarinda is much better and altho' still quite helpless is thought to be out of danger & in about a fortnight may be able to quit her Chamber.

It is evident that not only the Forde family but also another friend of Calcutta days, Mrs. Davis, had suffered considerable financial loss from Hancock's unsuccessful attempts to invest and manage their funds for them. There is no surviving reply from Hastings to Philadelphia, but his account book, later on, shows that he made a small payment to Mrs. Davis, which was presumably as a result of receiving this letter.

Mr. Woodman told Hastings, on 1st April 1780: 'Mrs. & Miss Hancock are at this time at Paris the young Lady is almost as tall as her Mother'; and at last Eliza herself comes into the limelight, her own voice now heard in the first of her surviving letters, which in effect constitute her autobiography. These letters were all addressed to her cousin Phylly [Philadelphia] Walter (1761–1834), her exact contemporary, and the youngest child of Mrs. Hancock's half-brother William Hampson Walter. Mr. Walter is a rather shadowy figure on the edge of the Austen family circle; for the latter part of his life, at least, he seems to have been employed as a steward or land-agent by Mr. Henry Lyell, a landowner of Swedish ancestry (the name was originally spelt Leijell) whose main estates were in Cambridgeshire; and, presumably in the course of his duties, over the next few years he and his family moved from village to village in the Sevenoaks/ Maidstone area of Kent. In 1778 they were at Ightham, in 1781 at Borough Green, in 1783 at Stone Street, and from 1784 onwards at Seal, where Mr. Walter died in 1798.

Phylly Walter herself was something of a shy country-mouse, living alone with her ageing and demanding parents; her only sister had died ten years ago, and her four brothers had by now all left home – Weaver was the curate of Penshurst in Kent, William and George had gone to Jamaica, and James was studying at Cambridge University. No doubt this was the reason she cherished Eliza's bulletins of news from the wide world beyond the confines of her Kentish villages, and carefully numbered and dated the letters as she received them. This methodical annotation shows that in fact the first eight of this sequence of letters are missing; they must have covered the period from late 1777 onwards, and described Eliza's travels on the Continent, her arrival in Paris and entry into French high society.

The Revd Mr. Cole, who thought so poorly of Paris, had been horrified also by the lavatorial habits of the French, commenting in his journal on the

... dirty magnificence of Versailles ... I did not wonder at the Dirt & Confusion of the Part of the Garden before the Castle, as so many Workmen were making Reparations in it, taking the Opportunity of the Court's Absence, at that Time at Fontainebleau; no more than at that Squallidness & Dirt in the Salons & Staircases of the Palace, presuming that they were not so, when the Court was here, but .... even under the Palace Walls, nay even upon that very Stone Staircase which leads into the Gardens, & under the Windows of the Royal Apartments, people were suffered to lay their Nastiness in such Quantities, that it was equally offensive to the Sight & Smell, as well as difficult to avoid treading in it as you went down them.

However, Eliza, now eighteen and in her own eyes very worldly and sophisticated, ignores the smells and the dirt underfoot and sees only the magnificence of the French court:

A Paris le 16 May 1780 – My dear Cousin, I own myself much to blame in having suffered so much time to pass since I last wrote to You but hope You will think my fault in some measure diminished when I assure You it has been greatly occasioned, by my waiting for an opportunity of sending my letter without expence to You, as I am sensible my epistles can be by no means worth the postage; I feel however my silence is no ways entirely to be excused since it has caused you for a moment to doubt of my affection, which You may be assured, my dear Phila, is ever the same, & not to be lessened by either time or absence, circumstances which altho' generally supposed to change the sentiments, are far from having that effect on mine, & which therefore I hope in future You will not do me the injustice to doubt of.

I sincerely rejoice in the good account You have had of your Brother William as well in your Brother James' success at college. They have both of them most likely almost forgot their cousin, but I hope when You write

you do not omit to remember me to them.

Our stay in Paris has been much longer than we at first intended, Clarinda's long & dangerous illness has been in part the cause. She is at present much better, & we think of soon moving; it will not be however a great way we propose spending the summer, or at least a part of it a small distance from this place, at a Lady's country house about 20 miles from Paris. The country is pretty & I do not doubt spending some time agreably, besides I shall not be sorry to quit for a little while the dissipations of the Town, & to enjoy a little quiet. Paris is however the city in the world the best calculated to spend the whole Year in, it is not like London, where the summer months are insupportable. The walks and rides here, The amusements which continue the whole year round, The almost continual residence of people of Fashion, all these Things render it at all times agreable.

We were a few days ago at Versailles & had the honor of seeing their Majesties & all the royal family dine & sup. The Queen is a very fine Woman, She has a most beautiful complexion, & is indeed exceedingly handsome; She was most elegantly dressed, She had on a corset & Petticoat of pale green Lutestring, covered with a transparent silver gauze, The petticoat & sleeves puckered & confined in different places with large bunches of roses an amazing large bouquet of White Lilac, The same flower, together with gauze, Feathers, ribbon & diamonds intermixed with her hair. Her neck was entirely uncovered & ornamented by a most beautiful chain of diamonds, of which She had likewise very fine bracelets; She was without gloves, I suppose to shew her hands, & arms, which are without exception the whitest & most beautiful I ever beheld. The King was plainly dressed, he had however likewise some fine diamonds. The rest of the royal family were very elegant, & indeed I may say The court of France is I believe upon the whole one of the most magnificent in all Europe.

There is perhaps no place in the world where dress is so well understood & carried to so great a perfection as in Paris & no wonder it should be so since people make it the chief business & study of their Lives. Powder is universally worn, & in very large quantities, no one would dare to appear in public without it, The Heads in general look as if they had been dipped in a meal tub; Hats likewise (which are called English but which do not bear the least resemblance to those of our nation) are much the fashion. The hair is cut in shades, not worn high at all. It was with reluctance, I conformed to the mode in this article, as my hair was very long on my arrival, & I was obliged to have it cut to half its length; but what will not All powerful Fashion effect & so much for the modes let us now speak of something more interesting.

I am happy to find You are so well pleased [with] Ightham, it is certainly an agreeable thing to have [?good] neighbours; I know not my dear friend whom You can have seen that have given You such accounts of me, but of this You may be assured that You or Whoever else expects a phenomenon or anything very accomplished in me will be much disappointed when ever they see me, & indeed to have had so much said in my favor is enough to make me afraid of ever presenting myself, as I am sensible how very very far The reality will fall short of people's expectations. You are very good in saying You wish for my return to England, be assured there is no one whom I should be more happy in seeing again than yourself. It is a pleasure however which seems to be at present very uncertain when I shall have. As to my settling abroad it is not at all likely, altho' not absolutely impossible as it is a thing that at this moment depends entirely on myself; I think like You that there are many worthy persons among my own countrymen, but I think likewise that worth is confined to no country or nation, & equally to be found in Germany, Flanders, or France. With all this do not imagine that I have left my Heart in either of those places, You may be certain I never was more mistress of it than at this moment & that I do not doubt keeping it whole for many years to come. Indeed it is so well filled up by friendship, that there is no room for any other sentiment. I am certainly much flattered at the assurance You give me of your confidence in me, but do not desire You to prove it at the expence of your liberty. All badinage apart I hope you will long preserve it & to tell you the Truth I don't think either You or I very likely to lose either our gaiety or peace of mind for any male creature breathing.

Adieu my dear cousin do not follow my example but let me hear from You soon; Mama joins me in every kind wish Love &cc to yourself My Uncle & Aunt & all your family; be assured how sincerely I am yours most affectionately, Eliza Hancock.

I believe you will be troubled to read my letter as it is most abominably wrote, indeed I have been in such a hurry as I am obliged to go out & be dressed & send my letter before noon that I hardly know what I have wrote.

By the same gentlemen who are so good as to take charge of this I send my picture in miniature done here to my uncle G. Austen. He will most likely shew it you, pray tell me in your next if you think it at all like what you remember me. It is reckoned here like what I am at present. The dress is quite the present fashion & what I usually wear.

The miniature referred to here has been preserved in the Austen family, and shows a piquante little face with large dark eyes; her hair is piled up and powdered and she wears a white dress, with blue ribbons decorating the dress and more blue ribbons casually threaded through her coiffure. Although Eliza apologises for her handwriting, in fact her father's insistence upon good tuition in this respect had clearly borne fruit, since her writing is beautifully small, fine and legible, with the lines entirely regular and the paper filled from margin to margin.

As planned, Eliza and her mother left Paris for a trip to Comblaville, near Fontainebleau:

Comblaville le 27 juin 1780 – My dear Cousin, I received your kind & entertaining Letter a few days ago, & cannot but confess the justice of the gentle rebuke You give me for having suffered so much time to pass before I answered yours, I own myself much to blame but hope to behave better in future, & to shew You by my exactness, my sincere intentions of amendment.

Your account of the Ball gave me much pleasure, as I was happy to find You had been so well amused, I doubt not my dear cousin's being distinguished wherever She goes & therefore am not at all amazed at her attracting the notice of the smartest Man in the room; I am not much acquainted with my countrymen, but your account gives me a good opinion of their taste. Upon the whole your ball must have been a very agreable one. The circumstance however of not being able to dance with the person You wished must have lessened your amusement. It is a vexation You would not have had in this country as it is the custom to change your partner every dance, by which means you have an opportunity of accepting & refusing as You please, of dancing with every one & the comfort if You are engaged to a person disagreeable to You of knowing it is not for the whole evening; in short it is a fashion attended with so many agréments that I am astonished it is not adopted in England. I should think it must be the most tiresome thing in the world to have the same partner (& may be a bad one) the whole evening while perhaps there were twenty others in the room whom you would have preferred. I am quite of your opinion that the plenty of beaux must have rendered your dance infinitely more agreeable, as in things of that sort nothing is so insupportable as to see Ladies sit by for want of Partners. It is what seldom happens in this country, on the contrary You have generally more on your hands than You know what to do with, I have frequently been engaged for more than 15 dances the same evening, & for 8 or 10 for the next ball. I am not surprised You should be so fond of dancing as it is an amusement perfectly suited to that gaiety, I have ever known you possessed of.

I am happy my account of Versailles could afford You any amusement; You wrong her Majesty however when you suppose her entirely indebted to art for her complexion. She has really a beautiful natural one, rouge is I acknowledge much worn here, but not so universally as you imagine, no single ladies ever make use of it, & were they to do it would be much disapproved of; When once married I own in general they make themselves ample amends for this denial; There are however many, many exceptions, & several could I cite amongst my own acquaintance who never made use of the least art in their Lives. The comtesse de Tournon in particular one of my best friends never wears rouge no one indeed can have less occasion for that or any other addition to her beauty as nature has done enough for her, not to render all art superfluous.

We are not at present at Paris, it is about three weeks since we exchanged the hurry & dissipation of that gay town, for the tranquillity of the country. This place, where I believe we shall spend the summer is called Comblaville about 7 leagues from Paris. The house we are in belongs to an acquaintance of the Lady I just mentioned to You. It is really a pretty place, very retired & very rural, we see but little company, now and then a visit from Paris & that is all; I amuse myself with walking, reading, music, work &cc I have here both an harpsichord and harp (The latter is at present the fashionable instrument). There is a large Garden & plantation belonging to the House, & I am generally out of an evening from 7 till past 9; How happy should I be could I enjoy your company in my evening rambles.

Mama has had a letter from my uncle G. Austen which informs us the picture is safe arrived. I own I had not reflected on your distance from Steventon, when I said you would see my picture; You will however most likely have a sight of it one day or other & You will then tell me if you find any resemblance of what You remember me. I imagine you are very tall at present pray let me know your height, that I may see whether You have outgrown me.

You do not at all approve then of my settling in this country, I have friends here as much for it as you can be against it; was any such <u>*arrangement*</u> *however to take place it would not banish me from England, I should certainly pay you a visit; how should you like it my dear was I to introduce* <u>*un cousin francais*</u> *to your acquaintance should you receive him very cordially or are you persuaded like [most of] our nation, that nothing good can come from France. With all this [be] assured I only joke & am far from having any serious thoughts of marr[ying in this] country, no, no, you will most likely see me return to England without [having] changed my name. True it is as I have already said I have friends here who are so good as to desire to keep me with them, & who therefore do every thing in their power to prevail on me to accept offers which would attach me to this country. You assure me you have yet no confidence to make me & that you have never experienced any soft emotions, I believe you My dear cousin & do not think either You or I very likely to have our peace disturbed by tender sentiments, as to me I begin to be persuaded, my heart is entirely insensible to any but those of Friendship, but in them be assured no one is warmer than myself. I have at present a particular friend in a convent at Paris, & my absence from her is almost the only thing that makes me regret that place, we however write to one another once a week; She has given me her picture & has mine, nor is our attachment of a short date it is now near two years since we first became acquainted, you see therefore I am constant in my friendships, my dear Phila may be assured that I bear her will never vary & that to hear of her welfare will always be one [of] my greatest satisfactions.*

I am happy to hear my cousins Weaver & James are well I beg to be remembered to them. Mama joins me in best Love &cc to my uncle Aunt yourself & Family & I beg you to be assured of the sincerity of the regard with which I remain, My dear cousin most affectionately yours, E. Hancock.

My letter is so wrote or to use a fashionable term si griffonée that I am afraid you will have some trouble to read it. I hope to have the pleasure of hearing from you soon, consider I have been a very good girl this time as it is not a week since I received yours.

It will perhaps amuse You to have an account of a new manner of dressing the hair which is lately all the taste. The hind hair instead of being turned up or plaited as usual is curled at the ends, fastened with a small comb, & suffered to wave over the shoulders in three or four large curls. The hair in general is worn exceedingly low before, young people who have good hair in an undress go without a cushion or any thing to raise it. Hats of all sorts are worn, chip in particular of all colours something in the form the English gentlemen wear them of a morning. Large gold earrings, that is to say a ring with a single drop in the form of a pearl are much the ton, they are not at all like what I have seen in England, in short was I to give you an account of all the different modes I should never have done. They have more taste & more whims in this country than in any other. Once more adieu my dear cousin, je vous embrasse de tout mon coeur.

Direct yours, A Mademoiselle Hancock au soin du Chevalier Lambert a Paris.

It will perhaps give You pleasure to hear, Clarinda who has been dangerously ill all the winter is much better, tho' still entirely helpless.

There is no further mention of Clarinda in Eliza's correspondence, so it must be assumed that she probably died not long after this letter was written.

Despite Eliza's assurances of being uninterested in matrimony, she had probably by now met her future husband, Jean-François Capot de Feuillide, who was a captain in the Queen's Regiment of Dragoons, and about ten years her senior. He liked to be known as the Comte de Feuillide, though in fact he was only the son of a provincial lawyer who had risen to become the mayor of Nérac, a town in the province of Guienne, in the south-west of France, where the family owned a small estate. By the summer of 1781 they were engaged, to the disapproval of Mr. Woodman, who wrote to Warren Hastings from London on 7th August 1781:

Mrs. & Miss Hancock are yet in France & likely to continue there the young Lady being on the point of Marriage with a French Officer which Mrs. Hancock writes is of good family with expectation of good Fortune, but at present but little. Her Letter was to Mr. Austen & Self on the Subject and she seems inclined to give up to them the Sum which was settled on her for Life, and wants the Money to be transferred into the French Funds which we have thought prudent for her sake to decline and Mr. Austen is much concerned at the connection which he sais [*sic*] is giving up all their friends their Country, and he fears their Religion.

The precise date of the marriage is not known, but Mr. Woodman wrote again to Hastings on 26th December 1781:

I wrote Mrs. Hancock ... who is in France, where I believe she intends to end her Days, having married her Daughter there to a Gentleman of that Country, I am afraid not very advantageously, although she sais [*sic*] it is entirely to her satisfaction, the Gentleman having great connections, and expectations. Her Uncle Mr. Austen, and Brother dont approve of the Match, the latter is much concernd at it; they seem already desirous of draining the Mother of every Shilling she has.

Mr. Hancock of Charing Cross being become a Bankrupt, and there being a Debt I believe of fifteen Hundred pounds due to his Brother Mr. Tysoe S. Hancock besides Interest, it became necessary for Mr. Baber to administer to the Will, in order to lay the claim which has been done, by which some Money will be received here from that Debt. I wish you could contrive it to be Paid to Miss Louisa, the Daughter of the late Col. Forde in part of the fifteen hundred pounds of hers which was in Mr. Hancock's hands at the time of his Death, for it really is a very hard case it being the whole of that young Lady's fortune.

In her next letter to Phylly Eliza sounds perhaps a little on the defensive, laying as she does such emphasis on the worldly benefits of her marriage:

Paris 27th March 1782 – I should never have the courage to address my dear cousin Philly, if I had not the greatest confidence in her friendship, & the greatest desire to convince her that I have never ceased to think of her with real affection; I am nevertheless not altogether so blameable as I may appear to be, as I did not receive your letter till long after its date owing to the neglect of servants, & my being out of town. As to the two former epistles you mention they never came to my hands; I imagine a letter I wrote you a short time before my marriage must likewise have been lost, as you speak of not having heard from me for above a twelvemonth; this would imply a neglect which I never can be guilty of where you are concerned, for be assured my dear cousin, you can have no friend more sincerely attached to you than myself & neither time nor absence can affect the regard I have ever felt for you.

The accounts which your letter brought me of the health and welfare of you & yours, gave me infinite pleasure. I am only sorry to find that you have met with so disagreeable a circumstance as the being obliged to quit a house with which you were satisfied.

As I know the affection you have borne me, I doubt not but you will expect & wish I should give you some account of myself. My Uncle Austen acquainted you with my marriage soon after its taking place. This event, the most important one of my life, was you may imagine the effect of a mature deliberation, & as it was a step I took much less from my own judgment than that of those whose councils & opinions I am the most bound to follow, I trust I shall never have any reason to repent it; on the contrary, if I may be allowed to judge of the future from the past & present I must esteem myself the most fortunate of my sex. The man to whom I have given my hand is everyways amiable both in mind & person. It is too little to say he loves, since he literally adores me; entirely devoted to me, & making my inclinations the guide of all his actions, the whole study of his life seems to be to contribute to the happiness of mine.

My situation is everyways agreeable, certain of never being separated from my dear Mama whose presence enhances every other blessing I enjoy, equally sure of my husband's affections, mistress of an easy fortune with the prospect of a very ample one, add to these the advantages of rank & title, & a numerous & brilliant acquaintance, amongst whom I can flatter myself I have some sincere friends, & you will unite with me in saying I have reason to be thankful to Providence for the lot fallen to my share; the only thing which can make me uneasy is the distance I am from my relations (among whom I beg you to be assured there is no one I regret more than yourself) & country, but this is what I trust I shall not have always to complain of, as the Comte has the greatest desire to see England, & even to make it his residence a part of the year. We shall certainly make you a visit as soon as possible after the peace takes place.

Your request for the picture flatters me exceedingly as it proves the share I have in your affection; I comply with it with pleasure, & will sit for the picture as soon as possible, but I fear I shall not be able to send it you very soon as I must wait for a safe conveyance which in this time of war is not easy to be met with; however be assured I will do my utmost in this particular as in every other to comply with your wishes.

I am happy to hear that you have had good accounts of your brothers Weaver & William; they seem to be successful & happy in their situation. I sincerely wish they may ever continue to be so. I can easily imagine how much satisfaction my cousin William's return would give you; what you tell me of your brother James gives me great pleasure. I suppose he is much grown since I saw him; I do not think we should either of us know one another again, I fancy we are both a little altered since the time when he made verses on me in which he compared me to Venus & I know not what other divinity, & played off fireworks in the cellar in honour of my charms. This happened as you may recollect in a visit I paid to Tonbridge some years ago.

In your last you gave me a description of a ball you had been at, I suppose you have been to more than one since. It is an amusement you seem to be fond of, & I doubt not but you have reason to be so, as I daresay you never go into publick without being distinguished. You mention your desire of being well dressed. It is a very natural one & usual to young persons as I know by experience. I have since my marriage endeavoured to find out some pretty silk which I might send you for a gown, as I have long wished to give my dearest Cousin this small mark of my regard but the not knowing exactly your taste & the great difficulty & risk of sending unmade silk has at last induced me to beg you to accept a draft on Mr. Hoare, Mama's Banker & which she will put into my letter, in its stead. You may in this manner make purchase of what is most agreeable to you. I hope my dear Philly will not be offended at this freedom. It is far from my heart & intentions to do anything that can give her pain; on the contrary there is nothing I wish more than to convince her how truly I love her & that in every circumstance of my life she will find my friendship & regard for her the same.

As for me I have danced more this winter than in all the rest of my life put together. Indeed I am almost ashamed to say what a racketing life I have led, but it was really almost unavoidable, Paris has been remarkably gay this year on account of the birth of the Dauphin. This event was celebrated by illuminations, fireworks, balls etc. The entertainment of the latter kind given at court was amazingly fine. The Court of France is at all times brilliant, but on this occasion the magnificence was beyond conception. The ball was given in a most noble saloon, adorned with paintings, sculpture, gilding etc. etc. Eight thousand lights disposed in the most beautiful forms shewed to advantage the richest & most elegant dresses, the most beautiful women, & the noblest Assembly perhaps anywhere to be beheld; nothing but gold silver & diamonds & jewels of all kinds were to be seen on every side. Her Majesty, who is handsome at all times had her charms not a little heightened by the magnificence of her adjustment. It was a kind of Turkish dress made of a silver grounded silk intermixed with blue & entirely trimmed & almost covered with jewels. A sash & tassels of diamonds went round her waist, her sleeves were puffed & confined in several places with diamonds, large knots of the same fastened a flowing veil of silver gauze; her hair which is remarkably handsome was adorned with the most beautiful jewels of all kinds intermixed with flowers & a large plume of white feathers. The king had a gold grounded coat entirely embroidered with jewels, the Comte d'Artois & the Princesses were dressed with equal magnificence, & the persons of the Court by no means fell short of them. In short altogether it was the finest sight I ever beheld, & I cannot give you a better idea of it than the one which struck me at the time, which was this: it answered exactly to the description given in the Arabian Nights entertainments of enchanted palaces.

Besides this ball we have had many others, but luckily for me they are now nearly over, as so much dancing, altho' perfectly to my taste, does not agree quite so well with my health, which tho' pretty good is not strong, that is I am seldom or ever ill, but my constitution is naturally delicate. I hope to spend this summer quietly. I do not think I shall quit Paris for more than a week or fortnight at a time. The Comte has an estate, but as it is at a great distance & as I have an elegant & convenient house here in an airy situation with a large garden, I prefer spending the summer where I am, especially as I have a number of acquaintances whose country seats are at a few miles distance, with whom I may spend as much time as I like; besides Paris is not like London, which is entirely empty during the summer, on the contrary it is all the year round full of company, there are a thousand amusements & I think it preferable if anything at present to what it is in winter.

I hope I shall soon have the pleasure of hearing from you, I promise you I will answer you directly, & that you shall find me in future a better correspondent that I have been hitherto. Pray do not forget to give me your address. I shall direct this according to the date of yours, but I much fear its not reaching you. I beg you will say a thousand kind things from me to my Uncle & Aunt & cousins, assure them of my kind love & best wishes in both of which Mama & their new cousin join; the latter to whom I communicate the kind things you say on his account is exceedingly flattered by them; he begged that I would assure you how much he wished the continuance of your regard as well as the pleasure of knowing you which he hopes one day to have. I begin to think that if ever you meet I may have some reason to be jealous. Consider, my dear, you are young & pretty, he is young & reckoned handsome, in the Military & a Frenchman besides – how many reasons to doubt his constancy; be that as it will, I assure you I shall take the matter very patiently; I am not of a jealous disposition, & you & I are too good friends ever to quarrel about our conquests.

I have wrote you quite a volume. It is time to have mercy & to leave off, besides I am forced to end my letter as I am obliged to leave room for the draft. I have had it put in such a manner as for you to be able to cut it off & give it to your Father to receive when he goes to London, as I imagine you would not much chuse (nor should I myself wish it) to give my letter out of your hands, I end therefore over leaf.

Adieu, my dearest cousin, let me hear from you soon, do not doubt my attachment, on the contrary be assured I am & ever will be your most affectionate friend & relation, Eliza Hancock, Countess de Feuillide.

The Walter family had now moved from Ightham to Borough Green; Mrs. Hancock's account at Hoare's Bank shows that Eliza's gift to Phylly was six guineas, which was paid out to William Hampson Walter on 18th April 1782. Another miniature of Eliza, with some of her dark brown hair enclosed at the back, and with the inscription 'Amoris et Amicitiae' ('Of Love and Friendship') was in the possession of Phylly's collateral descendants in 1908, but its present location is unknown. It was presumably painted in response to Phylly's request as mentioned in this letter.

The Dauphin referred to here is not the little boy who was so briefly Louis XVII and died wretchedly in prison during the Revolution, but his elder brother, the first son of Louis XVI and Marie Antoinette, who lived only from 1781–89.

The Walters now moved again, apparently from necessity rather than choice, to Stone Street, near Wrotham, in Kent, where they stayed for a year or two; and after another long interval Eliza wrote again:

Paris 1st May 1783 – Had I consulted my inclination alone I should long since have assured You my Dearest Cousin of the pleasure I received from your kind & entertaining Epistle but the hopes of conveying my letter in a manner less expensive to You than by the post induced me to wait for an opportunity of sending it which I have been at last happy enough to meet with.

You inform me of your having once more changed your abode & I think it not unlikely but your next may contain a similar intelligence from the account You give me of your habitation which seems to require a mind no less contented than your own to be in any degree satisfied with. To judge from your description Stone Street can have no other recommendation than that of its vicinity to Fair Lawn both itself & its environs being equally unpleasant. I can easily conceive the trouble & inconvenience such frequent removals must be attended with. I have experienced such a situation too often in my Life not to be well acquainted with all its disagreeable consequences.

It was with much concern I learnt the accident my Cousin William had met with. I hope however that his presence or the News of his perfect recovery have by this time made You amends for all the anxiety You have suffered on his account.

I have some idea You may have My Uncle & Aunt Austen with You at present as in a letter Mamma has received from them they mention their intention of paying You a visit about this time. They were to set out on a little tour at Easter & to take Kent in their way; The journey You purposed has doubtless taken place long since, I wish much to hear whether You were satisfied with your stay at Spring Grove & whether itself and its inhabitants answered your expectations.

The peace has at last taken place, little to the Satisfaction of the political world but much to mine. The evils of war are so numerous & so dreadful that in my opinion we can hardly pay too dear for their cessation. This event likewise affords me the greatest pleasure as it will hasten my return to my native country, a moment I look forward to with much joy as it will give me an opportunity of assuring My Dear Phila, my relations & all those who are kind enough to remember me that neither time nor absence have weakened my affection for them. I had once hopes of seeing England this Autumn but I fear that will not be in my power as I cannot well avoid making a journey into Guienne before I leave France. The Comte's Mother who inhabits that province & who is far advanced in Years having the greatest desire to see me, My first project must therefore be subordinate to this latter & cannot take place before it has been put into execution.

Paris has been very gay this winter a great number of private Balls have not a little contributed to enliven it. A new & elegant Opera house has been built since the dreadful accident which destroyed the other two winters ago, but the Public who are rather hard to please are not satisfied with it, & there is therefore a much finer one fitting up at the Thuillieries [sic]. *You may judge of its extent when I tell you that I have been assured of its having had Operas represented in it in which appeared a troop of five hundred horse for this theatre has been built for some years, by an Italian named Servandoni in imitation of those of Italy. I have not yet seen it & therefore cannot judge of the truth of the above report but in my opinion the most agreeable circumstance is its being situated in the midst of so fine a Garden as the Thuilleries as by this means people will be able to take the air both between the Acts & after the Opera a thing necessary in this place where the theatres are open the whole year & as much frequented in the midst of summer as at any other time.*

The gay world have lately been taken up with Longchamps, a kind of fashion which I will endeavor to give You some account of. Longchamps is a Monastery situated in the Bois de Boulogne a delightful wood I have already mentioned to You in the environs of Paris. It was formerly the custom to go thither to hear Vespers the three last days of Passion Week, but Devotion has given place to Vanity, Every Body now goes to Longchamps not to say their Prayers but to shew their fine Cloaths & fine Equipages. They do not even enter the Convent but content themselves with parading in the Avenue that leads to it in the stile of the Coaches in Hyde Park of a Sunday, their Appearance is however much finer for the number & magnificence of the Carriages are incredible. Most People have new & elegant ones on this occasion with four or six fine horses, as many Lacqueys as possible behind sometimes to the number of eight & often running footmen. The Elegants or fashionable young men are in general either on horseback or in open carriages. The Queen & Royal Family are generally there & what much contributed to the beauty of the Shew this year several of the Princesses made their appearance in open

Calashes drawn by six horses; the most elegant were the Dutchess de Chartres Cousin to his Majesty & the Princess de Lamballe whose natural beauty does not want all the additions it had received on this occasion for all the Ladies are very much dressed. You may imagine that the Coup d'oeil of the whole must be striking.

Whilst I am speaking of fashionable follies I cannot avoid mentioning the changes in the toilette. The hair instead of being turned up behind has been worn for some time past in two or three Clubs, but it is said this mode will not continue as it does not meet with her Majesty's approbation. Large yellow Straw Hats such as I believe You may have seen worn by the Hay Makers are universally adopted, they are called a la Marlborough as well as every thing else of late. This great General certainly could never have imagined that so many years after his Death his name [would] have been borrowed to set off all the frippery of Dress, Ribbands [and] Silk. [All] is a la Marlborough & the prevailing colour, is la mort de Marlbor[ough], the [death of] Marlborough, which is a kind of Pompadour shot with black the f[inest] tha[t can] possibly be imagined. The cause of this <u>Marlborough rage</u> is [the] most [curious in] the world. The Dauphin's Nurse was one day singing an Old Ballad [to] put him to sleep called the Death of Marlborough; The Queen happened to hear her was pleased with it & of course the whole court had it by heart the next day; The people who like to ape their betters followed their example, a Pantomime appeared on the subject, verses without number were composed, & the Fashion became general in a very short time.

If the weather is as fine on your side the water as on ours, You must greatly enjoy the Country. As to me I am at present writing to You in the midst of a little grove in my Garden which is very large for town as you may judge when I tell you that it supplies me with a vast quantity of flowers, Peaches, Melons &cc. It is what I shall most regret in quitting this House which however I mean to do as it is too small.

Mamma has I thank God had much better health this year than last, She is however very thin & that sometimes makes me uneasy; Her presence is one of the greatest & enhances every other blessing I enjoy. I am happy to hear My Uncle & Aunt are well, May they long continue so both for their sakes & your own. I am sorry My Cousin James is not yet settled to his wishes. It was with surprize that I heard of Mr. Hall's being married to a second wife. I hope to have the pleasure of hearing from You as I wish much to know whether Your Brother William is arrived, I think it besides a great while since the date of your last letter. You have no doubt spent some time in London this Year, I hear it has been very brilliant.

Adieu My Dearest Cousin a thousand loves & good wishes from all here to yourself & family be assured of their sincerity as well as of that of the Affection with which I remain eternally yours, Eliza Csse. de Feuillide.

I fear You will be troubled to make out my letter, I am sensible it is cruelly scrawled, but I have been much hurried & it is so near dark that I can hardly see to guide my pen, once more adieu my dearest friend.

The Revd George Austen and his wife did indeed visit Kent that spring, taking with them two of their young sons, Henry and Francis, to introduce them to their various cousins in the county. Fairlawne was an estate between Wrotham and Shipbourne, then owned by the Duke of Cleveland's family, so Eliza was evidently hoping that Phylly might find some benefit from having rich and aristocratic neighbours; Spring Grove, near Wye, was the home of the more plebeian Brett family. In the wider world, preliminary Articles of Peace between Britain and France had been signed at Paris on 20th January 1783, and the final Treaty of Versailles, which also recognised American independence, was signed on 3rd September 1783.

In the late summer of 1783 Paris went wild with excitement over the sudden invention of aerial balloons – in August a M. Charles, aided by the Robert brothers, ascended in a hydrogen-filled 'Globe', and the Montgolfier brothers made several ascents in the following months in hot-air balloons. Eliza wrote to tell Phylly of this incredible conquest of the skies, but her letter, 16 in Phylly's numeration, has not survived, and is just tantalisingly referred to in her next, No. 17:

Paris 7th May 1784 – I have alas so often begun my letters to You My aimiable Cousin with Apologies for long silence that altho' there never was more occasion for them than at this moment, I think You will allow me to omit them, in the first place because I look on a set of insipid excuses as a poor amends for having neglected writing & lastly because I flatter myself You are too well persuaded of the pleasure I feel in assuring You of my attachment, to need any protestations on my part how little my will is concerned whenever I defer answering your kind Epistles.

I experienced much pleasure from the account You give me of my Uncle Geo: Austen's Family. Each of My Cousins seems to be every thing their parents could wish them. Such intelligence would have given me the completest satisfaction had it not been accompanied by the melancholy news of the death of the valuable Mrs. Cooper, I sincerely lament her Loss & sympathise with the grief it must have occasioned. Both Mamma & myself were very apprehensive of the influence of this event on my Aunt's Health but fortunately the last accounts from Steventon assure us that the whole family continue well.

I am infinitely flattered by the kind impatience You express to see me in England. Be assured I partake it, & that the moment which restores me to my country will appear to me one of the happiest of my Life. I trust this period is not far distant as I am on the eve of a Journey which I have ever considered as the forerunner of that I so much wish to engage in. The latter end of this month is fixed for my setting out for Guyenne; I promise myself much pleasure from this excursion as it will not only make me acquainted with my husband's family & possessions but give me an opportunity of seeing the finest & most considerable part of France. You will stare perhaps when I tell You this <u>*excursion*</u> *I talk so coolly of removes me only about Six hundred & fifty miles from Paris. A Less frequent Traveller than myself would shrink at the thoughts of such an undertaking, but it occasions me none but agreeable Sensations. I have my share of the* <u>*wandering spirit*</u> *our Countrymen are in general possessed with which together with my being so early accustomed to a* <u>*vagabond*</u> *Life makes me seldom regret a change of scene, besides I am delighted at the thoughts of visiting Spain from which I shall be removed a few days journey only, I have not however the least inclination to fix my abode at Madrid, most Ladies would prefer the manners of the capital I at present inhabit.*

I gave You some account of the Globes or Ballons in my last; The attention of the public has been once more awakened by an improvement attempted in this discovery by a M. Blanchard who undertook by means of wings & a rudder to direct the course of the <u>*Ballon*</u>*, on the Day appointed for the experiment a most prodigious concourse assembled to witness it, but alas the obstinacy of one individual soon overset their expectations. It had been agreed that M. Blanchard & a Benedictine Monk should ascend with the Globe in order to regulate its motions, but at the instant they were seating themselves in the car fixed under this machine for the purpose of their conveyance one of the young Men belonging to the Ecole militaire (or military Academy) insisted on being of the party nor could the strenuous opposition he met with prevail on him to relinquish his design, a violent scuffle ensued & the wings & rudder were soon demolished. M. Blanchard had however the courage notwithstanding the shattered condition of his vehicle to set out alone for the aeirial regions, he ascended to the height of 1500 fathoms & returned from thence in perfect health & safety to the astonishment of most of the Spectators.*

I imagine You must long before this have been relieved from the anxiety You express in your last at not having heard from your brother William,

Montgolfier's ascent of 19 September 1783 at Versailles.
Blanchard's less successful attempt followed on 2 March 1784.
British Library 8755 bbb49

I sincerely wish You may have had favorable accounts & that he is entirely recovered from his lameness. I am happy to find my Uncle & Aunt enjoy so good a state of health & hope neither them nor your self suffered in this particular from the uncommon severity of last wint[er. I] am told the weather in

England much resembled that on the con[tinent]; I do not remember ever to have experienced such intense cold, [the streets] of Paris were for some time almost impracticable from the snow & ice with which they were filled, nor had we the comfort of being warm in our own houses to make us amends for being obliged to stay there, one froze by the fireside & never did I so much regret the Stoves of Germany & Flanders. Dancing was the only effectual method of rendering one's existence less uncomfortable, & such I conclude to have been the general opinion since the number of Balls this Year greatly surpassed that of the preceding ones.

It is still the fashion to translate or rather murder, Shakespear; Romeo & Juliet, Lear, Macbeth & Coriolanus have successively made their appearance on the French stage, in my opinion they make but an uncouth figure in their foreign attire. You are without doubt acquainted with the Spanish Barber a piece taken from the French, its author has just given us the sequel of the story entitled Marriage of Figaro, this production meets with very great success. In the musical way we have at present some celebrated performers, Madame St. Huberti first singer at the opera enchants every one by her voice as well as her inimitable talent for tragedy. On her performing the part of Dido before his Majesty he immediately settled an annual pension of 2000 Livres on her besides her usual appointments. There is likewise a Mademoiselle Paradies whose infinite skill in Music & particularly on the Harpsichord appears still more astonishing from her having been totally blind from her infancy.

Should You let me have the pleasure of hearing from You before the expiration of this month You will be so kind as to direct to me as usual but in case You make it longer before You write You will then address your Letter, to me, to the care of Miss Hinchliffe Woodstock Street Hanover Square London. This Lady is an intimate friend of Mamma's has frequent opportunities of sending to France & will not fail of forwarding your Letter to me. Adieu my dear friend, Mamma joins me in affectionate compts. to my Uncle Aunt & all your family, believe to me [sic] *most sincerely & unalterably yours, Eliza de Feuillide.*

The family news Phylly had passed on from England was that Mrs. Cooper, the sister of Mrs. George Austen, had died unexpectedly on 25th October 1783. The balloon ascent to which Eliza refers was that made from the Champ de Mars by Jean-Pierre Blanchard (1753–1809), one of the pioneers of ballooning, on 2nd March 1784. The 'Spanish Barber' is now better known as 'The Barber of Seville', by Beaumarchais; Mme. St. Huberti married in

1790 the Comte d'Antraigues, a professional diplomatic intriguer, forger, and double agent. He and his wife came to England in 1806 with credentials said to be from the Emperor of Russia, and something of their subsequent history is given in Chapter V.

Unfortunately Eliza's next two letters are missing; they must have described her journey to the south of France and her first meeting with her husband's family. The Comte de Feuillide had a widowed mother, a younger brother Jean-Gabriel and two sisters, Dorothée and Augustine; whether they welcomed this strange young foreign wife, with her mother in tow, can only be a matter for conjecture. In Eliza's surviving letters, there is only one brief and formal reference to her mother-in-law, when the latter died the following year.

Eliza's husband was now anxious to turn himself into a prosperous landowner; the French Government was eager to encourage the improvement of agriculture, and in 1782 the Comte de Feuillide had obtained a royal licence to take over and reclaim 5000 acres of swamp land, Le Marais, near Nérac, which could be held tax-free provided it was drained and made productive. He at once set labourers to work digging dykes across the swamp, and until such time as the ground dried out sufficiently for a new house to be built, he and Eliza rented the little Château de Jourdan in the village of Ste. Meille, near Gabarret, a country villa with dormer windows and pepper-pot turrets at the corners of its stone façades. It stood on a hilltop, looking out over woodland to miles of flat countryside and wide skies.

A sidelight on Eliza's life in Guyenne now comes from another source. In 1784 the Austens' wealthy Kentish cousins, Mr. and Mrs. Thomas Knight of Godmersham, set out on a leisurely tour of France for the sake of Mrs. Knight's health. She wrote home regularly to her sister-in-law Jane Knight with news of their travels, and by the spring of 1785 they were on their way back northwards from the Riviera:

Tonnières, 2nd April, 1785 – We left Montauban yesterday & slept at Agen. Mr. Austen having sent us word that the Comte de Feuillides house was near Agen, Mr. K. wrote to Mrs. Hancock, from Nice, informing her of our design of visiting them in our return, & desiring an answer to meet him at Toulouse or Montauban, but at neither of those places did he find any; I make no doubt but she has written, but her letter is perhaps sent on to Bordeaux: at Agen we enquired the distance of this house, & our Hostess happening to come from their neighbourhood, we got good information, but Mr. K. finding it was forty miles off, & a cross road, did not think it worth while to go; he therefore wrote a Letter of excuse to Mrs. Hancock.

Bordeaux, 10th April, 1785 – Mr. K. has had a letter here from Mrs. Hancock, in answer to one he wrote to her from Agen, & the Comtesse has been so obliging as to send me recommendations to some Shops at Paris: her billet was written in a very elegant style, & in a language much better adapted for Notes than our vulgar one, but I own I shou'd have thought her less affected, tho' perhaps less genteel, had it been in english: Mrs. H. mentions their design of visiting England next Spring, but as the Comte is ingaged in the cultivation of a large tract of Land, I shou'd imagine their coming must be uncertain – It is impossible for any thing to be civiler than her letters, or the messages she has sent from her Son & Daughter respecting our visit to them.

Eliza wrote again to Phylly, this letter being also in a very elegant style, and demonstrated the benefits of her education by tossing off a quotation from Alexander Pope's poem 'Eloisa to Abelard':

Chateau de Jourdan, 25th July 1785 – My Dear Cousin, I received too much pleasure from the perusal of your entertaining Letter, to defer any longer thanking you for it, & assuring You I rejoice too sincerely in every account of your own & estimable Family's Welfare, not to have experienced much Satisfaction from the particulars You give me, relating to your Brother & Sister, whom I congratulate as well as yourself on so pleasing an acquisition as your little Nephew, but at the same time I cannot help regretting that the decided Taste for nursing, you express, should not have an Opportunity of exercising itself on objects still more interesting than even so charming a Godson, as the little Henry, but I comfort myself with the reflection that the more you deliberate, the surer You will be of your choice, & besides I entertain the hope of the possibility [of] arriving time enough in England to dance at your Wedding.

I am sorry to find My Aunt has been indisposed, but flatter myself She has long before this got the better of her troublesome Complaint, which from your account I take to be much of the same nature with the Fevers which have prevailed in this part of the World, & which have affected every part of our

Family excepting Mamma & myself, As to M. de feuillide his Health, already very precarious for some time past, has not been able to withstand the severe Shock he received from the Loss of his Mother about Six Weeks ago; whose sudden Death preceded only by three quarters of an Hour illness, was a great addition to the grief for a Parent who adored her Son, & whose affectionate behaviour to me entitled her to my sincerest regrets.

The Physicians agree in prescribing the Waters of Bagnères to Monsieur de Feuillide, which has decided us to put the Plan we had long had of visiting them in execution as soon as Possible, We purpose spending August & perhaps September at this place, which is about two days journey from hence I mean with our own Horses, & I am assured to be one of the most delightful in the World. It is situated at the foot of the Pyrenean Mountains (very near neighbour of course to Spain) & abounding in all the amusements water drinking places generally afford & particularly has the advantage of assembling a number of my Countrymen, for I am told there are already fifteen english Families established there. A change of Scene is indeed I think indispensable for us all, & can alone dispel the Gloom the Mind contracts from such repeated strokes as I have had to acquaint You with of late, but let me not omit the acknowledgements I owe You for the kind concern You express for the melancholy event my last informed you of, & which has caused me too much real Grief not to be very sensible of the part You take in it.

The unusual want of Rain which you assure me has been complained of in England has not been less sensibly felt on the Continent, but we have been fortunate enough not to have our harvest suffer very materially from it, for thus far self interest brings me acquainted with farming concerns, which otherwise I confess I might chance never to trouble my Head about, since I am far from having the same partiality for this kind of occupation which those of the Nursery inspire You with; However, unworthy, & incapable as I am, of tasting the Pleasures which result from the Study of Agriculture, I cannot be indifferent to the Success of an undertaking which not only considerably adds to my Husband's Fortune, but in a manner immortalises himself; I have without doubt already mentioned to You a Donation made by the King to Mons. de Feuillide & his heirs for ever, of 5000 Acres of Land little distant from his Paternal Estate, at that time & for many preceding Ages entirely covered with Water. Very considerable & expensive Works carried on for eighteen Months past, have entirely drained this large extent of Ground & nothing can equal the Public Surprise at the accomplishment of what was deemed impracticable; at the same time I have the Pleasure of seeing My Husband looked upon as the Benefactor of a whole Province, from the Salubrity its Air has acquired by being freed from the pernicious exhalations of such an extent of stagnant Water, very advantageously replaced by a fertile plain not less agreeable to the view than I flatter myself it will be profitable to [its] owners.

The Public News must long ere this have acquainted You with Mr. Hastings' arrival in England, a circumstance which gives great Satisfaction to his Friends, that is to say to a very extensive circle, for who that is neither blinded by interest nor biassed by Party can possibly refuse Esteem & Admiration to a Character too much the ornament of the present Age not to be consigned in the Records of succeeding ones.

I have lately had the Pleasure of hearing from my Friend Mrs. Farhill, late Miss Wilson, who has made as good use of her time as my new Cousin, for it is now six weeks since She became Mother of a Daughter not less welcome than your little Nephew.

But I must not forget to answer your enquiries concerning the justness of your ideas of a Cloister especially as I am the better able to satisfy them, since I perfectly remember Bourn; Was I only to consult Gallic politeness, I should tell You the moments I had passed there with You could never be forgot, but I yet have so much Old English Sincerity left, as to confess, the Toys purchased at the famous Fair we visited together & the frequent remonstrances I experienced for not being able to resist the Sour Apples this delightful Mansion afforded greatly contributed I believe to impress it on my Mind. You are right in judging it in many respects resembling a Monastery, but it wants the high Walls & the double iron Grates, often armed with Spikes, which attend the latter; & yet my Dear Cousin dismal as such an Abode may seem I can believe it sometimes is that of Happiness, as some good Nuns who wanted me to increase the Sisterhood once endeavored to persuade me, & tho' I must confess I have not shewn much deference to this Opinion, which the difference of Religion & many other powerful motives would never have suffered me to conform my Conduct to, yet I make no doubt there is here & there, but only here & there, a Recluse to be met with who enjoys that Serenity of Mind which must result from a perfect indifference to the World, a freedom from all its Cares, & the elevating (tho' mistaken) idea of having made the most acceptable of all Sacrifices to her Maker & the brightest rewards awaiting her in another world, for all She has given up in this; such a frame of mind is too difficult to attain, for more than one in a thousand to compass it, but I look upon her to be a fortunate being to whom may be applied the charming Lines

> *'How happy is the blameless Vestals lot*
> *The World forgetting by the World forgot*

> *Eternal Sunshine of the spotless mind*
> *Each Prayer accepted, & each Wish resign'd.'*

I beg You will not deprive me of the Pleasure of hearing from You soon, continue I beseech You My Dear Cousin to give me every particular relating to yourself & Family & be assured the distance I am at, altho' it prevents my sharing your pleasures & occupations in Person, does not any ways influence my Sentiments nor render me indifferent to your Welfare for which you will always have my sincere wish, I beg you to make it acceptable to my Uncle & Aunt as well as a thousand Loves & Compliments from Mamma M. de feuillide & myself to them & to You, Adieu My Dear & Aimiable Friend I remain most affectionately yours, Eliza de Feuillide.

You mention your expectation of a Visit from Mrs. & Miss Depasso. Pray tell me whether the Beauty & accomplishments of the latter are equal to the very great praise I have heard of them.

Phylly and her parents had now moved to Seal, a village near Sevenoaks; local tradition says that they lived in the cottage known as The Grey House, opposite the church, but so far documentary evidence to support this claim is lacking. Phylly's youngest brother James had now taken Holy Orders, married a distant cousin Frances-Maria Walter, and gone to live in Lincolnshire, where he became Headmaster of Brigg Grammar School and also Vicar of Market Rasen – the 'little Henry' referred to here was their first son, born on 28th January 1785. Bourn Hall, in Cambridgeshire, was the seat of Mr. Henry Lyell, the employer of Phylly's father, though the date when Eliza and Phylly visited there is unknown. Other home news to which Eliza refers is that Warren Hastings had finally returned to England on 12th June 1785, after 35 years service in India; and on a more personal level, her friend Mrs. Farhill, who had been married on 8th July 1784, had given birth to a child before the first anniversary of her wedding. Eliza may have received the news of these two births with mixed feelings, since the 'melancholy event' in her own life must mean she had just recently suffered a miscarriage. Now that the work on her husband's estate was beginning to show results in the form of permanent drainage canals, new buildings, and reclaimed land laid out in fields with the promise of woodlands and vineyards, it was obviously desirable that there should be an heir to enjoy this property and her disappointment would therefore be all the greater.

Chateau de Jourdan 17th January 1786 – I really My Dear Cousin dare not venture to look at the date of your last Letter, for I am sensible it is a most shameful time since I ought to have acknowledged its receipt but heinous as my offence appears, I still venture to hope that my sincere contrition for having committed it, & the manner in which my moments have really been taken up, will obtain me my pardon, for a two months stay at Bagnères (the Water of this place having been as I mentioned to You in my last presented to M. de F.) & a Visit on my return from thence have literally not left me a leisure hour for this great while past.

I flatter myself You will partake my Satisfaction in being able to inform You that the purpose of the abovementioned Journey has been entirely answered, & your outlandish Cousin's Health & good Looks perfectly restored indeed I have every reason to be pleased with my excursion which has brought me acquainted with one of the most beautiful Spots in the World. The Town of Bagnères is tolerably extensive & makes no inelegant appearance from the quantity of Marble its environs afford having been taken advantage of for its construction. It is situated at the foot or rather in the midst of the Pyrenees, part of which are cultivated & bear the strongest marks of fertility & abundance while the rest are covered with eternal snows. This uncommon & striking Landscape is added to & heightened, by literally chrystal streams such as I had till now imagined to exist no where but in a Poets Brain, Vines formed into festoons more regular & more beautiful than the Decorations of any Theatre ever exhibited, Villages dispersed here & there, & a thousand other objects still more picturesque, concur to finish the Picture & render the Environs of Bagnères really inchanting.

The Amusements the place itself affords resemble those to be met with at Bath, Tunbridge Wells, &cc, a Theatre open every Day & frequent Balls are the principal publick Diversions, but what the most contributed to my spending my time in a very agreeable manner was my meeting with a most charming Society, chiefly english, amongst others Lord & Lady Chesterfield now on an Embassy to the Court of Madrid, who kept open House & whose aimiable manners contributed not a little to the agréments of Bagnères, the marks of Friendship I received from this Family and from the Ambassadress in particular, are such as I can never forget, this latter is indeed one of the most charming Women, I have ever met with; in short My Dear Cousin here am I once more restored to rural quiet & tranquillity but which I believe will be but of short date, for I am on the point of undertaking a new ramble, I have promised to spend the Carnival which in France is the gayest Season of the Year in a very agreeable Society who have erected an elegant Theatre for the purpose of acting Plays amongst ourselves, & who intend having Balls at least twice a week but the pleasure I expect from this jaunt is very inferior to that which I promise myself from a much longer journey which there is some prospect of my shortly undertaking.

It is now in agitation whether I shall or shall not set out for England next june; My husband votes for the affirmative but I am not myself quite determined from some reasons which You will be a better judge of, when I have let You into a little piece of my <u>family history</u>, namely My Dear Friend, that [it] is now two months since I have had a prospect of giving You an additional relation, should a Son be <u>in store</u> for M. de Feuillide he greatly wishes him to be a native of England for he pays me the Compliment of being very partial to my Country; but I own I have some repugnance to undertaking so long a journey in a situation so unfit for travelling. This important question must be determined in the course of a few months, & I am the more impatient for its decision as that of a visit I have entertained hopes of, depends in a great measure on it. I know not whether You have already heard that my Cousin James Austen has thoughts of spending some months with me next Spring I fear he will not think it worth while to undertake a journey of such a length should [I quit the] Country so soon as I apprehend, & You may easily judge how great a plea[sure this] change in my Cousin's plan would deprive me of.

The account You give [me of] your Brother William afforded me both pain & pleasure, I admire his fortitude & sincerely regret the occasion he has of exercising it, there are few men of his age who could support themselves as he does under such a tryal – may it therefore be the only one himself or any of his Family will have to undergo; indeed I sincerely rejoice whenever I reflect how much reason my Uncle & Aunt have to be satisfied with the Situation & Disposition of each of their Children. You my Dear Cousin contribute as much as any one of them I am sure to the Happiness of your respectable Parents by your chearful & charming Temper & affectionate Behaviour which can leave but one wish to form, that of seeing You united to some one worthy of You, but however should you still persist in reserving the exercise of your talent for <u>nursing</u> for your friends & not have any employment of this sort on your hands on your own <u>account</u> on my arrival in England I shall <u>supplicate</u> your aid for the brat I mean to introduce to You & which I am sure I shall be much at a loss what to do with as never was a being less qualified, nor one who had less taste for the cares of a nursery than your humble Servant.

Mamma who has been some what indisposed of late but is now perfectly recovered sends a thousand Loves & compliments to yourself & Family in which her Daughter & Son in law join her as well as in good wishes, the Compliments of the Season, & the desire that You & all that are dear to You may be witness of many happy returns of it. Adieu My Dear Cousin let me have the pleasure of hearing from You soon, I own I do not deserve it but we are taught to return good for evil, en attendant so agreeable a moment as the perusal of your entertaining Letters always proves to me, I remain my Dear Friend most sincerely & affectionately yours, Eliza de Feuillide.

The Lord Chesterfield whom Eliza met in Bagnères was not the 4th Earl (1694–1773), famous for his *Letters*, but his distant cousin and godson Philip Stanhope (1755–1815), who became the 5th Earl as his kinsman had no legitimate heir. The 5th Earl was appointed Ambassador Extraordinary and Minister Plenipotentiary to Madrid on 1st January 1784, and resigned this position in 1787, having been so lazy as never to succeed in crossing the Spanish border. It was said of him that he had a fair measure of shrewdness and affability, but that his tastes and manners were unaffectedly bucolic.

Guyenne 23rd May 1786 – I will not attempt, My Dear Cousin, to make You any apology for not having sooner answered your last kind Letter, since I trust You are too well convinced of my affection, to attribute my Silence to any other cause than its real one, that is to say, numberless avocations, & that precarious state of Health, too frequent an attendant on such a Situation as my present one, wch. (it is literally true –) has hitherto rendered all sorts of application & writing in particular too painful to me, not for my Correspondents to excuse my having somewhat neglected them.

It was with the truest concern that I received the account of the dreadful accident which had nearly proved so fatal to You & no less sincerely do I congratulate You on your almost miraculous escape from so great a danger. I flatter myself you are by this time entirely free from all its disagreeable consequences, & no longer undergo the heavy penance which confinement must prove to one of your lively disposition, but for which however You have had some sort of amends made You, since as You observe yourself, it is to this inability of quitting your seat, that You owe an opportunity of becoming acquainted with the interesting particulars You are so kind as to communicate me.

I much approve my aimiable Friend of your rejecting the Suitor whom both ill nature & Stupidity render unworthy of your choice, but I own I feel somewhat inclined to favour the humble Servant to whom there is nothing more material to be objected than his bordering on forty, & wearing a Wig, as to the first of these objections I think it a small one, & such as the good qualities You enumerate, amply atone for. The wearing a Wig I own is a circumstance of a more serious nature, but would it not be possible for You to prevail on your admirer to relinquish a part of Dress so little suited to your Taste? I had forgot You mention his inhabiting the City, but since he has a fortune sufficient to admit of his quitting a part of the Town which You with reason object to, I should think it would be very easy for You to make him chuse a more eligible situation. You see my Dear Cousin, I am very desirous of your entering a state which I am sure You would do great honor to; I fear however that I plead in vain in favor of the unfortunate being You seem determined to reject, but as You must have a very numerous set of humble Swains at your disposal, I flatter myself that some one amongst them will still give me an opportunity of assisting at your Wedding before I quit my native Country.

You will infer from hence that my visit to England mentioned in my last is no longer a matter of doubt & indeed notwithstanding my reluctance to quitting home in my present situation, & my still greater regret at a separation from the Comte de feuillide at a period when I could the most have wished for his presence, I purpose setting out on this long projected journey the 30th or 31st of this month; but in all probability I shall not reach England before the latter end of June or beginning of July, since it will be impossible for me to avoid making some stay in Paris. I mean to spend a very few Days in London, & if my health allows me, immediately paying a visit to Steventon, because my Uncle informs us, that Midsummer & Christmas are the only Seasons when his Mansion is sufficiently at liberty to admit of his receiving his Friends.

You will easily imagine how much my Thoughts & Time must be taken up at this moment since independant of the fatigue & Bustle inseparable from the preparations for such an expedition as I am about to undertake, my spirits are constantly agitated, & alternately raised & depressed by the idea of once more meeting friends that are very dear to me, & quitting the best of Husbands whose extreme concern at parting with me in my present situation adds greatly to my feelings on this occasion. Had it been possible for him to have quitted the important Works he is carrying on in this part of the World, he would certainly have accompanied me but he has promised to join me as soon as his Affairs can permit him so to do I must endeavor therefore to make myself easy en attendant & look forward only to the satisfaction which I promise myself in being once again an inhabitant of a Country wch. the presence of my friends & Family must ever endear to me. I feel howe[ver] mortified at making what may be termed my first appearance amongst [those] whose approbation I am so ambitious of, in a situation so thoroughly unfa[vourable to] good Looks as that I at present labour under; & my vanity is not a little hurt at the idea of presenting myself in my native Land after so long an absence, with a visage of a comfortable length at all times, but which my being grown extremely thin since I have aspired to the honor of being a Mother, has added about an ell to, whilst my waist is as You may suppose much more increased in circumference than ever my face in Length; add to all this a very tolerable share of Tan with which I have contrived to heighten the native brown of my Complexion, during a two Years residence in the country, notwithstanding all these disadvantages I yet flatter myself my friends will receive me kindly, since after all the qualifications of the heart & not those of the exterior are what are most to be attended to.

Adieu My Dear Cousin till the happy moment when I can assure You in Person of my attachment, for neither my Health nor Time will admit of my conversing any longer with You on Paper for the present, I trust the uncertain state of the one & the manner in which the latter has been taken up for I have had about twenty different things to attend to whilst writing this wretched Scrawl, will apologize for its incoherence & the innumerable faults it abounds with, but my strongest claim to your indulgence consists in the sincere attachment with which I beg My Dear Cousin to be assured I shall ever remain her most affectionate Eliza de Feuillide.

Mamma desires a thousand kind things in which I most sincerely join to My Uncle Aunt yourself & Family.

CHAPTER III

A racketing life

1786–92

✡

ELIZA AND HER MOTHER set off for England as planned, but either she had miscalculated her pregnancy or else the long journey from the south of France brought on a premature delivery, because her son was born at Calais on 25th June 1786. He was given an impressive string of Anglo-French names – Hastings-François-Louis-Henri-Eugène – though he was not actually baptised until a year later, 1st June 1787, when Eliza took him to the fashionable London church of St. George's Hanover Square for the purpose. This delayed baptism is unusual for the period, and the fact that the baby was made a member of the Church of England rather than the Church of Rome also seems odd, given that his father was a Frenchman and little Hastings might be expected to inherit the Le Marais estate in France. There was however a strong Protestant tradition in Nérac, and it may be that the Capot de Feuillide family conformed outwardly to Catholicism and were prepared to accept the Anglican wishes of the Comte's foreign wife.

After the necessary time for her recovery, Eliza, with her mother and new baby, arrived in England in July 1786, staying at Lothian's Hotel in Albemarle Street ('one of the hotels chiefly for the accommodation of Families recently arrived in London'), and immediately began renewing acquaintance with old friends from Indian days. In London they called on Sir William and Lady Burrell in Harley Street; the Burrells were very rich, and Sir William, a scholar and antiquary, who was considerably older than his wife and in rather poor health, had just acquired The Deepdene, a fine estate on the outskirts of Dorking, in Surrey. Lady Burrell's father Sir Charles Raymond was one of Warren Hastings's friends; she herself had some literary talent, and in later years published several volumes of poems and plays. She now wrote a charming short poem in welcome:

To Eliza – When you no more have power to please / By artless elegance and ease; / When that dear guileless heart shall grow / Cold as the Pyrenean snow; / Light and inconstant as the wind, /Artful, capricious, and unkind, / Devoid of honour, virtue, sense, / And ev'ry claim to excellence, / Then will Eliza cease to be / Thus tenderly esteem'd by me; / (Whose friendship ev'rything defies, / But cold neglect – and mean disguise.)

From London Eliza and her mother travelled in August to Berkshire for a three-week visit to Warren Hastings and his wife Marian, in their newly-purchased house, Beaumont Lodge, near Windsor. Perhaps Eliza named her son Hastings in the hope that her godfather might then be inclined to set up another trust fund in the baby's favour, but if she had had this hope, she was disappointed. In October they were in Surrey, visiting the Woodmans in their country villa at Ewell, and probably calling too upon the Burrells at The Deepdene, to admire not only the mansion house but also the pleasure grounds, which were already well-known for their planned woods and shrubberies, decorative canal of water, pathways winding between alcoves, grottos, caverns and other 'rural retirements', and for having extensive views from the terrace in front of the house over the surrounding countryside. By December they were back in London, and then went to Hampshire to spend Christmas with the Austen family. Mrs. George Austen wrote to Phylly Walter on the last day of the old year, with news of the festivities at the rectory:

Steventon 31st December 1786 – My dear Phylly, I am much obliged to you for your last agreable Letter, & the good news it contain'd, and hope your dear Father & Mother together with yourself continue in as good health as they were at that time, and also your Brother & Sister in Lincolnshire and their two little Boys – I hope your next will inform us that your Brother Weaver is again settled in some place as much to his satisfaction as when he was at Penshurst – We are truly glad to find that our Nephew Williams circumstances are such as to enable him to purchase an Estate; but surely my dear Phylly, if he can afford to do that, he may afford to make a visit to his friends in England during the summer months, and return to his Warmer climate at the approach of Winter. We will not give up all thoughts of seeing him again, and pray tell him as much in your next Letter.

We are now happy in the company of our Sister Hancock Madame de Feuillide & the little Boy; they came to us last Thursday Sennet ['sennet' is the abbreviation of 'seven-night', an old expression meaning a week] & will stay with us till the end of next Month. They all look & seem to be remarkably well, the little Boy grows very fat, he is very fair & very pretty; I don't think your Aunt at all alter'd in any respect, Madame is grown quite lively, when a child we used to think her too grave. We have borrowed a Piano-Forte, and she plays to us every day; on Tuesday we are to have a very snug little dance in our parlour, just our own children, nephew & nieces, (for the two little Coopers come tomorrow) quite a family party, I wish my <u>third niece</u> could be here also; but indeed, I begin to suspect your Mother never intends to gratify that wish. You might as well be in Jamaica keeping your Brother's House, for anything that we see of you or are like to see.

Five of my Children are now at home, Henry, Frank, Charles & my two Girls, who have now quite left school; Frank returns to Portsmouth in a few days, he has but short holidays at Christmas. Edward is well & happy in Switzerland. James set out for La Guienne, on a visit to the Count de Feuillide, near Eight weeks ago, I hope he is got there by this time and am impatient for a Letter; he was wind-bound some weeks in the little Island of Jersey or he would have got to the end of his long Journey by the beginning of this Month. – Every one of our Fire-side join in Love, & Duty as due, and in wishing a happy 87 to our dear Friends at Seal – I am my dear Phylly your affecte. Aunt C. Austen.

This visit to Steventon by Mrs. Hancock and Eliza was their first since October 1776, when Jane had been only a few months old; and it must have been with her eleventh birthday in mind that they brought with them the twelve little volumes of Arnaud Berquin's *L'Ami des Enfans*, a series of simple pious stories and dramatic scenes, intended to teach children French and morality at the same time, and which bear her name on the fly-leaves. Both Jane and Cassandra had been boarding at the Abbey House school in Reading for the last eighteen months or so, but now, as Mrs. Austen said, had come home for good. Of the other Austen children, the eldest, James (1765–1819), was on his way to France, since the Comte de Feuillide seems to have been quite willing to receive his wife's cousin even though she herself was absent; Edward

(1767–1852) was already several months into his Grand Tour of Europe, from which he would not return until 1790; Henry (1771–1850) would soon go up to his father's old college at Oxford, St. John's; Frank (1774–1865) had started his studies at the Royal Naval Academy in Portsmouth; and Charles (1779–1852), as the youngest, was still being taught at home. The 'two little Coopers' were Edward and Jane, the children of Mrs. Austen's deceased sister, and now aged 16 and 15 respectively.

Eliza's next two letters are missing, in which she presumably told Phylly of her recent visit to Steventon, and suggested they should meet in either London or Kent. Letter No. 25 is from her rented house in Marylebone, which was then a newly-developing fashionable residential suburb on the north side of London.

[3] Orchard Street, 9th April 1787 – I am much mortified My Dear Friend that You cannot give me your Company at the Times I mentioned in my last, especially as it will not be in my Power to receive You the latter end of the Month, which My Cousin Henry Austen is to spend with us, & this Visit cannot be deferred because it is most probable he will soon be obliged to residence [sic] *at Oxford. I find therefore I must not flatter myself with seeing You before the latter end of May or beginning of June & will let You know which as soon as I myself can determine, I am really quite provoked I should have been so long in England without seeing You. I am happy to find My Uncle is so much better & that yourself & every part of your Family are in good health, I have likewise much pleasure in finding You pass your Time so much to your Satisfaction, & enjoy those Amusements suited to your Taste & Time of Life, I know that Dancing holds the first place amongst these.*

As to me I have been for some Time past the greatest Rake imaginable & really wonder how such a meagre creature as I am can support so much fatigue, of which the History of one Day will give You some idea, for I only stood from two to four in the Drawing Room & of course loaded with a great Hoop of no inconsiderable Weight, went to the Dutchess of Cumberland's in the Evening, & from thence to Almacks where I staid till five in the Morning, all this I did not many days ago, & am yet alive to tell You of it. I believe tho', I should not be able to support London Hours, & all the racketting of a London Life for a Year together.

You are very good in your inquiries after my little Boy who is in perfect Health, but has got no Teeth yet, which somewhat mortifies his two Mamma's I long to introduce him to You but still more to see You myself. Adieu My

Dear Friend for I am so straightened for time I cannot indulge myself in conversing with You, Pray let me hear from You, as your Letters always give Me the greatest Pleasure. Mamma desires to be most affectionately remembered to You & yours, in which I most heartily join, & beg You to be assured of the sincere attachment with which I shall ever remain your most affectionate Friend & Relation Eliza de F.

Once again Eliza had managed to enter the highest social circles in the land, for her reference to the 'Drawing Room' shows that she had donned the elaborate Court fashions – a richly-decorated dress with tight bodice, huge hooped skirt, and be-feathered tiara – and attended one of the daytime receptions held at St. James's Palace, the official royal residence in London; from there gone to a party given by the Duchess of Cumberland, wife of George III's younger brother; and then to Almack's assembly rooms, where the most exclusive balls were held.

Later in the summer Eliza and Phylly finally succeeded in meeting at the inland spa town of Tunbridge Wells, in Kent. The Wells had been very fashionable earlier in the eighteenth century, since the town was conveniently less than forty miles south of London, but were now being overtaken in popularity by the seaside resort of Brighton, which had become the favourite summer residence of the Prince of Wales. However, the belief in the medicinal qualities of the iron-impregnated drinking water ensured that visitors seeking health as well as a country holiday continued to patronise the Wells for several more decades. As the guidebook explained, the town was built partly in a sandy valley

> closely surrounded by steep hills, and partly on two charming elevations, called Mount Ephraim, and Mount Sion. ... The position of the hamlet proves very inviting, the houses appearing like a large town in a wood. The turf on the common is covered during the summer with flocks of sheep ... The Wells, is the centre of business and amusement, because here rise the springs, here the markets are held, and here the chapel, the assembly-rooms, and the public parades are situated. The parades, usually called the Upper and Lower Walk, run parallel to each other, and are much frequented ... the bandstand, or orchestra, is in the centre of the Upper Walk, which is also known as the Pantiles. ... A species of portico, supported by wooden Tuscan pillars, runs the entire length of the principal walk, and affords an agreeable shelter from the

sun and rain. Below this are shops for jewellery, Tunbridge wares, &c. A row of trees, of luxuriant growth, also contributes to the amenity of the place; and, under the shade, the company meet, sit, or walk, during the hours of general resort. There are parties to the High Rocks, and

Paul Amsinck. *Tunbridge Wells and its neighbourhood, illustrated by a series of etchings and historical depictions... The etching executed by Letitia Byrne.* London, 1810.
British Library L.R.297.a.15

other romantic scenes, with which the whole neighbourhood abounds. These rocks are about a mile and a half southward from the Wells, and consist of a great number of rude eminences, several of which are above seventy feet high, though their average may be taken at forty. Being situated among woods, by the side of a gentle murmuring stream, they are at once romantic and sequestered.

The company generally repair to the parade pretty early in the morning; and, after drinking from the spring, and spending an hour or two in walking, during which they are serenaded by the band, frequently assemble in parties to breakfast. Subsequently to this repast, it is customary to walk, ride, or read, according to the predominant disposition. Dinner over, the musicians again ascend the orchestra, and the evening promenade commences, which is only interrupted by tea, the theatre, card-assemblies, or the public rooms. The Master of Ceremonies has two balls in the season, which are generally very brilliant. Excursions to the noblemen's and gentlemen's seats, and many remarkable places in the adjacent country ... furnish another pleasurable employment of time at Tunbridge Wells.

Now that James Walter was married and settled in Lincolnshire, Phylly wrote regularly to him with news of her life in Kent; in the following letter she told him of her first meeting with these long-lost relations, and her unaccustomed round of social gaieties:

Seal, 19th September 1787 – I came home on Tuesday from Penshurst to which place my aunt and madame brought me the day before. I had spent ten days with them at the Wells. They came here and staid one night when I returned with them and lived a gayer life than I ever before experienced, engagements for every hour; for the first few days I was miserable, and wd. have given anything to have got away to any retired corner, but their very great kindness, affection and attention to me soon reconciled me to the dissipated life they led and put me in mind that every woman is at heart a rake. ... I will just relate a few of the particulars from my journal.

We all left Seal at 5 o'clock the 6th inst. in an elegant coach and four, as they seldom stir without, got to the Wells and went directly to the Rooms, for the benefit of two celebrated Italian singers: after they had done singing some gentlemen proposed dancing which was readily agreed to and we kept it up till past twelve.

On Friday morning the Comtesse and I hunted all the Milliners' shops for hats: She presented me with a very pretty fancy hat to wear behind the hair, on one side, and as a mixture of Colors is quite the thing I chose green and pink with a wreath of pink roses and feathers; but the taste is all the most frightful colors. Her dress was new – as it is a compliment generally paid to Mr. Tyson the master of the ceremonies ball – most truly elegant, quite distinguished as the richest in the Rooms – I danced almost all the Evening and kept it up till past two o'clock concluding with a French dance which, as I can't write it, is in English the Baker's wife – only 6 couple and something in the Cotillon style, the figure changing every time. We danced it full an hour and a half.

Saturday morning, went to see a horse race rode by Lord Sackville & Mr. Cumberland, the former beat. In the evening to the play which my cousin bespoke and was Which is the Man? and Bon Ton; the house crowded. Sunday morning went to Chapel, then took an airing, paid several visits by leaving cards; in the evening drank tea at the Rooms. Monday by myself to Frant; my aunt fetched me home & all went to the play, Percy and The Maid of the Oaks. Tuesday my aunt and I went to the Rocks and rambled there; in the evening to the Ball. Wednesday took an airing, paid a visit, and was let in to the Play again. Thursday almost all day on the Pantiles ... to the Rooms in the evening. My aunt and cousin never touch a card. Friday dined at Major York's with a large party but left them at 7 o'clock to go to the Ball. Saturday all dined at Mr. Motley Austen's at Lamberhurst, a very pleasant situation and such worthy people that I enjoyed the visit exceedingly; returned to the play which was The Drummer and Robinson Crusoe. Monday morning I went to Penshurst.

You will expect my opinion of my friends. To begin with my Aunt, I do not know a fault she has – so strictly just and honourable in all her dealings, so kind and obliging to all her friends and acquaintance, so religious in all her actions, in short I do not know a person that has more the appearance of perfection. The Countess has many amiable qualities, such as the highest duty, love and respect for her mother; for whom there is not any sacrifice she would not make, and certainly contributes entirely to her happiness; for her husband she professes a large share of respect, esteem and the highest opinion of his merits, but confesses that Love is not of the number on her side, tho' still very violent on his; her principles are strictly just, making it a rule never to bespeak anything that she is not quite sure of being able to pay for directly, never contracting debts of any kind. Her dissipated life she was brought up to, therefore it cannot be wondered at, but her religion is not changed. Her partiality to me was very great. I do not believe she has a thought she would wish to keep from me, tho' I took the liberty of differing in opinion on many subjects; we often kept up a dispute for some time. They were very desirous of keeping me longer with them, and as they had some thought of going for a week to Brighton wished me to be of the party, but I declined it upon my mother's account.

They go at Xmas to Steventon and mean to act a play Which is the Man? and Bon Ton. My uncle's barn is fitting up quite like a theatre, and all the young folks are to take their part. The Countess is Lady Bob Lardoon in the former and Miss Tittup in the latter. They wish me much of the party and offer to carry me, but I do not think of it. I should like to be a Spectator, but am sure I should not have courage to act a part, nor do I wish to attain it; it's agreed I am to spend some time with them in Town after Xmas; they do not go abroad till the spring.

The dance that Phylly could only call The Baker's Wife had originated in the mildly improper French popular song, 'La Boulangère a des écus', which suggested that the baker's wife acquired her monies in other ways than by the sale of bread. It remained a favourite for years, and Jane Austen herself danced it in 1796 and also mentions it in Chapter III of *Pride and Prejudice*. Mr. Motley Austen (1747–1815) was the eldest son of Mr. Francis Austen of Sevenoaks, and so a first cousin of both the Revd George Austen and Mrs. Hancock. At this time he was living at Court Lodge, Lamberhurst, but later bought the Kippington estate on the outskirts of Sevenoaks.

Eliza returned to the topic of amateur dramatics later in the year:

Orchard Street, 16th November 1787 – Your Aunt has already apologized for her Daughter's silence My Dear Cousin & therefore I will only allow myself to add on this Subject that nothing but the real impracticability of my writing could have prevented my doing it, & made me deprive myself of the Satisfaction I ever feel in addressing You, & now to the subject of this epistle.

I have a favor to ask of You My Dear Friend a Favor which I trust You will not refuse me – You know we have long projected acting this Christmas in Hampshire & this scheme would go on a vast deal better would You lend your assistance You may remember when You was at Tunbridge my expressing a very earnest & a very natural wish to have You with me during the approaching festival, & on finding there were two unengaged parts I immediately thought of You & am particularly commissioned by My Aunt Austen & her whole Family to make the earliest application possible & assure You how very happy You will make them as well as myself if You could be prevailed on to undertake these parts & give us all your Company. Indeed My Dear Cousin your Compliance will highly oblige me & your declining my proposal as cruelly mortify me. I know You have engagements but if You love me put them off to another Year consider it is the only Christmas we may pass together for many many Years, whereas You have it always in your power to be with your other Friends, who I am sure are too reasonable to object to your taking this only opportunity of being with an affectionate Relation from whom the Sea will very shortly divide You. As to any diffidence in regard to succeeding in the Parts, I beg it may be sent to Coventry, for I assure You they are neither long nor difficult, & I am certain You will succeed in them, Your accomodations at Steventon are the only thing My Aunt Austen & myself are uneasy about, as the House being very full of Company She says She can only promise You 'A place to hide your Head in' but I think You will not mind this inconvenience, I am sure I should not to be with You. Do not let your Dress neither disturb You, as I think I can manage it so that the Green Room should provide You with what is necessary for acting.

We purpose setting out the 17th of December, so that if You can come to me in Orchard Street the Day before, I shall be happy to have You go down with me & when once the Plays are over, if You are determined to quit us we will consent however reluctantly to part with You; I assure You we shall have a most brilliant party & a great deal of amusement, The House full of Company & frequent Balls, You cannot possibly resist so many temptations especially when I tell You your old Friend James is returned from France & is to be of the acting party.

I shall be very impatient for your Answer & must take my leave en attendant as I really am hurried to Death To-Day Adieu My Dearest Cous[in, how] happy I shall be to spend so much Time with You, [my] Love attends My Aunt & Uncle as well as a thousand [kind] things on the part of my Mother, I send You a kiss from Little Hastings whose Teeth plague him a good deal, believe me ever your most sincere & affectionate Friend & Relation, Eliza.

Remember I must have a favorable answer.

However, Phylly took fright at the idea, and wrote on 21st November making excuses to refuse the invitation, which brought a swift response from Eliza:

Orchard Street, 23rd November 1787 – I received your Letter Yesterday My Dear Friend & need not tell You how much I am concerned at your not being able to comply with a request which in all probability I shall never have it in my power to make again. The not leaving your Mother alone is certainly very essential, but would it not be possible to engage some Friend or Neighbour to come & stay with her during so short an absence, or might She not spend it with her Son Weaver at Penshurst? for I know my Aunt's Good Nature too well to imagine She would object to any scheme of this kind which would facilitate ours, however My Dear Cousin You are the best judge of all this, nor will I teaze You with any further importunities, but cease to press You on a Subject which You beg me not to urge.

I will only allow myself to take notice of the strong reluctance You express to what You call appearing in Publick. I assure You our performance is to be by no means a publick one, since only a select party of Friends will be present, and as to your very great apprehensions of not succeeding, You may be well convinced they are totally groundless. I think a consciousness of the many advantages which distinguish You might assure You of this, & besides if You do justice to my Friendship You cannot suppose I would press You to do any thing in which You could possibly appear either in an improper or a disadvantageous Light. As to the other Persons You mention, they are totally out of the question, as I would not have any thing to do with them for the world, for the society of such formal gothic beings by no means suits me, I could not help laughing at your idea of the eldest of the three shining in any character, how was it possible My Dear Friend that You should not recollect her Time of Life & appearance would make her appearing on such a Stage as ours the heighth [sic] *of Absurdity?*

You wish to know the exact Time which we should be satisfied with & therefore I proceed to acquaint You that a fortnight from New Years Day would do, provided however You could bring yourself to act, for My Aunt Austen declares 'She has not room for any idle young people' — Shall I be candid & tell You the Thought which has struck me on this occasion? — The insuperable objection to my proposal is, some scruples of your Mother's about your acting — If this is the case I can only say it is Pity so groundless a prejudice should be harboured in so enlightened [and] *enlarged a mind. I believe I have not told You that* [the] *parts allotted You were so very short that You would no*[t have] *Time for this terrible panic which seems to have taken possession at Seale to have manifested itself, but it is Time to have done with these unnecessary repetitions.*

I am very much obliged by your kind enquiries after little Hastings who is greatly better within these two Days He has really suffered incredibly for these two months past, I hope however he will be quite stout again by the Time You see him in Town. Adieu My Dearest Cousin, I cannot at present indulge myself in writing any longer to You, as I expect Company & must dress. My Mother joins me in Love & every good wish to yourself & Family Do not doubt my sincere & tender regard for you since it is that makes me so much regret the being deprived of your Company —

Believe me ever your most affectionate Friend & Relation, Eliza.

I beg as a very particular favor that You will not communicate that part of my Letter which contains my surmise concerning your Mother's objections to her or any part of your Family.

Eliza's reference to a trio of old-fashioned and apparently middle-aged ladies is puzzling, because none of the Austens' immediate neighbours in Hampshire seem to have had family members at this date who would fit such a description. Despite the original plans to act 'Which is the Man?' and 'Bon Ton', the plays performed at Steventon over the Christmas and New Year holiday were 'The Wonder' and 'The Chances'. These were romantic comedies set in the sixteenth century, the one in Portugal and the other in Italy, with plots involving plenty of confusions and misunderstandings between disguised ladies and jealous gallants, and no doubt Eliza enjoyed playing the leading female role in both.

In the spring of 1788 Eliza invited Phylly to come and stay with her in London, and from there Phylly, very much the wide-eyed country-mouse, wrote as usual to her brother James to tell him of her doings:

Orchard Street, 21st April 1788 – I never experienced so thorough a racketing life and had no idea that it cou'd be equal to what I now find it. This is the 3rd week I have been in town. Our mornings are spent in ridiculous sort of calls from one door to another without ever being let in, shopping and by way of treat to me sometimes a walk in Kensington Gardens. ... My dear friends are all affectionate kindness to me, and do everything for my pleasure. I have even the coach with a coronet always at my command, but when able to find my way I prefer walking. ... The opera we went in style to, as we sat in Mrs. Hastings' box. I have had the pleasure of seeing a great deal of the Hastings. ... I have drunk tea at his house in St. James' Place – everything more elegant than I ever saw before. Mrs. Hastings I admire exceedingly, very affable, lively and pleasing. ... I have once been to the Trial which, because an uncommon sight, we fancied worth going to, and sat from 10 till 4 o'clock, compleatly tired, but I had the satisfaction of hearing all the celebrated orators, viz. Sheridan, Burke & Fox. The first was so low we cd. not hear him, the 2nd so hot and hasty, we cd. not understand, & the 3rd was highly superior to either as we cd. distinguish every word, but not to our satisfaction as he is so much against Mr. Hastings whom we all here wish so well. ...

I have seen Mr. Hampson several times. He is married to a young woman of Fortune, but not pleasing in my eyes; he is very much respected. ... I called on Mrs. Freeman; Mr. Freeman left a will to give everything equally between his widow & sister Stella, no legacies. Mr. Hampson was very much disappointed.

This letter was heavily edited prior to its first publication, and although it begins in April, the reference to Mr. Hampson's marriage to Jane Hodgson on 25th June 1788 suggests that the text as it now stands may be in fact a conflation of two or more of Phylly's epistles; unfortunately all the manuscripts are lost, so it is impossible to check the accuracy of the transcripts. Mr. Hampson (1765–1820) was a maternal cousin of both Eliza and Phylly; he was in fact a baronet, *Sir* Thomas Hampson, but as he had republican principles preferred not to use his title. The Freemans were also cousins, hence Mr. Hampson's disappointment at being overlooked in Mr. Freeman's Will.

The trial of Warren Hastings, impeached by his political opponents for supposed maladministration and corruption during his years in Bengal, had begun on 13th February, with public sittings in Westminster Hall; after seven years of delay and procedural incompetence, it eventually terminated in his acquittal in April 1795.

Mrs. Hancock and Eliza brought Phylly home to Seal and stayed again at Tunbridge Wells for a few days, probably going on to Ramsgate thereafter for the benefit of little Hastings's health. His teething troubles, perhaps exacerbated by the medical treatments of the time, had brought on convulsions; and Phylly passed this worrying news on to her brother:

Seal, 23rd July 1788 – Madame de F. and my aunt are returned to London. Poor little Hastings has had another fit; we all fear very much his faculties are hurt; many people say he has the appearance of a weak head; that his eyes are particular is very certain; our fears are of his being like poor George Austen. He has every symptom of good health, but cannot yet use his feet in the least, nor yet talk, tho' he makes a great noise continually.

The disturbances abroad I fancy will keep them longer in England than they intended. They propose consulting the French Ambassador, and acting according to his advice. I have some hopes they will visit the Wells again.

Henry Austen is sadly mortified at one of the Fellows of St. John's choosing to marry or die, which vacancy he is obliged to fill up, and wd. totally prevent his accompanying his cousin to France, wh. was particularly harped upon on both sides. ...

Yesterday I began an acquaintance with my two female cousins Austen. My uncle, aunt, Cassandra & Jane arrived at Mr. F. Austen's the day before. We dined with them there. As it's pure Nature to love ourselves I may be allowed to give the preference to the eldest who is generally reckoned a most striking resemblance of me in features, complexion & manners. I never found myself so much disposed to be vain,

Jane Austen – engraving made in 1869
from a watercolour sketch by Cassandra Austen, ca. 1810,
and used as frontispiece to her nephew's *Memoir of Jane Austen.*
British Library 10855.e.8

as I can't help thinking her very pretty, but fancied I could discover she was not so well pleased with the comparison – which reflection abated a great deal of the vanity so likely to arise, & so proper to be supprest. The youngest (Jane) is very like her brother Henry, not at all pretty & very prim, unlike a girl of twelve; but it is hasty judgement wh. you will scold me for. My aunt has lost several fore-teeth which makes her look old; my uncle is quite white-haired, but looks vastly well; all in high spirits & disposed to be pleased with each other. ..

I continue to admire my amiable likeness the best of the two in every respect; she keeps up conversation in a very sensible & pleasing manner. Yesterday they all spent the day with us, & the more I see of Cassandra the more I admire – Jane is whimsical & affected. They all say a violent deal about my visiting Steventon next Xmas ... They leave Sen'oaks this Evening.

The bells at Sen'oaks ring merrily for the prodigal son's return. Mr. Frank Austen's son, John, from the East Indies, arrived last night; he has been rather a wild youth & left his Father rather displeased, but his wrath is subsided by a long absence, & his utmost wishes have lately been to live till his return ...

Madame de F. my aunt etc. are all packing for their departure in about a month.

This letter also was evidently edited prior to its first publication, and it seems likely it may be another conflation of different texts and that the events related took place over several days if not weeks after the apparent date of 23rd July. The Revd George Austen's second son, George junior (1766–1838) had suffered from fits in his childhood and had grown up in some way disabled, possibly deaf and dumb – hence Phylly's gloomy comparison of his case with that of little Hastings. The rest of the family news she mentions is that Henry Austen had matriculated at St. John's College on 1st July 1788; and that Cassandra and Jane, aged respectively 15½ and 12½, had been brought by their parents to be introduced to their rich old great-uncle Francis Austen, their father's benefactor, who lived at The Red House in Sevenoaks. He had reached the age of 90, hence his wish to live long enough to welcome home and forgive his scapegrace youngest son, Captain John Austen of the 36th Regiment of Foot.

The disturbances in France to which Phylly refers were the riots, sparked off by fears of French national bankruptcy, that had taken place during May and June 1788 in Rennes, Dijon and Pau, with the French army being called in to restore order at Grenoble. Though Eliza's plans may have been delayed, she was not as yet unduly perturbed by this civic unrest in her adopted country, and was busy buying furniture and fittings for the new house which her husband was building at Le Marais.

Orchard Street, 22nd August 1788 – I hardly dare look at the date of your Letter My Dear Cousin, however what gives me some degree of comfort is that You begin it with excuses for not having wrote; I confess my silence has been much longer and infinitely more inexcusable than that You apologize for, however as You know my Heart & know how sincere an affection it will ever retain for You, You will not be inexorable, I trust, but pardon an omission which has I assure You by no means been voluntary.

Hardly a Day has past in which I have not both wished and intended to write to You, but a constant bustle and an insufferable number of avocations of every kind have ever interfered & prevented my following my Inclinations. Our Uncle & Aunt whom You have so lately seen must have told You how great a hurry & worry they left us surrounded with, none but those who have experienced it can form a just idea of the plague & fatigue of mind and Body which ever attend such a removal as ours. Articles of every kind to purchase, furniture to bespeak & the packing of the whole to attend to, in short dust & litter and confusion has my existence consisted of for these last two months, however my business is now drawing to a conclusion, but I do not think that for all that I shall be able to get away before the first Week in September. If possible we mean to contrive a meeting at Hayes Grove before we quit this Island I need not tell You how much my inclination is for it, but I am not quite so sure of the ability as the will to realize this Scheme.

I am sure the meeting our Steventon Friends gave You great pleasure, They talked much (for they dined with us in their way back to Hampshire) of the Satisfaction their visit into Kent had afforded them. What did You think of My Uncle's Looks, I was much pleased with them, and if possible he appeared more aimiable than ever to me, What an excellent & pleasing Man he is, I love him most sincerely as indeed I do all the Family – I believe it was your first acquaintance with Cassandra and Jane.

What has contributed to hurry me and take up my time is my having been obliged to pay some Visits out of Town, We spent a little time at Beaumont Lodge and I am but just returned from an excursion into Berkshire, during which we made some little stay at Oxford. My Cousin James met us there, & as well as his Brother was so good as to take the trouble of shewing us the Lions, We visited several of the Colleges, the Museum &cc & were very elegantly entertained by our gallant relations at St. John's, where I was mightily taken with the Garden & longed to be a Fellow that I might walk in it every Day, besides I was delighted with the Black Gown & thought the Square Cap mighty becoming. I do not think You would know Henry with his Hair powdered & dressed in a very ton-ish style, besides he is at present taller than his Father.

We spent a Day in seeing Blenheim I was delighted with the Park and think it a most charming place, I liked the outside of the mansion too, but when I entered it I was disappointed at finding the furniture very old fashioned & very shabby, there are many fine pictures, and a most noble Hall, The Library too is a fine room. We meant to have seen Nuneham, belonging to Lord Harcourt but his Majesty without consulting us most unkindly chose to breakfast there, the very Day we intended to have visited the place, so that we were obliged to defer that scheme till my next journey to that part of the World, that is to say some few Years hence.

We returned to Town on Sunday and of all the dreadful storms of Thunder Lightning & Rain I ever remember, I think that we experienced on that aimiable place called Hounslow Heath was the worst, however I believe it saved us from being robbed as we afterwards heard that two Highwaymen were at that very moment in waiting for their Prey & nothing but the violent storm prevented their stopping us. The town is now most completely empty & of course very melancholy, How much You are to be envied who enjoy Shade & pure air, instead of the smoke & Dust which surround us. I have but very few acquaintance here at present & one of them is preparing for a very long voyage. I mean Madl. de Pinto whom You know I have a great regard for, She embarks for Lisbon next Thursday.

You mention the troubles in France but You will easily imagine from what I have said concerning my app[roaching] journey that things are in a quieter state than they were some month[s ago]. Had they continued as they were it is most probable M. de F. would have been ca[lled up] & it would have been a very unpleasant kind of Duty because he must have borne arms against his own Countrymen.

I was much grieved to hear a very indifferent account of your Brother Weaver's Health, for our Steventon Friends told me he had not got the better of his Ague, but I hope he is by this time quite recovered. I was likewise informed it was not impossible but You might visit Bath and I sincerely wish this Scheme may take place as I think it would afford You much amusement.

You will say I am very unconscionable when I beg You to write soon, but indeed My Dear Friend I want to hear all how and about it & pray let me have a full & particular account of all your Flirtations. I cannot give You much intelligence concerning any of your Town acquaintance; What is become of Mr. E– I know not, our Louisa has long since been at Tunbridge, which

She writes me word is some what stupid. Captn. & Mrs. Churchill are just gone there & Miss Birch who has been till now on a visit to Mrs. Bissett at the Isle of Wight. Mrs. Farhill I believe I have not seen three times since You left me but I know She is once more in Louisa's Way, as is Mrs. Hampson, who with her Husband is still at Broad Stairs. They have taken a large & very excellent House in Wimpole Street not many Doors from Mrs. Lawrell's. I have seen Mrs. J. Freeman very frequently, She still inhabits her House in Charles Street, Mrs. Freeman means to reside altogether at Langley. Mr. & Mrs. Hastings whom you enquire about are now at Malvern in Worcestershire, but I believe they will soon return, Mrs. H. has been very ill but is now much better. I have not heard whether the aimiable Mr. W. is married, I suppose You know Miss Lydia Mathews has changed her name, She is married to a Mr. Botham an East Indian. As to our Friends, those sweet creatures called Jack & Tom F– I know but little of them & I think I need not add that I care still less about the matter I am sure your Sentiments perfectly coincide with mine in this particular.

I dont know what other Beaux I can give You a more satisfactory account of unless it is a young Gentleman whom You recollect there was some little scandal about during your stay in Orchard Street, don't be alarmed for I mean your morning visitor little Hastings, He now sports twelve Teeth 8 of which he has acquired since Ramsgate & what is still better he has cut the last without Convulsions, upon the whole I think He is much the better for Sea bathing, He acquires some new Accomplishment every Day & his last is a very elegant one, He doubles his prodigious fists & boxes quite in the English style.

I have yet twenty things to say to You, but my paper will not allow of it, Have You seen the agreeables lately or are there any new agreeables that have rivalled them. Is not there a certain Clergyman some where in your neighbourhood that You contrive to flirt with a little? Adieu My aimiable Friend think of me & think of me with some affection, since notwithstanding all my faults I love You most sincerely & shall ever remain your faithful Friend & affectionate Relation, Eliza.

Eliza's next letter shows the problems of arranging visits at short notice in an era when mail coaches travelled at an average speed of six miles an hour:

Tunbridge Wells, Sunday 31st August [1788] – My Dear Philadelphia, You will perhaps be somewhat surprized at receiving an Answer to yours dated from this place, but the earnest solicitations made me by Lady Rous & Louisa have prevailed on me to spend a few Days here. I wish much to avail myself of this opportunity & hope we shall contrive a meeting. If you cannot get as far as the Wells, Louisa & myself will take a ride over to Penshurst in order to see You there any Day You will fix, but Lady R. is so good as to request You will come & dine with us here as there is a moon She thinks You will not be afraid of returning in the Evening. You know there is a Ball on Friday, if You should like to come & dine with us that Day, we can all go to the Ball together & if You will accept half my Bed (for I occupy the only spare apartment in the House) You need not return till Saturday. I can answer for My Friends here being very glad of your Company if You think this scheme practicable, & I need not assure You of the pleasure it will afford me.

As I am very much straightened for time I cannot answer your entertaining & welcome epistle so fully as I could wish however I hope to be able to answer it soon in Person. I have a notion this Letter will go to Town & if that is the case You cannot receive it before Tuesday, nor I your answer till Thursday, therefore if You should not approve of the Friday scheme, I think You had better come over to us either Wednesday or Thursday, or else contrive to let me know You will meet me some Day before Saturday at Penshurst. I am not sure but what I shall be obliged to return to Town on Saturday, but that will not interfere in the least with the Ball plan which I shall be rejoiced if You can accomplish; I should think You might easily contrive it for You may either come here ready drest, or else bring your Gown for You will have my apartment to dress in, & miss Rosalie will be very happy to give You all the assistance She can. The Dinner Hour in this Mansion is a quarter past four, but You should come early that I may have the more of your Company, I think we shall be very snug; As I have already told You if You cannot make Friday convenient, come & dine with us, either Tuesday, Wednesday or Thursday You will certainly find us at home.

This is quite a Letter of Business, Adieu My Dear Cousin for I am forced to quit You. The Wells are most comfortably stupid tho' I ought not to tell you so for fear it should prevent your coming, however I own I trust your Friendship for me will induce You to overlook such deficiencies. Once more Adieu believe me ever with sincere regard your most affectionate & faithful Friend & Relation, Eliza de F.

Remember me affectionately to all your Family, I congratulate You on the Birth of a Niece but [I would] be very sorry to give You as many Cousins as You have acq[uired] nephews & nieces of late. I know You will be glad to hear that both your Aunt & Puggy are well, as I have just heard from the former & She forwarded your Letter to me. Adieu, it rains most aimiably, a pleasing circumstance as one can't stir out of Doors, & You know how much I love staying at home. Make no ceremony about accepting the invitation for Friday because I know My Friends here will be happy to see You.

Lady Rous was the widow of Sir John Rous, and mother of Louisa, who married Mr. John Birch in 1791. Phylly's new niece was Frances, first daughter of her brother James, born 28th July 1788. Eliza's French maid Rosalie may have been subsequently seduced by an English baronet, Sir Thomas Champneys, or so a reference in one of Jane Austen's letters some years later would seem to imply.

Mrs. Hancock and Eliza went back to France, probably in the autumn of 1788, and spent the winter in Paris. In the following spring Mrs. Hancock wrote to Mr. Woodman:

Paris, 5th February 1789 – Dear Sir, I did myself the pleasure of writing on the 16th Ulto, acquainting you that Messrs. Harman & Co. would settle the affair of the Bond whenever you would call on them, & yesterday I received a Letter from them dated the 27th Ulto. wherein they tell me they are in daily expectation of your calling but that they had not yet had the pleasure of seeing you, I shall be glad to have this affair settled as soon as possible, as my Bankers will send my Accounts immediately after.

When I left England I flattered myself I should see it again in about three years, I may possibly now enjoy that pleasure much sooner, tho' for a very short time, some affairs I have to transact will I fear, make it necessary for me to visit England in the Month of June & should Mons. de Feuillide join his Regiment about that time my Daughter will certainly accompany me; you was kind enough when I was last in England to offer me the use of your House in Cleveland Row; if your Family should be removed to Ewell before our arrival and attended with no inconvenience to either Mrs. Woodman or yourself, you will infinitely oblige me by giving me an Apartment in it during my stay which will not exceed a Month & perhaps not three Weeks. We shall want only two Beds & one of them for our Maid Rosalie the only person we shall bring with us as we wish to travel as light as possible; We shall want so small a part of your House that it will not prevent you or any part of your Family coming to Town, and I should not have made you this request if I thought it could be attended with any inconveniency to you, but I may be mistaken, & in that case beg you will excuse me & be assured I shall not take a refusal unkind, I have too often experienced yours & Mrs. Woodman's Friendship to doubt your inclination to oblige me when in your power, and many things that I can't foresee at this distance, may make your compliance with my request inconvenient & perhaps impossible.

It was with real pleasure I learnt from yours that you were all well at Ewell, you are by this time in Cleveland Row &, I hope, enjoying there the same Blessing of Health. We have not been [quite so] fortunate here, the Ct. de Feuillide has an intermitting Fever which he [brought] from the Country hanging about him for some time, he is now better but I cannot boast of his Wifes Health, who is thinner than ever & much troubled with Headaches & little feverish complaints, She is however much better than She has been. I was also much indisposed during the very Cold Weather so that our dear little Boy was the stoutest person amongst us, he is thank God quite well and we are all daily getting better, and unite most sincerely in affectionate Compliments & best Wishes to you & all yours believe me to be Dear Sir, your much Obliged & most Obedient Humble Servant, P: Hancock.

Eliza also wrote at the same time, still trying to convince herself that her son, now nearly three years old, was developing normally; and delighted to hear that Phylly had fallen in love with a naval officer.

Paris, 11th February 1789 – Indeed My Dear Cousin, I am very very much ashamed of my long silence, and hardly dare look at the date of your letter, but believe me, and do not think this assurance is dictated by the common place stile of apology for omissions of this nature believe me I say when I tell You that my heart has not been in fault. I have a very sincere affection for You which I trust You are persuaded of and which has never varied and I think never will if I know any thing of my own heart and its feelings, after reminding You of this truth I need not add its necessary consequence, I mean the impossibility of neglecting what we love, a moments reflection on which must convince You that my will has had little to do with the apparent want of attention which it should seem that I had been guilty of.

A series of occupations, a total derangement in my plans, and much ill health on M. de F–s and my own part is what has interfered with the use I ought to have made of my pen, and if I dared I would add, that perhaps Your own example had somewhat authorized my own dilatoriness, Indeed My Dear Friend I thought your letter a long while on the road and was anxious for accounts from You – but to return to that so important thing (I mean, important to myself) called Self; M. de F– who desires his best respects to my charming Cousine, M. de F– I say has been very ill, and You who have so high an opinion of conjugal Duties will easily guess that my mind was much engrossed at such a period. He is now perfectly recovered, but I have since been very much indisposed myself, a sort of feverish Complaint has hung about me, & do not laugh when I tell it You My Nerves are still most exceedingly disordered.

As You mention accounts from Steventon having informed You of my being detained in Paris I need not repeat what You are already acquainted with, but I know not whether You was also told the cause of this change in my arrangements, which was my receiving letters from M. de F– in which he informed me that a malignant fever raged at the Marais and of course he did not think it safe I should come there and preferred joining me in Paris as soon as possible. You will imagine that I do not think of returning to the South yet a while, and indeed it must be allowed that one may patiently abide a future season in such a place as Paris, however I have not as yet had much to do with the gay world or its pleasures as my health has been so indifferent as hardly to admit of my quitting my fireside, a circumstance I am the more grieved at as it renders me totally unable to send you any amusing or interesting intelligence –

You must therefore for the present My Dear Cousin content yourself with Family News, and as I know You are not like a Gentleman of my acquaintance who says 'that Family News and Family Parties would have exhausted the Patience of Job himself' as I know Your feelings are different and as I flatter myself You are really interested in me and mine, You will not perhaps think an account of my little Household so very insupportable. I will proceed in a most matronly manner, for You know I am a very matronly sort of body to tell You all the wonderful endowments of my wonderful Brat, whom I think You would allow to be much improved. He endeavors to chatter both french and english, says a great many words and tries to say still more, is most comfortably rude and riotous, hitherto somewhat spoilt, but his Grand Mamma declares that as soon as he can be made to understand & hear reason, he shall cease to be indulged – as it would be very unnatural to disparage one's own offspring in a friends opinion and as I have shewn You the worst side of the picture and pointed out its blemishes, it is but justice likewise to make you observe its perfections; I must therefore tell You that this said Son of mine is notwithstanding what I have already said most exceedingly good tempered and I do not think he will ever be either Alderman or Lord Mayor as he has not the least of the greediness and Love of Dainties which children usually shew, and will absolutely offer his half muncht apples or cakes to the whole company altho' I have remonstrated on the impropriety of the proceeding. To crown all his accomplishments I have taught him to say Cousin – Philly, is rather too difficult but I trust it will be accomplished in Time and so much for little Hastings, let us now proceed to some other subjects.

One in particular which your letter contains, is a very interesting one – And so, that same blind urchin has found his way to your heart but not so very blind neither, for I think your choice seems to do great honor to your discernment. Be assured My Dear and aimiable Friend that I am infinitely obliged to You for the mark of friendship You have given me & that I feel the value of the confidence You repose in me – if possible it has made You dearer than ever to your Eliza – It is, as You observe somewhat peculiar that You who are not fond of travelling should have fixed your affections on one who seems destined, at least for some time, to lead an unsettled Life – Pray let me know in your next a great deal more a[bout] all this, and answer all the questions which You think [I would put] to You if present, one of the most material of which You [can] guess to be whether there is any probability of your shortly changing your name, and if such a change should take place what part of England you will become an inhabitant of. I want too of all things a description of his person, is he tall or short, fair or brown, & particularly are his eyes black or blue? in short would he be to my taste, which I think You must be pretty well acquainted with. What will become of the poor black [coats now] You have forsaken them for Blue, I would advise your young Conquest Mr. Richard All- to determine on the latter or he must wear the willow which I do not think at all suited to your Brow, Besides I cannot think a Lover blessed with your approbation sufficiently wanting in taste, or so deprived of discernment as not to feel the values of the treasure he possesses and forfeit it by his inconstancy; seriously My Dear Friend & without any sort of compliment I think the Man happy enough to obtain you will be a very fortunate mortal and his lot a most enviable one. I imagine You have spent a very gay and very pleasant Christmas at Mrs. Pickarts and danced a great deal. Pray what will become of the poor forsaken agreeables when once they find you have really made a choice.

Louisa informed me You corresponded, I receive very frequent letters from Her & She has sent me her picture beautifully done to set, it is the most striking likeness I ever beheld and a performance of the languishing Mrs. B–s, I do not mean J.B. Louisa expresses much pleasure at the idea of seeing You at the Wells this Summer, Perhaps when You are strolling arm in arm on the

Pantiles a thought of Your absent Eliza will obtrude itself – Be assured I am often with You in idea, at least you are often with me, that is in my Thoughts. Your account of Miss Depasso's dread of taking the air is very extraordinary, I had heard of her engagement to Mr. Whitehead as a thing which had been entirely put an end to.

I suppose You have had frequent accounts from Steventon, & that they have informed you of their theatrical Performances, The Sultan and High Life below Stairs, Miss Cooper performed the part of Roxelana, & Henry the Sultan, I hear that Henry is taller than ever.

Adieu My Dear and aimiable Friend, I have still a thousand things to say to You, but my perverse paper will not let me. Do not treat me as I deserve, but charitably bestow an immediate answer on this scrawl, How are your good Father & Mother & absent Brother & Sister? Remember My Mother & myself most affectionately to every part of your Family & accept your Aunt's Love particularly addressed to You, once more Adieu, continue to love me, be assured of my sincere affection & that at all times and in all places you will ever find a faithful friend & relation in your Eliza.

On 7th July 1789 Eliza and her mother arrived in London to consult with their lawyer Mr. Cruise regarding the trust fund that Warren Hastings had set up for the Hancock family. It seems that the Comte de Feuillide had been trying to take control of this, because Mr. Cruise advised that the Comte could have no claim except to the interest of the £10,000 until after the deaths of Mrs. Hancock, Eliza, and Hastings, and therefore could not alienate it.

Although Mrs. Hancock had spoken of paying only a short visit to London, the riots which broke out in Paris on 12th July 1789, culminating in the storming of the Bastille on 14th July, heralded the onset of the French Revolution, so it seems probable that Eliza and her mother found themselves willy-nilly staying in England. They may have visited Steventon during the next few months, because one of Jane Austen's funniest pieces in her collected *Juvenilia*, the mini-novel 'Love and Freindship', was finished on 13th June 1790 and bears the dedication 'To Madame la Comtesse De Feuillide this Novel is inscribed by her obliged Humble Servant *The Author*'. Perhaps Eliza had told her of the motto 'Amoris et Amicitiae' which she had used on the miniature presented to Phylly in 1782.

Eliza's next letter to Phylly, No. 31, written some time in 1790, is missing – this would have told her that Eliza intended to spend some time at the seaside resort of Margate, on the north coast of Kent, again for the benefit of Hastings's health. Letter No. 32, in the New Year, takes up her account of events:

Margate 7th January 1791 – Alas My Dear Friend, for with both Sorrow and Shame do I speak it – it seems to be decreed that I should ever be faulty in regard to you – That Fate must have something to do with it I am the more convinced as my Heart bears testimony it has had no share in it nay that my inclination dictates very different proceedings, remember therefore the Lines of the Poet who affirms that 'If weak women go astray / Their stars are more in fault than they' [a slight misquotation of a line from Matthew Prior's poem 'Hans Carvel'] *and once more graciously extend your mercy and pardon to me. I will not tease You with a tedious and insipid detail of the many avocations by which I have been engrossed, the odious letters of business which have not suffered me to devote my pen to more agreeable correspondents &cc &cc it would be taking up your time in no very entertaining manner and therefore I think it better to plead guilty in every thing but what relates to my affection for You and throw myself entirely on your lenity for a remission of my transgression.*

You will find by the date of this I am still an inhabitant of M. for altho' much pressed to spend my Christmas in Surrey, the inconvenience of removing so numerous a family and the great Benefit Hastings has received & still reaps from Sea Bathing made me think it better for us all to remain where we were and put off jaunting till another Year. The place as You will easily imagine has long since been divested of its principal attractions, No longer any Rooms Balls or Plays and hardly any agreeables does it afford, As I can however always make up my mind to retirement, as well as to its reverse when it falls in my way, I contrive by reading, Music Drawing and different kinds of study to fill up the twenty four Hours so as not to find them tedious, and as there is a small circle left of my particular acquaintance some degree of society occasionally varies the scene. I had fixed on going to London the end of this Month, but to shew You how much I am attached to my maternal duties, on being told by one of the faculty whose Skill I have much opinion of that one months bathing at this time of the Year was more efficacious than six at any other & that consequently my little Boy would receive the utmost benefit from my prolonging my stay here beyond the time proposed, like a most exemplary parent I resolved on foregoing the fascinating delights of the great City for one month longer and consequently have determined on not visiting the Metropolis till ye 28th of Febry. Was not this heroic?

M. de F. had given me hopes of his return to England this Winter but the turn which the affairs of France have taken will not allow him to quit the Continent at this Juncture. I know not whether I have already mentioned it to you My Dear Friend, but my spouse who is a strong Aristocrate or Royalist in his Heart has joined this latter party who have taken refuge in Piedmont and is now at Turin where the french Princes of the Blood are assembled and watching some favorable opportunity to reinstate themselves in the Country they have quitted; I am no politician but think they will not easily accomplish their purpose, time alone can decide this matter and in the interim You will easily imagine I cannot be wholly unconcerned about events which must inevitably in some degree influence my future destiny.

I sincerely hope You have spent your Christmas in an agreeable manner and that a sufficient portion of your favorite amusement dancing, has exhilarated your spirits, I will not ask you whether they have received a more powerful cordial for You have informed me You could not hear from a certain aimiable Traveller before the Spring; Whenever those wished for accounts arrive may they make You ample amends for the tediousness of expectation and the painful state of suspense it always occasions. Why should You, so chearful in all oth[er matters] seem to see this subject in a gloomy light and declare that ['Happiness?] never will be your lot'; I hope and trust many Years of Felicity [lie] in store for You, and that I shall ere a very considerable period is elapsed hear You are comfortably settled in the way most agreeable to your wishes; your good Parents conduct in this respect is a fresh proof of their affection for You & the solidity of their judgement, it must be allowed however that it was somewhat hard hearted in You to treat the admirer who so repeatedly sued for your Favor with so much severity, I really pity him, especially if he is a man of sense as in that case he must feel the extent of his Loss more sensibly.

I had the pleasure some time since of hearing You were in good health as my Mother received a letter from Steventon which informed us E. Austen had seen You in a visit he paid to your part of Kent, Did I tell you that he spent a few days with us here and that I thought him a very pleasant young Man.

I believe I have not a scrap of news to send you, not even a flirtation to give you an account of, tho' indeed You well know that to be the last thing I would meddle with, I must therefore I believe confine myself to domestic occurrences, in the first place therefore I have the pleasure of informing You my Mother is in good health, indeed She has not for some time experienced any complaint except a slight attack of the Rhumatism. Hastings grows much &

begins to lisp english tolerably well, his education is likewise begun, his Grandmamma having succeeded in teaching him his letters. The Sea has strengthened him wonderfully & I think has likewise been of great service to myself, I still continue bathing notwithstanding the severity of the Weather & Frost & Snow which is I think somewhat courageous.

Have you heard lately from your Brother in Lincolnshire, how is my Cousin Weaver, and are my Dear Uncle and Aunt in good Health, remember me most affectionately to them, my mother joins in this request as well as in Love to yourself; I hope You will not punish me as I deserve for my misdeeds, but indulge me with one of your acceptable epistles before it is long, Adieu I conclude in haste for it is late & I fear missing the post, continue to love me in spite of all my faults & be assured, My dearest Phillida that You have not a more truly affectionate Friend nor one by whom You are more sincerely beloved than by your faithful Eliza.

Charles d'Artois (1757–1836), the youngest brother of Louis XVI and later King Charles X of France, had fled to Italy in the autumn of 1789 and gathered other royalist émigrés around him at Turin, in the hope of organising a counter-revolution, but without success. He later sought refuge in England, only returning to France in 1814.

The Revd. George Austen's third son Edward had returned from his Grand Tour of Europe in the autumn of 1790 and was now living at Godmersham in Kent with his adoptive parents Mr. and Mrs. Thomas Knight II. Eliza's comment that she is being pressed to go to Surrey suggests that she had just received another of Lady Burrell's poems:

And will Eliza then return? / Shall I once more behold her here, / And from her eyes, delighted learn / Her generous heart is still sincere? // Shall we retrace those happy days / When first we knew each other's mind, / When first I spake Eliza's praise, / When first I found her good, and kind? // Ah! friend, so lov'd – so long deplor'd, / Welcome again to Britain's shore! / May health, may peace, their sweets afford; / May ev'ry blessing crowd thy door. // And when thy many friends have shar'd / The language of thy tuneful tongue, / Let a few hours to me be spar'd, / At distance from the busy throng. // If you can love our beechen trees, / Sequester'd cells, romantic views, / I court you to such scenes as these, / Dear to your friend, and to the muse. // While the gay birds their carols sing, / and to the sun their plumes display, / We will enjoy the sweets of spring / As grateful, and as blest as they.

Later in the Spring Phylly Walter stayed with Eliza in London, and while she was there the first signs of Mrs. Hancock's terminal illness appeared – cancer of the breast. Following Phylly's return to Kent, Eliza sent an updated bulletin on her mother's condition:

[Orchard Street, London] 23rd June 1791 – My Dear Cousin, I fear You have thought me very remiss, but besides my having been much hurried, I wished to have it in my power to inform You of some change for the better; My Dear Mother's general Health continues, Thank God, pretty good and her Breast I trust is in a more promising state than when You quitted Town. You know She had just then put herself under the care of a person who then gave and still continues to give us the most flattering hopes of a perfect cure. She however always declared her remedy would be slow in its operations nor did She expect any visible effect from it in less than three weeks, About a fortnight has now elapsed, and I think both the swelling and hardness in some degree abated so that having already reaped more benefit than we had been taught to expect in so short a time, I venture to indulge great hopes that I shall at length have the unspeakable happiness of seeing my beloved parent restored to Health. You who know of what importance this event is to My peace of mind must also be convinced of the trembling anxiety with which I await it indeed what I have suffered for this last month beggars all description and has convinced me that tho' I thought I had met with many troubles before, they were all trifles compared to this last heavy affliction. Never will the Year 1791 be effaced from my memory for from the first Month of its commencement to the present period my feelings have constantly been exposed to some fresh trial.

I sincerely hope You all reached your peaceful abode in perfect Health and greatly the better for your Journey. I have no News to entertain you with as you will easily imagine, for besides the Town growing emptier every Day, I have as you may suppose renounced all intercourse with the gay World and find infinitely more satisfaction in endeavouring to amuse My Mother, and if possible render her present Situation less irksome, than any other way of passing My time could possibly afford me.

The family at Steventon were perfectly unacquainted with the present state of things, till the receipt of a letter which I wrote my Aunt last Saturday, and on Sunday Edward Austen called and was much surprized at finding we had so much cause for anxiety; He is now proposing to visit the Lakes with Mr. & Mrs. K. and a large party as I understood, no less than twelve in number, but his beloved alas is not to bless him with her presence on this occasion. I asked him how he would be able to exist? which enquiry he answered with that calm smile of resignation which his Sex generally wear under circumstances of this nature.

I suppose You have long since heard Sr. Nelson Rycroft is going to take unto himself a Mate; I h[ear the] Lady is a Miss Read, a fine Woman and a fine fortune, I [had] the intelligence of the match and its speedy conclusion from M[rs. Read] the Mother of the Lady, so that there can be no doubt of it.

My Mother desires to be most affectionately remembered to You & yours in which I beg to join as also in particular enquiries concerning your Father's Health which I heard with concern was but indifferent when you quitted London, I hope he is now quite recovered. I know You will be glad to hear Hastings is well and also that your Aunt's Spirits continue good, She declares that the Pain She at one time suffered is greatly abated since She has made use of the remedy on which our Hopes are now founded, She is allowed to take a little Air once a Day but all violent exercise is forbid. Adieu My Dear Friend excuse this wretched scrawl and believe me what I can never cease to be your truly attached & affectionate Friend & Relation, Eliza.

Edward Austen was now engaged to Elizabeth Bridges (1773–1808), the third daughter of Sir Brook Bridges, Bt., of Goodnestone Park, near Wingham, Kent. Sir Nelson Rycroft, Bt. (1761–1827), of Farnham in Surrey, married Miss Charlotte Read on 11th July 1791.

Orchard St. 1st August 1791 – My Dear Cousin, I should have been earlier in my acknowledgements for your last kind letter, but have had my time and thoughts of late, more engrossed than it is possible for me to describe. You know my inclination perfectly agrees with my duty in making me My Dear Mother's constant Companion, and using my utmost endeavors to amuse and divert her Thoughts, so that there are few moments in the Day which I can devote to any other employment, and besides I really at intervals have been a prey to such racking anxiety, that all the faculties of my mind have been as it were totally absorbed, and myself literally incapable of using my pen.

You will perhaps infer from this that the dear Patient is worse, but I thank God, that, notwithstanding what I have been saying is not the case, on the contrary I flatter myself She is upon the whole better as the swelling is somewhat softened, and the inflammation entirely gone, however She still at intervals suffers such acute pain, and the progress of her amendment is so very slow, that in spite of all my endeavors my spirits sometimes sink, and I shudder at the possibility that all our efforts may be ineffectual – Oh My Friend how dreadful it is to experience even the shadow of uncertainty where those we love are concerned! My Mother's Doctress is steady in her declaration of the certainty of time and perseverance accomplishing a perfect cure, and fortunately my Mother is persuaded of it so that her spirits continue good, indeed her Courage and resignation under all the pain, inconvenience, and confinement which She suffers is wonderful and a fresh proof of the happy disposition and excellent way of thinking which all who know her must long since have been convinced She was endowed with.

I was very certain your good Father & Mother would very sincerely participate in my anxiety, as I know their regard for the valuable cause of it, It gave me much satisfaction to find my Uncle was so much better and I hope soon to hear his Health continues good. A Visit from your Brother James would certainly have been an agreeable Surprize both to My Mother and myself, but we are far from taking it ill he did not call, as we are vain enough to suppose it was not want of inclination but ability to follow that said thing called inclination, which prevented us from seeing him. I hope You have had good accounts of himself and family since they quitted You, but talking of Visitors there is one that I have been and am still in hourly expectation of seeing and that is yourself my fair Cousin, for You gave me hopes of seeing You in Town ere long and I trust You will not disappoint me whenever Your projected visit to Mrs. Robinson takes place, You will most undoubtedly meet with us for we do not stir out unless for a gentle walk or airing, My Mother laments much being detained in London which You know is her Aversion and sorry am I for her sake that there appears no probability of a removal being practicable for some time to come. M. de F. has promised me the favor of a visit in Septr., and should it take place and Mamma's Health admit, we shall then go to Bath, a journey from which I promise myself much pleasure, as I have a notion it is a place quite after my own heart, however the accomplishment of this plan is very uncertain, as from the present appearance of things France will probably be engaged in a War which will not admit of an Officer whose services will certainly be required, quitting the Country at such a period.

I have no news, at least nothing but Home News as Swift says, to send You, the most remarkable occurrence of this nature is that my son and Heir who promises to be as great a pickle as any who ever deserved that appellation, has laid aside his feminine Garb and now makes a most manly appearance in a jacket and trowsers, my reason for making him adopt this habiliment is that I think it will make him hold himself more upright and walk better now he has got rid of that terrible incumbrance called petticoats.

My Mother has this very morning received a Letter from Steventon where they all enjoy perfect Health, The youngest Boy Charles is gone to the naval Academy at Portsmouth, As to the young Ladies I hear they are perfect Beauties and of course gain 'hearts by dozens', James you know has got the living of Sherborne.

I was all astonishment on finding Mrs. Fermor had been so slightly remembered in Mr. F. Austen's Will, and my Mother immediately said no wonder herself should have been entirely forgot if that was the case; I must say however it was extremely unkind, as I find the old Gentleman left 6000 pr Annum behind him, It all goes to Mr. M. Austen who was immensely rich before, his younger Brother Captn. John Austen I understand has only 12000 Pounds left him.

I did smile, to be sure when you said that the All— were the attraction to Eltham, flirtation's a charming thing, it makes the blood circulate; Adieu My Dear Friend be assured no one can be more sincerely attached to You than your affectionate Eliza.

Pray have You had any accounts of the absent Your heart will help You to My meaning.

Old Mr. Francis Austen of Sevenoaks had died on 21st June 1791, aged 93, leaving the bulk of his estate, as Eliza says, to his eldest son Francis-Motley Austen, and only one hundred guineas (£105) to his widowed niece Mrs. Elizabeth Fermor who had lived with him as hostess and housekeeper since his wife's death. He did however leave £500 apiece to the Revd. George Austen and to his other nephews. James Austen had just been presented to the vicarage of Sherborne St. John, near Basingstoke in Hampshire, which was in the gift of the Austens' friends Mr. and Mrs. Chute of The Vyne.

Eliza wrote again at the end of August, and also during September, with further details of her mother's illness. Phylly did not keep these letters, but passed on the news to her brother James in Lincolnshire, half-sympathetic and half-censorious:

Seal, 4th September 1791 – I heard yesterday from Eliza de F.: I am sorry to say a melancholy account of my poor Aunt; she has lately suffered violently ... Poor Eliza is compleatly miserable and has the hard task of being forced to appear cheerful when her heart is ready to burst with grief & vexation. My aunt privately exprest to me how much she felt for her, & that she endeavoured to stifle her pains to avoid her the concern of seeing her mother's sufferings.

Seal, 9th October 1791 – Poor Eliza must be left at last friendless & alone. The gay and dissipated life she has long had so plentiful a share of has not ensur'd her friends among the worthy; on the contrary many who otherwise have regarded her have blamed her conduct and will now resign her acquaintance. I always felt concerned and pitied her thoughtlessness. I have frequently looked forwards to the approaching awful period, and regretted the manner of her life, & the mistaken notions of my poor aunt's intended, well–meant kindness; she will soon feel the loss & her want of domestic knowledge. I have just wrote to assure her she may command my services.

Although Phylly's letter to James has an unpleasant tone of smug spitefulness, she did at least have the tact to write more warmly to Eliza, who gratefully acknowledged her professed sympathy:

Orchard St., 13th October 1791 – The very day after I received your's, My Dear Friend, that is to say two days ago, I sat down to answer it, but the innumerable interruptions I experienced, really forced my pen out of my Hand, and till this moment I have not been able to resume it. It would be difficult for me to express all I felt in perusing your very kind letter, but I beg you to be assured that the affectionate, the soothing expressions it contained, and the real regard by which I am sure it was dictated, afforded me the greatest consolation I can receive under my present anxiety of mind, for which I find no Balm like the kind sympathy of a sincere Friend – How rare are those who deserve such an Appellation! and consequently how highly should we prize the very few on whom we can bestow it!

I am sure you are impatient for some account of your Aunt and therefore I will proceed to inform You that for some days past She has been mending in point of Bodily Health; What I mean by this is, that She has better nights, that She now can take a small quantity of Sustenance (for I believe I told You that She loathed every species of Food that could be offered her) and that She is much free-er from pain. She also has somewhat recovered her Strength, so far at least as to quit her Bedchamber for some Hours in the Day, at the same time I see no change whatsoever in the appearance of the Tumour & there has been a return, tho' a very slight one of the Bleeding. Her Surgeon however says that the time has been too short to have effected any alteration in the above particulars, & that it is a great point to have in any degree re-established her Health in other respects. In this I acquiesce and most thankful am I to see even the Slightest change for the better; Her relief from the agonizing pain She suffered is alone such a Blessing as I can never be sufficiently grateful for to that Almighty Power who accepted yours & my earnest supplications, for You told me My Dear Friend that You had joined in those I offered up. She is also free from a Fever, which had not left her for many Days before Mr. Rooss was applied to, in short Her Health is certainly considerably amended & that leads me to hope that tho' there is not any visible change in the Swelling, yet still these favorable Symptoms denote that if the disorder is not subdued, it certainly does not gain ground; I know you will hasten to communicate these particulars to My Dear Aunt & pray at the same time say every thing that is affectionate from me. Tell her also how much both my Mother & myself were obliged by her kind offer of coming to Town, My Mother desires me also to say that as there is not a person breathing for whom She has a sincerer affection, her presence consequently would at a time when She was able to enjoy it afford her the sincerest Satisfaction, but She would not for the World put her to the inconvenience which such a Journey must occasion her especially as it wd. be useless at the present juncture when She is not allowed to converse with any one for more than ten minutes a time, & sees no one but myself. Mr. Rooss's strict orders are that She should be kept as quiet as possible & that every thing that is likely to agitate her in the smallest degree should be avoided. Our punctually observing these directions he says is the most probable method of avoiding any violent return of those Bleedings which have been so very alarming.

On Monday, as You had informed me, I had the pleasure of seeing your good Father & was happy to find him so well considering the severe attack he underwent so lately. My Mother expressed a particular wish to see him so that I indulged her & suffered him to remain with her a few moments, He declared She looked much better than he expected. I mentioned having heard from You that very morning & he in his joking way asked me if You was married, in answer to which question I asserted that it was probable he knew more of that matter than myself, He however persisted in declaring that in such affairs young Ladies were much more explicit with those of their own Age & Sex than with Papa's & Mamma's; but I was not less obstinate in maintaining that however that might be in general, I was notwithstanding convinced that whenever You changed your name Your Parents would be the first persons apprized of it, & that I never expected to hear of your having taken the road to Gretna; I must tell you that this edifying Discourse past before Edward Austen, who had just called in, and who se[emed] greatly entertained by it.

And now My Dear Friend let me congratulate [you] on the proof DBB has given of the excellence of that Heart in which you have so large a share. The little Anecdote you mentioned does him the highest Honor & proves a degree of real Bravery & Humanity very rarely possessed & which I believe very few of his Sex would have evinced; I shall be happy to hear you have met, as I know that circumstance must afford you infinite Satisfaction.

I have scratched this letter in such haste that I fear you will not be able to read it, there is one part of yours however which I have not yet answered, but 'tho last be assured it was not least' in my thoughts I mean your very kind offer of coming to me which I cannot sufficiently thank you for making, or my Aunt for being willing to consent to so great a sacrifice as that of your Company; but as You have already said, all protestations on this subject are I trust needless between us because You will know my heart & the sincere affection it bears You. I will therefore only say that notwithstanding the gratification your Society must ever afford me my Situation is not at present such as to render it possible for me to avail myself of your friendly offer, which indeed I should at any time be very delicate of accepting because I know how necessary Your presence is to your good Mother's comfort; but really independent of this consideration, as I have already told you your Aunt at present is not able to see any one but myself, and I endeavor as much as I can not to let her feel the want of any other nurse. I would fain chat with you a little longer, but my time is not my own just now & therefore I must bid you Adieu in the hope that e'er long I shall resume the pleasing employment of informing you My Dear Mother's Health continues mending; in the meanwhile let me hear from you My Dear Phillida & do me the justice to believe that no one can be more affectionately & more sincerely attached to You by all the pure & sacred Laws of real Friendship than your Eliza.

Phylly's admirer Mr. DBB unfortunately defies identification; the *List of Commissioned Sea Officers of the Royal Navy, 1660–1815*, shows several sailors of the time whose initials are D.B. or D.-.B., but none with the particular combination of D.B.B. It can only be guessed that he had not yet attained the rank of Post-Captain, and so could not afford to marry and keep a wife and family.

Orchard Street, 14th November 1791 – My Dear Friend, You had not heard when You wrote last to me, how very ill My Dear Mother was at the period I saw your Brother, but he must since have informed You of the very dreadful attack She was then labouring under. It is now three weeks since She was taken so much worse than I had yet seen her, that my Apprehensions (which I did not think admitted of any addition) were proportionably increased and I immediately called in a Physician, a Dr. Austin whose skill is reckoned very great. He agreed with the Surgeon, that is to say Mr. Rooss in whose Care

I told you that my Mother was, in thinking her in the most immediate danger & for the three following Days it was not expected She could live as many hours; what my distress was for indeed I was in a state nearly bordering on distraction, You will easier conceive than I describe to You. It pleased the Almighty however to alleviate it and contrary to all expectation the excellence of My dear Mother's constitution supported her thro' the severe Conflict, for this fortnight past She has been recovering her strength; there is also a great alteration in her Complaint for considerable portions of the swelling are now continually detaching themselves, whether this change is for the better or the worse I am too ignorant to determine, but yet I cannot help hoping the whole of the Tumour will thus be removed in time. As to Mr. Rooss, it is very difficult to find out his real opinion, but I think he seems better satisfied than he was, indeed he has ventured to say that if there was no return of the Bleeding, it was possible all might yet be well. What is one great Comfort is that my Mother's Spirits are surprisingly good, and that She has so far recovered her natural rest, that She is able to leave off the Laudanum which has been administered to her for some time past; in short the Agitation of my spirits alternately elevated by a glimmering of Hope & then again sunk by Despair is not to be expressed. However I endeavor I assure You to preserve as much as possible both my Composure and my Health, because I am sensible that were I totally deprived of either I could no longer be useful to the dear Sufferer.

I congratulate you on having seen DBB but am sorry to find he thinks of quitting England again so soon. You certainly must know best but I confess I cannot help wishing your union with this happy man of your choice no longer deferred. You say You are determined to have no other, then why not take him at once? for surely it is almost the same thing? & I don't see why DBB should not make his voyages and take every step his fortune may require just as well as a married man as he could as a single one indeed as his mind will be more at ease from being secure of the object of his affections and he will have an additional incentive to the acquisition of fortune it may reasonably be supposed his efforts will be so much the more successful. Perhaps My Dear Cousin you think all this very impertinent, but remember You have more than once kindly given me leave to communicate my thoughts to you without disguise. I am sure the Ball which was in agitation when you last wrote must have proved very pleasant, for what can a fair one experience more delightful than to enjoy the society of the man of her Heart? unless indeed it be, what some would think a still more exquisite gratification, that is to say teazing the Man of their Hearts; but you I know, are much too good ever to deal in such wicked amusements, which indeed seriously speaking can never be thought of where there is a real regard. I am greatly obliged to your good Friend for the kind interest he took in my situation, I hope one of these days to thank him for it, and at the same time wish him & myself Joy of having acquired a new Cousin.

I saw in the Papers this very Morning that one of Mrs. Wynch's Sons is married to Miss Perfect of West Malling – [I ho]pe the Lady does justice to her name. Edward A. I believe will also in [an]other month or two take unto himself a spouse, He shewed me the Lady's picture which is that of a very pretty Woman; as to Cassandra it is very probable as You observe that some Son of Neptune may have obtained her Approbation as She probably experienced much homage from these very gallant Gentlemen during her Aquatic Excursions; I hear her Sister & herself are two of the prettiest Girls in England.

I believe I have no news whatsoever to send you which you will not be surprized at, as you know I do not mix much with the world at present. Did I tell you when I saw you in Town how very noble a House our Cousin Hampson has got, he has left Wimpole Street and is now in Cumberland Place, where he has purchased a really magnificent Mansion. Your old acquaintance Mr. & Mrs. J.B.B. have spent their summer on the Coast of France, but are now returned from thence & I hear talk still of India in the Spring. The Mother & Sister have been here to make their personal enquiries concerning my Mother; As to the Lady & Gentleman all the advances they have made or may make towards renewing their acquaintance with me, must ever be fruitless, as I should despise myself if I could be capable of the meanness of admitting people into my presence who have treated me as they have done.

Adieu My Aimiable Friend, present my most affectionate remembrance to all your dear relatives, continue me that share in your regard which I so highly prize & believe me ever most faithfully & affectionately yours Eliza.

Edward Austen married Elizabeth Bridges in Kent at the end of December 1791, and the young couple lived for the next few years at the village of Rowling, near Goodnestone. The Revd George Austen's youngest son Charles had entered the Royal Naval Academy at Portsmouth in July 1791, so perhaps the Austen family had escorted him there and taken a seaside holiday at the same time, with the eighteen-year-old Cassandra being admired by naval officers, as her elder cousins guessed.

By now Mrs. Hancock must have been well aware that she could not hope to recover, however brave a face she maintained towards Eliza, for on 14th December she made her Will; as her husband had done, she chose Warren Hastings and Edward Baber for her executors. Although Eliza must have known, or guessed, that her mother's lawyer and a neighbour from Orchard Street had been called in together for the purpose of witnessing the Will, she makes no reference to this in her next letter to Phylly:

23rd December 1791 – It was both my Wish and Intention to return an early Answer to my Dear Phillida's kind epistle, but it is unfortunately so much more difficult to carry good resolutions into execution, than to form them, that in spite of all my purposes to the contrary, day after day has glided by without my being able to accomplish the projected Letter. Literally My Friend, however strange the assertion may appear, I never had less leisure than at the present juncture; It is true I decline all engagements, I never stir out of the House, for it is above three Months since I have been over the Threshold of the Door, and yet what with my attendance on My Dear Mother, My Attempts to amuse her, the little matters of Business which now devolve on me, and the visits of those friends whom kind solicitude brings, my Time is more engrossed than ever it was, and the only portion of it which is not devoted to one or the other of the above mentioned avocations is the interval I now avail myself of, that is to say the moments between My Mothers Bed Time which is half past nine, and my own at nearer Twelve than Eleven – but enough on this Subject, I merely wished to account for my being so remiss a Correspondent to one whom I take so much pleasure in writing to, and now we will dismiss this theme for one which I am sure You are impatient for me to enter upon.

Your Good Father who kindly called on us some days since has undoubtedly told You how he found my dear Mother; Since his seeing her She has, in addition to the other evils She labours under, suffered much from a severe Cold which She has caught in spite of all precautions, and which has been attended by a violent Cough and complaint in her Bowels, a circumstance which in her reduced state was particularly alarming; however, I thank God She is better and I trust a few days will remove the remainder of this temporary indisposition, for such I hope it will prove. As to the cruel Disorder itself, from which She suffers so severely She herself seems to think there is some amendment, but to my unutterable Sorrow I cannot flatter myself into a similar Belief, and can only say that I do not think She gets worse, which however is certainly a great point in her Situation; it is also most fortunate that She has had no return of the dreadful bleedings, but these two circumstances alas, include all the favorable ones attending her Case. The Tumour remains in the same state and She experiences as much pain as ever, her appetite also is as bad as ever, and it is with the greatest difficulty I can prevail on her to take a sufficient quantity of sustenance for her Support. Notwithstanding all her Sufferings however her Spirits continue surprizingly good, and She appears (I say appears for perhaps She only seems thus in order to keep up my spirits) convinced that time & patience will accomplish her Cure. She has more than once declared that She hopes next Summer to be able to visit You at Seale and promises herself the greatest pleasure from realizing this scheme; May the Almighty grant its taking place and my enjoying the large share of Satisfaction which this Journey would on all accounts afford me.

It gave me sincere concern to find your worthy Friend DBB had been assailed by that severest of all Calamities, Sickness, but I trust he is, long ere this, perfectly recovered. I do not wonder that your visits should have contributed more to his restoration than all those which his Physician could pay, since there cannot be a more sovereign remedy for most Bodily Complaints than ease of mind, to which nothing can certainly be more conducive than the presence of that Being whom we prefer to all others – I am on my own Account as well as yours (for that said thing called self will intrude on all occasions) happy to find you are likely soon to enjoy some share of the Species of Satisfaction above alluded to, I mean in your intended Visit to Mrs. K: during which you tell me you are likely to be gratified with DBB's Society and I hope also to obtain some share of yours, indeed I look forward to that period with great pleasure and hope nothing will prevent your visiting London next month according to the intentions announced in your last.

I believe [I have] no News whatsoever to send you, but indeed how should I in my present recluse state; I have however this moment received an Invitation which I sincerely wish you could avail yourself of in my stead, it is to a couple of very elegant Balls which you are certainly well convinced that nothing could bribe me to go to at present. My mind is not tuned to Gaiety and I have no merit in renouncing every thing of the kind for with a Heart so cruelly agitated & depressed as mine it would be impossible for me to participate in any thing which the World denominates Amusement.

In answer to your enquiry concerning the Situation of Cumberland Place, a question which I assure you did not in the least surprize me, because it is a part of the Town which few People are acquainted with from its having been very lately built, in Answer I say to your wish for Information on the

Subject, I must inform You that it is at the End of Great Cumberland Street which runs into Oxford Street and is nearer Hyde Park than Orchard Street. Cumberland Place is built in the form of a Crescent and is not yet half finished. The Houses are extremely noble, and I know that one about two doors from our cousin's lets for fifteen Guineas a Week. Apropos Mr. Hampson is at present at Bath where he was ordered for his Health, which however I am glad to find is better. Do you know that I think it would be a very nice match, and that you might as well come & be my neighbour, I should think it delightful but what would DBB say?

I am almost ashamed to send you this stupid and almost unintelligible scrawl, I know however that you are anxious for intelligence concerning my dear Mother, and therefore my letter shall depart trusting to your indulgent Friendship to excuse all the deficiencies of the performance you will receive. Pray present mine and my Mother's most affectionate Love & Good Wishes together with those of the Season to your good Father & Mother & every part of your Family; Adieu my dearest cousin and be assured of that sincere regard with which I remain most faithfully & most affectionately yours, EF.

Their cousin Mr. Hampson was now a widower, as his wife had died on 6th May 1791, leaving him with one young son, hence Eliza's joking suggestion that Phylly ought to marry him and come to live in London.

The next two letters from Eliza, Nos. 40 and 41, are missing; they would have told Phylly of Mrs. Hancock's further decline and then her death in February 1792. It seems that in the New Year of 1792 Eliza took her mother to the village of Hampstead, on the northern outskirts of London – possibly for some desperate last-minute treatment, as Hampstead then had several resident doctors and was considered a very healthy place – because it is in the churchyard of St. John-at-Hampstead that she lies under a simple ledger-stone, which once bore the inscription:

In Memory of Philadelphia Wife of Tysoe Saul Hancock Esqr Whose Moral Excellence united the Practice of every Christian Virtue She bore with pious resignation the severest trials of a tedious and painful Malady and expired on the 26th day of February 1792 Aged 61.

Warren Hastings and Edward Baber called on Eliza early in March, to open Mrs. Hancock's Will in her presence. The Will showed that she had lent her entire capital of £6,500 to the Comte de Feuillide, as all her other arrangements (bequests to her goddaughter Louisa Forde and to her Hancock sister-in-law Olivia, with the remainder to Eliza and little Hastings) were dependent upon his repayment of this money to her estate. Nevertheless, her final wish was that her executors should not in any way try to force her son-in-law to honour this debt.

The Comte de Feuillide was able to visit England to comfort Eliza in her bereavement, and took her to Bath for recuperation, but his visit was cut short, as her next letter to Phylly explains:

[Orchard Street, London] 7th June 1792 – Such a length of Time has elapsed My Dear Friend since any Letters have passed between us, that I really know not which of us is most to blame for this interruption of our Correspondence, but be that as it may, I am too desirous of some account of You & yours to remain any longer silent.

As I have the Vanity to think You in some degree interested in what relates to me, I will proceed to give You an Account of Myself. I believe it is since I last wrote that my Journey to Bath has taken place, from which I derived little amusement, perhaps more owing to the state of my Spirits, than any thing else. After about a fortnights Stay we returned to London & M. de F. proposed remaining here some time, but he soon received Accounts from France which informed him that having already exceeded his Leave of Absence, if he still continued in England he would be considered as one of the Emigrants, & consequently his whole property forfeited to the Nation. Such Advices were not to be neglected and M. de F. was obliged to depart for Paris, but not however without giving me hopes of his return in some Months, that is to say when the state of Affairs will let him, for at present it is a very difficult Business for a military man especially, to obtain Leave to absent himself. Thus My Dear Friend am I once more a very solitary Being, the Acquaintance & Connexions however whom I have here are very kind and attentive to me and I endeavor on my part as much as possible to struggle with the melancholy which has taken deep root in my mind but which I know was I to give way to it would render me totally incapable of every Duty I have yet to fulfil.

I think of quitting Town about ye 15 or 16th of this Month & paying two Visits in Surrey, one to my very old Acquaintance Mrs. Farhill who has got, as I am told a very pretty place near Bagshot, the remainder of the Summer I believe I shall spend with our good Friends at Steventon, & hope the quiet & good Air will be of great service to my Health which indeed stands much in need of some such restorative; I have really been very ill for some days past, but that has been chiefly owing to a sudden alarm which I experienced. I suppose you have heard of the Commotions we have of late had in this Metropolis, and Tuesday last going thro' Mount Street in my Carriage I most unexpectedly found myself in the midst of an immense mob who were contending with a large party of Guards on Horseback, because these latter endeavored to disperse them & prevent their demolishing some Houses which they were determined, & had begun, to pull down. The noise of the populace, the drawn swords & pointed bayonets of the guards, the fragments of bricks & mortar thrown on every side, one of which had nearly killed my Coachman, the firing at one end of the street which was already begun, altogether in short alarmed me so much, that I really have never been well since. The Confusion continued all that day & Night & the following Day, & for these eight & forty Hours, I have seen nothing but large parties of Soldiers parading up & down in this Street, to which Mount Street is very near, there being only Grosvenor Square between. My apprehensions have been that they would set fire to these houses they were so bent on demolishing, and think if that was the case how soon in such a City as this a Fire very trifling in its beginning might be productive of the most serious Consequences.

I shall hope to hear from You soo[n with] a long account of all your goings on I suppose You have been [away on] Visits &cc & often, <u>very often</u> thinking of, & writing to <u>your o[ther] Brother DBB</u>, Have You had any accounts of him? I sincerely wish you may & those of the most satisfactory Nature. Adieu My Dear Cousin, your <u>little Cousin</u> is well & begs leave to kiss your fair hands remember me affectionately to My Uncle & Aunt & all your Family & believe me to be most truly your affectionate & faithful Friend, Eliza.

Continue to direct as usual, for if you should be so lazy as to suffer me to have left Town before You write, all letters directed to me here will be carefully forwarded to me.

The disturbances in Mount Street took place on 5th and 6th June 1792, and arose from the arrest of a party of servants who had been too freely celebrating the King's birthday on 4th June; as there was then no civil police force, it was the custom for soldiers to be called in to quell such rioting.

The grief and worries Eliza had recently experienced now resulted in illness:

Orchard St. 16th July 1792 – Nothing My Dear Cousin but real inability to write should have so long prevented me from answering your last, but for these two Months past I have been so great an Invalid as never to have been out of the faculty's hands, and am still taking Bark [quinine] *and I know not what odious things besides, all Day long, Indeed nothing but the impossibility of a removal should have kept me in Town so long.*

You will naturally expect to hear some particulars concerning the nature of my Complaints & tho' there are few things more irksome on most occasions, than accounts of this nature, yet as I am sure your Friendship for me will make you desirous of such intelligence, in the present instance I will venture to give it you; Primo, then, my regard for Truth obliges me to confirm the Account your good Father heard when he was in Town but as this little Accident was attended with no very serious consequences at the Time, I flattered myself my Health would not suffer materially; however in a very short Time I was attacked with a very violent fever & such a pain in my Head as I never had felt in my Life which for three Days & Nights nearly distracted me, at the end of this period a most violent eruption made its appearance and my Physician declared I had got the Small Pox. This I assured him could not be the case for I had had it, in short My Dear Friend for I would not quite tire you out with my dismal Story, my Disorder at length proved to be the Chicken Pox but which I had so severely that those about me all gave me the comfortable assurance that I must be marked & completely frightful for the rest of my Days. This prediction however has not been exactly verified, at least I am not much more frightful than I was before, for the only trace now left of my Malady is one single mark in my forehead which as you may suppose does not make any violent alteration in my appearance. I sincerely wish my Health had been as little affected but whether it was owing to my having two illnesses immediately after each other, or what other cause I cannot say, but I really have never recovered my last indisposition, I have a slow fever almost constantly, have lost my rest & Appetite and am altogether a very poor creature.

I flatter myself however that I shall receive Benefit from change of Air & mean to leave Town the Day after To–morrow, I am going to Mr. Woodman's who have [sic] *got a charming place between Ewell & Epsom. My stay there is very uncertain, and I believe I must make another Visit before I can reach Hampshire which I think I have already told you I mean to make my resting place for the remainder of the Year. I have been in great hopes of seeing You, as You mentioned being in Town some time this Month, but I fear my expectations in this particular will not be fulfilled.*

You will be surprized to hear that D.B.B. should have been mentioned in a letter I received from the environs of Durham some time since. You must recollect I think that I have a friend settled in that part of the world of the name of Egerton, She has a cousin on a visit to her & that cousin mentioned DBB in the way I doubt not he deserves, for She represented him as endowed with every valuable & aimiable quality, and added that he knew me, so that it was in [con]sequence of this assertion that my Friend spoke of him to [me and] enquired where we became acquainted; in Answer to which I [said] my personal knowledge was very small (You know it was only acquired on the Walks at Tunbridge) but that I had often heard from very good Authority that he was really the worthy and aimiable Being he had been represented to her. I hope my Dear Friend that you approve of my conduct in this transaction which trifling as it is I thought You would like to be informed of, as I think there is always infinite pleasure in hearing those we love well spoken of. I expect to be condoled with in your next & once more called sly, the former however You need not take much trouble about as I really bear the Loss occasioned by this said accidental occurrence with great christian patience, & the latter epithet I think, & so I am sure do you in your Heart, there never was any human being less entitled to than myself.

You may direct to me as usual for this whole month, for my letters will be carefully forwarded to me & when once August is begun direct to me at Steventon for I hope to be there by that time, remember me most affectionately to all your Family & believe me for Life your tenderly attached & faithful Friend, Eliza.

An 'accident' was the current euphemism for a miscarriage – Eliza's brief pregnancy was evidently the result of the Comte de Feuillide's visit earlier in the year. Her friend in county Durham was Catherine, the wife of the Revd Charles Egerton, who had held the living of Washington since 1786; their rectory was 'an elegant and commodious brick mansion, with good gardens annexed', as a contemporary local historian proudly described it.

Eliza went to stay with the Austens, and while she was there the political scene in France changed abruptly, for on 21st September 1792 France abolished its monarchy, and Year I of the new French Republic was decreed as beginning on 22nd September.

Steventon 26th October 1792 – My Dear Phillida, You know my Laziness in regard to Writing so well that I dare say My Silence has not occasioned You any Surprize, That it does not however the less need an Apology, I am well aware but indeed I had rather trust to your Good Nature for my Excuse than take up your Time with Attempts for my own Justification which I own

I flatter myself to be the less necessary, after all, as you must be thoroughly convinced that altho' my native Indolence may sometimes prevent my making the Use I ought of my Pen, yet that neither that or any other impulse can prevent me from being in the most comprehensive Sense of the Word your faithful Friend, and that as such My Heart must glow with sincere Affection for You in spite of all Appearances may seem to say to the contrary.

The many interesting particulars contained in your kind Letter were most acceptable – Happy indeed would it have made me could we have chatted in person on all these Subjects and most provoking was it that I should leave Town just as You entered it. I had flattered myself you would have visited London rather sooner, and that my being detained there would have afforded me at least a Glimpse of You, but these Expectations were not to be answered, and I have now nothing for it but to live in hopes that at some future Opportunity, when You come to buy your Wedding Cloaths perhaps, or in short whenever either Business or Pleasure brings You again to the Metropolis, I shall be more fortunate.

Yours found me as You expected quietly settled at Steventon, in regard to which place and its inhabitants I will endeavor to answer all your enquiries as well as I can. In the first place then I have the real pleasure of informing You that our Dear Uncle & Aunt are both in perfect Health, The former looks uncommonly well, and in my opinion his Likeness to My beloved Mother is stronger than ever, Often do I sit and trace her Features in his, till my Heart overflows at my Eyes. I always tenderly loved my Uncle, but I think he is now dearer to me than ever, as being the nearest and best beloved Relative of the never to be sufficiently regretted Parent I have lost; Cassandra & Jane are both very much grown (The latter is now taller than myself) and greatly improved as well in Manners as in Person both of which are now much more formed than when You saw them. They are I think equally sensible, and both so to a degree seldom met with, but still My Heart gives the preference to Jane, whose kind partiality to me, indeed requires a return of the same nature. Henry is now rather more than Six Foot high I believe, He also is much improved, and is certainly endowed with uncommon Abilities, which indeed seem to have been bestowed, tho' in a different way, upon each Member of this Family. As to the Coolness which You know had taken place between H. and myself, it has now ceased, in consequence of due acknowledgments on his part, and we are at present on very proper relationlike terms. You know that his Family design him for the Church. Cassandra was from home when I arrived, she was then on a visit to Rowling the Abode of her Brother Edward, from which She returned however some time since but is now once more absent as well as her Sister on

Portrait miniature of Henry Austen by an unknown artist,
made ca. 1820 after he had become a clergyman.
Jane Austen Memorial Trust

a Visit to the Miss Floyds who live at a place called Ibthorp about eighteen Miles I believe from hence, They both return on Monday next.

I suppose You have heard long since of the Death of poor Dr. Cooper, his Daughter came immediately here, I know not whether You are personally acquainted with Her, but I think You must recollect my having mentioned her (She was one of our Theatrical Troop). At the Time of her Father's Death She was on the very brink of Wedlock, The Day being fixed, but the abovementioned melancholy Event necessarily occasioned a Delay of the [nuptials which] are now fixed for some Time in December and are to be celebrated in this [house so] that I suppose we are to be mighty gay; indeed I am delighted with the Thoughts of it, for I never was but at one Wedding in my Life and that appeared a very stupid Business to me, I hope I shall be better amused at this. All this while I have not told you who the happy Man is, be it therefore known unto You, He is a Captn. Williams of the Royal Navy (I am sure You will now be much more interested about him). His present Fortune is but small, but he has expectations of future preferment. The happy Pair are to inhabit the Isle of Wight, to which they have kindly given me a pressing invitation, and which if I am alive next Summer I may possibly accept.

The little Sailor whom You enquire after, was perfectly well when he was last heard of, which however is now some time since. He is expected home in the Course of the next Year. I suppose you know that both Mrs. James & Mrs. Edward Austen are in the encreasing way, The latter I have only had a peep at, and the former I have not seen a great deal more of, as She is so much incommoded by her present Situation as to be confined to her Bed for whole Days; I think them both pleasant as far as I can judge.

I have still so much to say and so little room left in this odious paper that I know [not] how I shall manage, I should have done much more wisely had I followed your Example and taken a sheet of larger dimensions. I can readily believe that the Share of Sensibility I know You to be possessed of would not suffer You to learn the tragical Events of which France has of late been the theatre without being much affected. My private Letters confirm the Intelligence afforded by the public Prints and assure me that nothing we there read is exaggerated. M. de F. is at present in Paris, He had determined on coming to England, but finds it impossible to get away.

I most sincerely rejoice in your having hitherto had such Accounts from the deserving DBB as must upon the whole be very satisfactory. How fortunate that he preserved his Health, May You soon be restored to each other and meet, no more to part. Indeed it would give me most sincere pleasure to hear You were united, as I trust it would be securing your Happiness. Pray continue to inform me of every particular relating to this interesting Subject. Your Sister is indeed a notable Dame, and very few there are who could have dispatched such a Business so expeditiously, If She goes on at this rate Your Brother bids fair for having a patriarchal number of children.

I have no thoughts of going to Town for some Months to come but I may perhaps spend a fortnight at Bath in the Course of next Month; Mrs. Egerton whom I believe you know by name is there and presses me much to come to her – Louisa whom you enquire after sailed for India last August with her Spouse, She wrote to me repeatedly and made use of such very moving pleas for forgiveness, that I could not help granting it, She is I find in a bad state of Health.

As notwithstanding what you say of your disinclination to dancing, I cannot yet believe you totally indifferent to such matters I think I ought to inform You how we stand in regard to them in this part of the World. There has been a Club Ball at Basingstoke and a private one in the neighbourhood, both of which My Cousins say were very agreeable. As to myself I was too ill to go to them being confined to my Bed with a feverish Attack. There is to be another Ball the 4th of Novr. which I shall go to if I am able, but I do not think I shall dance, See how staid & Sober I grow. I know You will kindly wish for some account of Hastings, He has I think gained much Health & Strength from his residence here, He is the Play Thing of the whole Family. Adieu My Dear Cousin, luckily for you I am forced to end this slovenly scrawl, remember me affectionately to all at home, and do not doubt my being for Life faithfully and affectionately yours, Eliza.

Pray do not neglect burning this.

It seems rather odd that Eliza should have wished Phylly to burn this letter, as it does not appear to contain anything that might need to be kept secret, but merely brings Phylly up to date with the latest news of the Austen family and their friends and relations. Mrs. Lloyd and her daughters Martha and Mary [at that time 'Floyd' was an alternative spelling for 'Lloyd'] who had lived in the parsonage at Deane from the spring of 1789 until January 1792, had then moved to Ibthorpe, a pretty little village in northern Hampshire, where Jane and Cassandra were presently visiting them. Mrs. Austen's brother-in-law, the Revd Dr. Edward Cooper, father of Edward junior and Jane, and vicar of Sonning-on-Thames, Berks, had died on 27th August 1792, and Jane Cooper was married at Steventon, on 11th December 1792, to Capt. Thomas Williams, RN. The 'little sailor' was Francis Austen, now a midshipman on HMS *Minerva* and away in the East Indies. Edward Austen and his Elizabeth had their first child, Fanny, on 23rd January 1793; James Austen had married Anne Mathew on 27th March 1792, and their only child Anna was born on 15th April 1793. On Phylly Walter's side of the family, her sister-in-law Frances had given premature birth to her seventh child, George, on 28th August 1792, but three of her elder children had already died in infancy.

The tragical events in France were already casting long shadows across Europe, and with the end of this year 1792 peace also came to an end.

CHAPTER IV

A reasonable quantity of beaux

1793–97

✡

ONCE THE FRENCH had abolished their monarchical government, it was obviously only a matter of time before the royal family themselves were seen to be a political embarrassment which could not be allowed to survive, and after a trumped-up trial Louis XVI was guillotined on 21st January 1793. Marie-Antoinette likewise went to the scaffold a few months later, and their eight year old son, nominally Louis XVII after his father's death, was left in prison to die of tuberculosis. Some of the French nobility and clergy managed to flee to England, where they formed émigré colonies in London and other provincial towns and received welfare support from the Government. One such colony lived in Reading, some of them occupying a house next door to the school where Jane and Cassandra had been pupils in 1785–86, and made friends with the present schoolgirls, two of whom recalled in later years:

It was bright summer weather, and we lived more and more with the noble emigrants, talked with the ladies, and danced with the gentlemen under the trees in the Abbey garden to the sound of the harp. We were then as it were completely carried away with the spirit and feelings of France in the olden times ...

and:

Something wonderful and admirable it was to see how these Dukes and Duchesses, Marshals and Marquises, Chevaliers and Bishops bore up under their unparalleled reverses! How they laughed and talked and squabbled and flirted – constant to their high heels, their rouge and their furbelows, to their old liaisons, their polished sarcasms, their cherished rivalries! ... very many lived literally on the produce of their own industry; the gentlemen teaching languages, music, fencing, dancing; whilst their wives and daughters went out as teachers or governesses, or supplied the shops with those objects of taste in millinery or artificial flowers for which their country is unrivalled.

On 1st February 1793 the new French Republic declared war on Britain and Holland, a war which spread around the world and lasted for twenty years.

There is no definite knowledge of Eliza's movements for eighteen months after her letter of 26th October 1792; in March 1793 Phylly told James Walter that she supposed her to be still at Steventon, though she had not heard from her for six months. Did Eliza perhaps go to Reading and then to London to seek out the émigrés in the hope of getting news of her husband? In the 1780s the Comte's works of reclamation at Le Marais had been very successful, and as the land dried out crops were sown, cattle stocked and buildings erected. However, the local peasantry resented the loss of the fish and wildfowl which they had been accustomed to catch freely in the marsh and so turned against the Comte and began to attack his employees and damage the newly-created property. It may have been this hostility which made the Comte move to Paris in 1792 with the intention of coming to England, as Eliza had told Phylly, only to find himself trapped there. His name was placed on the list of émigrés and his goods were confiscated – some of the furniture from his new house at Le Marais, no doubt that which Eliza had bought in London in 1788, was sold in July 1794, and the rest carried off to the nearby town of Nogaro. In the meantime, the Comte had been traced to his lodgings in Paris and was arrested in February 1794. A friend of his, the elderly Marquise de Marboeuf, was accused of having hoped for the arrival of the Austrians and Prussians and of keeping provisions for them; the Comte tried to buy off her accusers, who took his bribe and betrayed him. At his trial he was described as a 'cultivateur' and former captain of dragoons, aged 43, and two of the witnesses who gave evidence were his housekeeper, 'la citoyenne Joubert', and 'la citoyenne Grandville, l'ancienne maitresse de Feuillide'. Both the Marquise and the Comte were guillotined on 22nd February 1794.

There was a family tradition amongst the Austens, lingering on until the late nineteenth century, that the Comte had made an attempt to save himself by claiming to be an impostor, a valet who had murdered his master and assumed the identity of de Feuillide. No record of such a statement appears in the proceedings of the trial, so if it were ever made it must have been recognised immediately as nothing more than a wild fabrication of despair and as such ignored.

Whatever happened to Eliza during these eighteen months must remain a puzzle; but in March 1794 she was certainly in London and reading a report, in one of the ephemeral newssheets which circulated amongst the émigrés in England, that the Comte had been condemned to death. Later that year she went to stay with her friends the Egertons in their rectory at Washington, co. Durham, and from there wrote to Warren Hastings:

Washington, 19th September 1794 – Dear Sir, I entreat You to accept my sincere Thanks for the few Lines with which You have favored me, and for your Care of the Letter enclosed in yours, which I am concerned to think should have occasioned you so much trouble. On seeing a foreign Post Mark I flattered myself with receiving some important information, and was much disappointed to find myself addressed from Corunna by a Person to whom I am almost a Stranger, and who writes merely to request my endeavors to obtain an english Passport.

In Answer to your kind enquiries concerning my Health, I have the satisfaction of saying, that I find myself much the better for the Northern Air of which I have now made some trial, having been at this place, that is to say on the borders of Northumberland, ever since July; I purposed returning to London some time next Month, but Mr. & Mrs. Egerton, the Friends to whom I have already paid so long a visit, kindly insist on my not leaving them till after Christmas. I beg to present my most affectionate Compts. to Mrs. Hastings, and sincerely hope her Health as well as your own is good; I trust too that You have had no return of the Complaint in your Eyes. To request an Answer on these Subjects would I am sensible be trespassing too far on your time, but if between the present period and January You will bestow a Line on me just to say how You are, it will afford me much Satisfaction, and add to the many favors You have already conferred on her who must ever be, Dear Sir, Your truly affectionate Goddaughter, Elizabeth de Feuillide.

My address is at The Revd. Charles Egerton's, Washington, Durham.

There is now another gap in Eliza's history; presumably she returned to London some time in 1795, and then probably went again to Steventon, for according to Austen family tradition it was in 1795–96 that her cousins James and Henry both started to court her. James's wife Anne Mathew died suddenly in May 1795, leaving him lonely in his parsonage with one little daughter, and it must have seemed most appropriate to him that a young widow and widower should console each other, especially as they had been friends since childhood. On the other hand, Henry had joined the Oxfordshire Militia in 1793, was tall and handsome in his lieutenant's uniform and, although ten years younger than Eliza, was nevertheless far more like her in character than was his serious and introspective elder brother. It seems that the impetuous Henry was the first to propose, some time in 1795, but Eliza refused him kindly and no acrimony arose between them. On the rebound he engaged himself in the following year to a Miss Mary Pearson, but within a few months the engagement was broken off, apparently by mutual consent.

Eliza's next surviving letter shows that by 1796 she was as cheerful and flirtatious as ever, on holiday again at Tunbridge Wells, and anxious to have Phylly's company once more.

Tunbridge Wells, Thursday 22nd September 1796 – My dear Cousin, I will not let another day pass without scribbling you a few Lines, tho' I must go out at half past twelve, but hurried as my scrawl will be, I flatter myself it will still afford you some pleasure, as the vehicle of the intelligence that I reached this place on Saturday night (about eleven) without having met a single Collector, or Mishap of any kind. The coolness of the Air & the Moonlight were delightful and nothing but your presence was wanting to complete the pleasure of my ride. On Sunday you were much missed and much enquired after on the Pantiles, I did not go to the tea drinking but spent the evening soberly with Mrs. Gaillier. Monday I experienced sincere satisfaction in the arrival of some Friends whom I believe you heard me mention, I mean Mr. & Mrs. Johnson and their two Daughters, as they are extremely intimate with Mrs. G. we have spent our evenings all together ever since their arrival and I have lost all my Money at Cassino. To-night I was engaged again to Mrs. Gaillier, but Mrs. Barton, Mrs. Keyleigh (another acquaintance who is just arrived) and the Eyles's have beset me to go with them to the Coronation Ball, I hesitated for some time, but at length consented, because I always find that the most effectual mode of getting rid of a temptation is to give way to it.

Let me now My dear Cousin remind You of my wish to obtain your

Company to Brighton – I am very sensible how unwilling your good Mother must be to part with You, but still I trust She will not refuse to do so on this occasion, as I know the pleasure She has in obliging, and She must also be sensible of the real benefit which your Health is likely to receive from Sea bathing – I am convinced it will set you up for the whole winter. Let me once more repeat that it will be conferring the sincerest pleasure and a real obligation on me to afford me your Society in this little Expedition, on which I do not however mean to set out quite so soon as I intended. The Johnsons' arrival & earnest wish to keep me here have induced me to add another week or Ten days to my stay but this I imagine will make no difference to you. Another motive for my remaining here somewhat longer is the benefit which my little Boy receives from the waters, and I am also frightened from a removal just at this Period by the information that Lodgings now let at Brighthelmstone for 16 & 18 Guineas pr. Week.

I will make particular enquiry as to conveyances between this place & Brighton, but my own idea in regard to your travelling is this – If I cannot send my horses to fetch you hither (which I fear, I shall not be able to do, as to tell you the truth one of them strained his Shoulder in his last journey to Seale in such a manner that he has been laid up ever since) you I imagine can easily reach me – From hence I will send one of my women Servants by the Stage, consequently there will be room in the Chariot for the rest of the Party – If I should return to London from Brighton, You may easily come home from London (to which I would carry you) by the Stage – but if I should go elsewhere on quitting Brighton I am almost sure You may reach Tunbridge or Sevenoaks by the Stage, and should it be otherwise it is extremely easy to proceed by the same conveyance to Town and from thence home – Do you understand all this? for I am afraid I have made a sad jumble of it.

I imagine that a certain Beau concerning whom it seems your prediction was not altogether erroneous has lost his way, or stuck fast in the deep roads for I have never yet set eyes on him – Perhaps his courage fails him as you have so barbarously refused him a Passport – I think his coming to B– may not be amiss, as some thing to tag after us will be rather necessary – Condole with me, for dear Baddy is gone – After some very friendly Chat, The Curricle was once more brought forward, and I in a luckless hour once more said [word missing], *on which the Gentleman wisely determined Yea, yea should* [word missing] *be in my power – I do most unfeignedly rejoice at his departure, for he is an imperious inconsistent wretch.*

There is to be a Tea drinking, Concert & Ball on Saturday by desire of the Dutchess of Gordon, it is supposed it will be well attended, and I and all my squad which now cuts no inconsiderable figure, mean to be there, How I wish you could join our Party! Lord & Lady Studley are come down and many more fine people, in short the Pantiles look very gay, notwithstanding which I amuse myself with abusing them all day long – Adieu my dear Phillida, let me hear from You and believe me ever very affectionately yours, E. de F.

Remember me very affectionately to your Father & Mother; I received your letter only this morning for it had been missent to Bromley.

A 'collector' was the current nickname for a highwayman; every town held a Coronation Ball annually to commemorate that of George III, on 22nd September 1761. Unfortunately, there is no way of identifying Phylly's 'certain Beau' or Eliza's admirer 'dear Baddy'. Despite Eliza's optimism that sea-bathing was beneficial for little Hastings, a few weeks later Phylly wrote gloomily to her brother: 'I'm afraid he is already quite an idiot.'

Eliza and Phylly did go to Brighton together, but whilst there Eliza fell ill, with what seems to have been an abscess or cyst in the breast, and their holiday had to be cut short as she sought medical treatment.

London, Monday 17th October 1796 – My dear Cousin, I have deferred writing to You that I might be enabled to give You more certain accounts of my Health, concerning which I know You are so kind as to interest yourself – I cannot however yet say any thing very positive – I think the swelling is decreased and is sunk lower, but the progress of this amendment is so very slow, and at times appears so dubious, that I would see Farquhar, if it was not for my horror of the medical tribe – at any rate, I think I must consult him or some one else if another week does not make a really evident alteration for the better.

I got here early on Wednesday Afternoon and found nothing ready for my reception, as my letter had been misunderstood, and it had consequently been concluded that I should not arrive till the following day – a Beau who occupied one floor was not yet gone out, and how to squeeze my family into a part of this small house when the whole hardly suffices for it, I knew not – at length after a great deal of bustle plague & fretting, we contrived to find sleeping room – The beau You may be sure was very accommodating on this occasion. The house is the nicest little Box You can imagine but I do not like the situation for it is quite at the world's or rather the Town's End, and I find it the most inconvenient thing imaginable to reach a Shop of any description.

As to my Acquaintance, it does not so much signify for I shall probably not see many of them – As yet, not one knows of my arrival in Town, and I have consequently been quite a recluse which was not necessary to make me regret the loss of your Society. Indeed My dear Phillida I do most sensibly miss it and after having known the comfort of a sensible & sweet tempered Companion, Solitude appears doubly forlorn & irksome to me. I hope You performed your little Journey with Ease & Safety, and did not suffer materially from the cold, which I trust You repelled according to my sage counsel, with your new fashioned Shawl – I fear however that you did not escape the Rain for I think you could not have reached home, before a heavy shower which I regretted much on your account. I hope You found your Father & Mother well, and renewed my Thanks to them for having indulged me with so much of your company which I do not ask if they were delighted to regain.

I can send you no London News, excepting that Mr. Dowton the Hero of the Tunbridge Wells Theatre has made his appearance at Old Drury and been received with much applause. I suppose you know that Lord Malmesbury set off on Saturday for Paris in order to treat for peace. I have received a long letter from Mrs. Barton who as I expected has given up the thoughts She perhaps never had, of coming to Brighton, She is to be in Town, for the Winter, the 25th of this Month; She says the Johnsons and Mrs. Keyleigh have left the Wells, and that your favorite Colonel & his Lady are preparing to do the same. Adieu My dear Cousin, let me hear from You for I much wish to know how you accomplished the remainder of [your] Journey, and believe me to be in the mean [time] your affectionate & obliged Friend, E. de Feuillide.

Hastings who often talks of you desires to be affectionately remembered, and that I will assure his Wife elect, that he is still determined on having three Children – This puts me in mind of my own increase of Family – Don't however be too much shocked, for I only mean to speak of an aimiable Terrier with which the Coachman has graciously presented George, I have not yet been able to obtain my much desired Pug. Direct to me No. 3 Durweston Street Baker Street Portman Square London.

The Durweston Street in which Eliza was lodging was at some time in the nineteenth century re-named Crawford Street, and the then Durweston Mews became the modern Durweston Street, but the area has now all been redeveloped. William Dowton (1764–1851) had been acting in Canterbury and Tunbridge Wells since September 1791; he made his first appearance in London at Drury Lane Theatre as Sheva in Cumberland's comedy 'The Jew' on 11th October 1796, and was an instant success. Lord Malmesbury had gone to France to negotiate a peace settlement, but his negotiations were broken off in December 1796. Pugs were originally a Chinese breed and were introduced to Europe by the Dutch in the seventeenth century as a result of their trading contacts with China. From Holland they gradually came to England and were very fashionable during the first half of the eighteenth century. By 1790, however, they had fallen out of favour, so it seems Eliza was anxious to re-start the fashion by acquiring one as a lapdog.

Eliza's next letter shows her courage in making a jest of her visit to the doctor's surgery, despite realising that her symptoms were all too similar to those which had caused her mother's agonising death:

7th November 1796 – I have been prevented writing to You My dear Cousin by being so thoroughly disheartened about my Complaint, as to dislike entering into any particulars concerning it – A few days after I wrote last to You I thought myself materially worse, and accordingly dispatched a Note to Farquhar requesting him to appoint a time for seeing me – This Note I addressed to Dr. Farquhar, whereas it should have been to Sr. Walter Farquhar Bart., but this impropriety he forgave, and appointed a quarter before four that day for our meeting. With a beating heart I repaired to my Rendezvous, and was told that Sr. Walter was not yet returned home – The Servant would have shewn me into a Parlour with a good fire in it, but on seeing two Smart young Men there, who opened eyes as wide as Barn Doors to view the Doctors female Patient, I desired to go into another Apartment and was accordingly shut into a Study where an empty grate announced the cold reception which I had to depend on. Here I waited nearly two Hours which gave me an opportunity of reading various physical Books filled with shocking cases, and also of inspecting two large presses (this part of the Story you must keep secret) where I expected to find Skeletons, but however met with nothing but crooked Scissors and other formidable Surgical Instruments, and a few Embryos in Spirits. At length the Doctor came, and the grave face which he put on sufficiently alarmed me – He told me the mercurial ointment did not agree with me, and desired I would immediately discontinue it, and that very evening apply four Leeches to the Swelling Not a moment he said was to be lost, for there was an unpleasant pulsation in the swelling which he trusted the Leeches would remove; at the same time however that his Looks and manner frightened me, his words afforded some Comfort for he said he made little doubt of curing me but that it was likely to be a tedious Business. A written Prescription for Draughts to be taken Night & Morning he also gave me and with this I set off to my Apothecarys in Pall Mall, both in order to bespeak the Leeches & have my Drugs made up –

The idea of these Leeches was very terrible to me, but I mustered up what courage I could, and the odious Beasts were stuck on – They obligingly staid with me above two Hours, and Sr. Walter who saw me again the next day was well satisfied with their effect, tho' I could not see any apparent difference in the Swelling – He desired me to continue my Medicines, and in the course of a few days the Leeches were again applied. They then favored me with their Company still longer than the first time, but they had not been taken off ten minutes when the places where they had been applied, and indeed the whole side of my neck up to my ear, swelled and inflamed in so terrible a manner, that myself and those about me were exceedingly alarmed, and I accordingly dispatched an Express for my Doctor, who soon quieted our fears, by an assurance that what I experienced was a very common occurrence, for that it often happens, and there is no foreseeing or preventing the circumstance that the bite of the Leech is venomous. He ordered Bread & Milk Poultices, and after feeling for a week as if I had been stung by four Wasps, the consequences of this accident subsided. Since the above mentioned period to the present I have continued my Medicines, and Sr. Walter says the Swelling is materially better, and that in one Month more, it will probably be removed. To the Eye however there is so little amendment that I often doubt whether there is any, but I endeavour to strengthen my stock of faith and hope my Doctor's Predictions will be fulfilled – I ought certainly to be thankful that my general Health is not in the least affected – indeed from my Looks no one would suppose that any thing ailed me. I ought to apologize for this tedious lamentable story of myself, but I know your Friendship is such that you will not feel uninterested in particulars with which I would not have ventured to have tried the patience of most others.

I rejoiced to hear that You found your good Father & Mother well, and was not only [pleased] but also proud of the good Looks on which your [parents] complimented you. If we had not been driven away from Brighton, and all my darling plans defeated, I am convinced you would have received the most lasting benefit from the Sea Air & Bathing – I hope however that I shall at some future period be made amends, and that you will honourably & punctually repay what I lost of your society – When I am quietly settled in that said domestic Retreat which you have talked of, you must charitably come

& prevent my spouse and self from going to sleep or quarrelling for want of other amusement. I am enraged beyond description at the indelicacy of the Beau, Naughty Man! I conclude you talked to him very seriously on the Subject when you next saw him.

I am so much of a prisoner, for I do not stir of an evening for fear of fresh cold, that I cannot tell how the world goes. I saw some of it however in the Park this Morning where the Princess of Wales & myself took an Airing – We were however so unsociable as to go in different Carriages. I have seen Mr. Hampson who enquired particularly after you – His Sister is just arrived from Jamaica, her Husband died a few days after they got on board of Ship, and She is to live with her Brother for the present; I have not seen her but I am told She is a pleasing looking woman. Mrs. Barton is come to Town and we have met several times; Mrs. Gaillier & Mrs. Johnstone do not yet know of my being in London, indeed I have avoided all my acquaintance as much as possible for I have not spirits to see them, and besides it teases me to be continually telling the same story about myself. I have however been found out by many, and have a fairly considerable Levee every morning and a reasonable quantity of Beaux the present hard times considered. I have seen Mrs. Freeman frequently; did I tell you that Mrs. Stanhope has been confined for several months in consequence of a miscarriage, I believe you do not like the word, but I could not think of another. Have I already told you that Mrs. Gaillier & Mrs. Johnstone have quarrelled and don't speak, This happened at Tunbridge just after my departure so that I think I was lucky to be out of the Fray.

Our Cousin Henry Austen has been in Town he looks thin & ill – I hear his late intended is a most intolerable Flirt, and reckoned to give herself great Airs – The person who mentioned this to me says She is a pretty wicked looking Girl with bright Black Eyes which pierce thro' & thro'. No wonder the poor young Man's heart could not withstand them.

I hope you will allow this letter to be thoroughly if not well filled, Let me hear from you soon and believe me to be with the sincerest regard My dear Phillida your affectionate Friend, E. de F.

I live in hopes of the dear Pug's arrival, Pray get him for me if possible.

Sir Walter Farquhar (1738–1819), a fashionable London physician, had been created a baronet on 1st March 1796 and thereafter appointed as one of the Prince of Wales's medical attendants; his consulting room was at 42 Great Marlborough Street. Mr. Hampson's sister Mary – another first cousin of Eliza and Phylly – had been married to a Mr. Samuel Stevenson.

It sounds as if Phylly had been teasing Eliza about James's courtship, and the possibility of her settling down in a peaceful country parsonage. Eliza also seems to have confided in Lady Burrell, for the latter wrote another poem: 'To Eliza, a Dialogue between Inclination and Prudence'. The argument between these personifications is that Inclination is all for Love, while Prudence is for Fortune; Inclination says she scorns

'the gilded bait, / The dull magnificence of state, / The sweets that luxuries afford, / The joys by trivial minds adored; / Gay coronets that cover care, / And pomps that make the vulgar stare, / Proud porticos, capacious rooms, / Expensive robes and waving plumes ...'

in favour of love in a cottage. Prudence in turn scorns both military and clerical husbands:

'Some quartered Captain you may wed, /A profligate, ferocious fellow, /As brave and brutal as Othello, / Whose paltry pay can scarce produce /Enough for regimental use; / Or if your fancy is not set/ On scarlet coat and epaulet, / Suppose you chuse a graver line, /And fall in love with a Divine! / ...The parsonage by yew trees bounded, / And with infernal roads surrounded, / Appears in sight – your reverend mate / There sees the whole of his estate, / And with his sermons and his wife, / Prepares to be a drone for life / ...Forth at the early morn you go, / And see the pallid primrose blow; / ...Meand'ring streams, enamell'd fields, / And bowers romantic pleasure yields / ...But when bleak winter shews his face, / And love moves on with slower pace, / When wither'd leaves are scatter'd round, / And vapours hover o'er the ground, / When whistling winds are heard to pass / Along the churchyard's fading grass / How chang'd the scene!'

Prudence goes on to point out that it would be all too likely a parson's income could not support a large brood of children, 'And matrimonial troubles prove / That indigence can conquer love.' Inclination ends the poem by saying she would still prefer to share a husband's troubles, and be poor but honest. Lady Burrell's advice therefore remained tactfully inconclusive.

Phylly's admirer Mr. DBB had by now disappeared from the scene, leaving her disconsolate, though Eliza did her best to encourage her hopes:

13th December 1796 – My dear Cousin, Lazy as I am in regard to writing I should ere this have thanked You for your entertaining epistle had I not been much engrossed by house hunting and moving – From various inconveniencies attending my late abode I found it impossible to remain in it, and my state of Health rendered it as impossible to quit London, so that I had no remedy but seeking a more commodious habitation in this said Town – After seeing some dozens of houses I determined on the one I have now occupied a week, and which is really very pretty & comfortable, besides its being situated in one of my favorite Streets, viz: Manchester Street, which you may perhaps recollect that I have already inhabited, but my present Mansion is on the opposite side of the way to my late one.

I think you wish for some account of my health and therefore I will no longer delay informing You that the swelling is about half the size you remember it, and has for some time past shewn a disposition to break, on account of which Sr. Walter in his last visit prescribed a bread & milk poultice to be kept constantly applied – This mode of treatment is excessively inconvenient as it confines me entirely to the house and prevents the admittance of any Visitors, a few insipid females excepted – How long this is to last I know not, but it bids fair for some weeks at least, so that I have great need of some of the patience in which I know you abound.

I was much entertained by your account of Mr. Streatfield's Ball which must have been a very elegant affair – I dare say Mr. S. was not inconsolable for the absence of his good Mother, but I can easily believe it somewhat embarrassed you tho' there are those who declare that it is less formidable to be the only female in a quartetto, than to share a Duet; be that as it may I have no doubt You performed your part exceedingly well, and greatly to the satisfaction of your Beaux – I really wish You would think a little more about one of them, and condescend to inhabit the comfortable Mansion which You must now have seen to so much advantage.

The Pacquet which you mention having found on your return home is an incomprehensible business – If it really did come from DBB, and I should think you could not be mistaken in his handwriting, he must have fabricated it in one of those inconsistent fits to which all his provoking sex are subject; or what is still more likely, he longed to hear of you, knew not how to write to you, and took this awkward way of extorting a few lines from You – I long to know what you have done, and whether you have heard any thing further from him – surely he will never let the matter rest here, and indeed my opinion that a reconciliation will one day take place is strengthened by this odd circumstance – Most sincerely do I wish that this said opinion of mine may prove founded, for I do believe that he yet has a larger share of your regard than any other of his Sex. Captn. Anderson's visit & conference with your good Mother were truly comic, and I hope You will have some future occasion of continuing so entertaining an acquaintance – The Man must certainly be deeply smitten, and little less brazen – perhaps however he does not deserve this latter imputation since potent Love will make a Lion of a Lamb.

The last day of my Liberty, mind I do not say my Widowhood, I spent at Mr. Hampson's, when Mrs. Stevenson & myself did our best to entertain eleven beaux – I thought the party remarkably pleasant – We talked much of You, and Mrs. S. says She would write to you if She was not at all times a very bad Correspondent, and just now too weak in spirits to engage in any undertaking where her feelings are concerned – her Brother is all kindness & attention to her, and I think She must find herself extremely comfortable, at least I know I should greatly enjoy a good house, and a nice carriage that cost me neither trouble nor money.

I am glad to find you have made up your mind to visiting the Rectory, but at the same time, and in spite of all your conjectures and belief, I do assert that Preliminaries are so far from settled that I do not believe the parties ever will come together, not however that they have quarrelled, but one of them cannot bring her mind to give up dear Liberty, and yet dearer flirtation – After a few months stay in the Country She sometimes thinks it possible to undertake sober Matrimony, but a few weeks stay in London convinces her how little the state suits her taste – Lord S's card has this moment been brought me which I think very ominous considering I was talking of Matrimony, but it does not signify, I shall certainly escape both Peer & Parson.

Mrs. Barton is very friendly, and very often sits an hour with me. I have dined once or twice with her & her Mother only – The tittle tattle which you informed me of amused me much – The beau is in Town, but he has kept himself, or others have kept him, out of my way.

I was concerned to hear of Marianne Austen's [dea]th which my Cousin Jane wrote me word of – I do not [re]member ever to have seen her but I feel for the shock which her parents must have sustained, and which must have been increased by the manner of her death.

I have not one scrap of news to send you, which I lament, and you will perhaps wonder at, till you recollect that I am as much a recluse in the midst of this Metropolis as I could be in your Brother's delightful Hermitage. The uncertainty of my Health has prevented my seeing either Mrs. Gaillier or Mrs. Johnson so that I hope they do not know of my being in London – If I ever get rid of my present incumbrances, the above mentioned ladies, and many more shall be indulged with my reappearance amongst them.

I once more thank you for your puggish intentions in my favor, and wish that you may be able to realize them, tho' to say the truth I am already possessed of one of these bewitching animals, but as he is yet in a state of infancy, and has something like a weakness in one of his hind legs, it is uncertain whether his future accomplishments may answer my fond expectations, and I consequently shall joyfully receive as many more Pugs as you can procure for me – you would laugh to see me consulting my Doctor about my Dog, and administering Vapour Baths which he has prescribed for him.

It will be extremely meritorious in you to return an early answer to this letter which certainly is not worth acknowledging, but when you recollect that I ever am desirous of hearing from you, and particularly desirous of hearing something more of the mysterious packet, I think you will write. Once more adieu, remember me affectionately to your fireside, and believe me with sincere regards your faithful Friend & Relation, E. de F.

I had well nigh forgotten to give you my address which is No. 33 Manchester Street Manchester Square London. How does the cold weather agree with you? It has given me Chilblains with which I had not been tormented since the days of my youth.

Manchester Street still exists, and as a whole has not changed very much since Eliza's day. She was in fact living amongst many of the exiled French nobility, for by this date nearly every house in the approximately square district bounded by Oxford Street, Portman Street, Harley Street and the Marylebone Road, was occupied by the richer of the émigrés, some of whom did not return to France until the restoration of the Bourbon monarchy in 1814. Eliza also took her next lady's maid, Manon, from within the refugee community, as well as finding housekeepers in the persons of a Mme Bigeon with her daughter Mme Perigord.

The Lord S– who called upon Eliza while she was writing this letter cannot be identified with any certainty, but the likeliest person would seem to be Charles Sackville-Germain (1767–1843), Viscount Sackville of Drayton, whom she had seen and probably met at Tunbridge Wells during her holiday there nine years ago, as Phylly Walter mentioned in her letter of 19th September 1787. Lord Sackville was described by a contemporary as 'a little, smart-looking man, and a favourite with the ladies'; later in life he succeeded his cousin as the 5th Duke of Dorset, but despite his wealth and rank and evident personal charm, died unmarried. Marianne Austen (1781–96) was the third daughter of Mr. Francis

Motley Austen of Lamberhurst and Kippington; the cause of her sudden and apparently tragic death is unknown.

30th December, 1796 – I will no longer defer thanking You, My dear Cousin, for your kind solicitude concerning me; I have suffered much since I wrote last, for all my Poultices proved ineffectual in breaking the Tumour, and about eight days since Sr. Walter told me I must submit to having it opened; the very operation I had always dreaded, and which you may perhaps remember my talking of at Brighton, however I had nothing for it but acquiescence, and the consequence has been the reduction of the Swelling to the size of a Pea – What now remains must be removed by a Caustic, under which application I suffer at this very moment, and am likely to do so at least a week longer; I have however leave to go out but have not availed myself of it on account of the severity of the Weather, tho' I must confess that I found some difficulty in <u>*prudently*</u> *giving up a brilliant Musical Party & Supper a few days since, but on New Years Day I mean to venture to Mrs. Gaillier's where I am invited to dine & sup with a large circle; I shall of course give your Love to the Colonel – Mrs. G. has just been with me and is not less friendly & goodhumoured than usual.*

I was most highly entertained with your account of Lady Frances B's <u>*modest attempt*</u> *on Mr. S. whom She will certainly carry by Storm, unless you kindly condescend to Chaperon him – Pray let me know how this affair comes on and whether her Ladyship is still handsome? She certainly pays a great Compliment to the married state by wishing to engage in it a fourth time – I am sure I find it difficult enough to determine on a second. Be satisfied My Dear Phillida that I cannot take amiss any thing that your Friendship may prompt on this subject, and that I am fully sensible of the truth & justice of the observations in your last, but* <u>*my impulse*</u> *in favour of Liberty & disfavour of a Lord & Master, is as irresistible as Mr. Merlin's.*

Has Cassandra informed You of the Wedding which is soon to take place in the family? James has chosen a second Wife in the person of Miss Mary Floyd who is not either rich or handsome, but very sensible & good humoured – you have perhaps heard of the family for they occupied my Uncle's house at Dean six or seven years since, and the eldest Sister is married to Mr. Fulwar Fowle who is Brother to Cassandra's intended; Jane seems much pleased with the match, and it is natural she should having long known & liked the Lady.

I am quite provoked with the silly young Man who has given you so much pain with his nonsensical Packet – I believe You act quite right in letting the thing rest as it is, but I think I should have been tempted in your place to have written a line of excuse for my mistaken suspicions, however as I said before it is perhaps best to refrain, but at the same time I am but too well aware that your feelings must be painfully tried, and that it requires all the Resolution & Philosophy you possess, to fulfil the task you have resolved on, Alas it is but too true that 'Of all afflictions taught a Lover yet Tis sure the hardest science to forget.' [Eliza quotes again from Alexander Pope's 'Eloisa to Abelard']. *I am very sorry for poor Mr. Kent's accident, but much diverted with his Plan and your Mother's mischievous wish for its accomplishment – I should have been somewhat surprized indeed at seeing a Pug of such magnitude, and I think I should have found it somewhat difficult to have nursed him on my lap or carry him about under my arm as I do my present puggish favorite. I hope you are satisfied with your new horse, and that he will afford you many pleasant airings, I hope too that he will enjoy a better state of health than his Predecessor.*

I have no London news to tell you, excepting that Mr. Pitt's Match with Miss Eden is much talked of, and that Wigs such as mine are all the rage – A very handsome young Man has just been with me who has adopted this stile of Headdress and it alters him so completely that I did not know him when he first entered – All the fashionable Belles have at least half a dozen of these Perukes. Altho' you are not passionately fond of Mrs. Delafield, I am sure you will be sorry to hear that She has just had a Paralytic Stroke from which however She seems likely to recover. I beg you will send Captn. Anderson to me with all speed for his £100,000 will suit me wonderfully well [it is] indeed very unfair in such a disinterested Being as yourself [to ma]ke such conquests, you ought to leave them to those females who like myself have a great relish for all the pretty things that are not to be had without plenty of Cash. How has this very cold weather agreed with you? I have suffered the less from it, from having been such a Prisoner – The cold on Christmas Eve is said to have been more intense than ever was experienced in England. I conclude you have had Balls & many other gay doings in which the Country abounds much more than London at this Season – Pray let me have a particular account of them.

I must bid you Adieu for Hastings chatters so intolerably that I know not what I write – He is putting the Map of England together and sticks Kent close to Durham, because he says his two best friends live in those Countries – Have I told you that I have begun teaching him to write and that he regularly comes to school to me every day, for that & French & English reading, you would laugh to see how grave we both are on these occasions.

Adieu My dear Cousin, a very merry Christmas & very many happy new years to you, believe me ever most affectionately yours, Eliza.

'Mr. Merlin' may perhaps be a reference to John Joseph Merlin, 'The Ingenious Mechanick', whose exhibition of clockwork inventions had become one of the sights of late eighteenth-century London. There was a later tradition in the Austen family that James had proposed to Eliza and she had rejected him on the grounds that he was a clergyman, but whatever the truth of the matter he had finally given up hope of being successful in his courtship, and married instead an old family friend, Mary Lloyd, on 17th January 1797. As Eliza reminded Phylly, Mary's sister had married her cousin, the Revd Fulwar Fowle, some years earlier, and Fulwar's younger brother Tom was engaged to Cassandra Austen. The young Prime Minister, William Pitt, never did marry Miss Eden – he 'had taken much pleasure in the society of Eleanor Eden, a daughter of Lord Auckland, but he explained to her father that his affairs were too embarrassed to allow him to make her an offer of marriage', since his debts at that time amounted to £30,000.

3rd May 1797 – Indeed My dear Friend I am quite ashamed of my silence and have little to offer in its justification unless you will accept the very busy Life of this Metropolis as such – It is indeed most certain that I have had very few leisure moments and there is another thing equally certain, viz: that I am the worst Correspondent in the World – This You will say You have long since been convinced of, and indeed it is but too true that from the indolence or perhaps the volatility of my temper it is always an effort in me to write a letter, and were it not for my sincere regard for yourself and a few more I should long since have dropped every Correspondent I have in the World – Do not however suppose that I dislike receiving letters, for nothing gives me more pleasure, and if my friends would be contented to write without requiring Answers I should like to hear from them seven times pr. Week.

I hope that You have had no return of the complaint in your Eye, and consequently no further occasion for Mr. K's <u>management</u> with the success of which he is doubtless much flattered. Your Leeches certainly behaved much better than mine, but this also I attribute to the aforesaid judicious <u>management</u>, in short when one is certain of meeting with so able & <u>tender</u> a Physician it must be quite a pleasure to be sick; notwithstanding which I very inconsistently wish to hear that You are now quite well & quite free from every Symptom of the Complaint which You seemed to apprehend, & for which the participation of the Princess Royal (for you know that her R.H. has lately *been afflicted with the Jaundice) would perhaps not appear to You to be an adequate Compensation.*

Great Preparations are now making for the Nuptials of the above mentioned Royal Fair, whose Intended is said to be the greatest Man in Europe – I am assured it is a fact that he cannot eat with any comfort if the Table has not been hollowed out in such a manner as to make room for what delicate Ladies

The Bridal Night, 18 May 1797, by James Gillray.
The wedding of the Princess Royal and the Prince of Wurttemberg on the 18th May was followed by a dinner for the party at Royal Lodge, Windsor.
British Library 2262 f.6

would denominate his long Stomach. The fashionable World are also much taken up with Miss Farren's union with Lord Derby – This lucky Woman from being Servant to the Public for the last fifteen Years is now going to be the second Peeress in England – A great number of simpletons have been to see her Wedding Garments which are superlatively magnificent – She has thirty Muslin dresses each more beautiful than the other, and all trimmed with the most expensive Laces, Her Wedding Night Cap is the same as the Princess Royal's and costs Eighty Guineas – I have no patience with such extravagances, and especially in such a Woman.

I have just received a letter from Steventon where they are all in great Affliction (as I suppose You have heard) for the death of Mr. Fowle, The Gentleman to whom our Cousin Cassandra was engaged – He was expected home this Month, from St. Domingo where he had accompanied Lord Craven, but Alas instead of his arrival news were received of his Death. This is a very severe stroke to the whole family, and particularly to poor Cassandra for whom I feel more than I can express – Indeed I am most sincerely grieved at this Event & the Pain which it must occasion our worthy Relations – Jane says that her Sister behaves with a degree of resolution & Propriety which no common mind could evince in so trying a situation.

I thank you for your communication of the Step which you have taken with regard to DBB, and I must also tell you how much I approve your conduct in this particular – Let the World in general say what they will, it is surely one of the noblest efforts of the human mind to own an error, and I am much mistaken in DBB's Character if he will not feel this, and consequently esteem you more than ever; besides You have satisfied your own internal sense of rectitude, and your mind will be easier whatever is the event – You think the matter will end here but I cannot be of the same opinion or doubt that a reconciliation will take place, for I have known a much more improbable one come to pass – Where two Beings thoroughly suit each other there is an attractive force which must ultimately bring them together.

I have been under some uneasiness on Hastings's account for he has had some fainting fits which were not however either preceded or followed by any illness, so that I endeavor to flatter myself they were only the result of the relaxation which the sudden setting in of the mild Weather has occasioned him – His spirits are extremely good, and he both sleeps & eats well. I believe it is since I last wrote to you that I have had accounts of my Property in France – The National Convention have laid their clutches on it as I expected but it seems they are so kind as to keep up the farms &cc and I am assured that a decree has passed which secures its [occupa]tion to me whenever I can claim it in a proper manner [however] to do this I am urged to go to France or to send Hastings but I do not feel inclined to do either one or the other while the War lasts.

I was last night at a Party of about Two Hundred at Mrs. Gaillier's, Your dear Colonel looked as captivating as ever – Apropos whom should I see in Hyde Park last Sunday but the charming Baddy in his still more charming Curricle – How my heart beat! but tho' I did all I could to be recognized, the ungrateful Monster would not look towards me. To morrow I dine with a Tunbridge Lady &cc by the bye I am more in Love than ever with this &cc,

and the provoking creature takes a thousand sly methods of making me understand he is as much smitten with me, but his allegiance will not let him avow it. I hope your Ball has taken place & that You were well amused; I am invited to one on ye 10th & another on the 17th & sincerely wish I could make them over to You. Captn. Austen has just spent a few days in Town; I suppose you know that our Cousin Henry is now Captain, Pay Master & Adjudant [sic]*, He is a very lucky young Man and bids fair to possess a considerable Share of Riches & Honours; I believe he has now given up all thoughts of the Church, and he is right for he certainly is not so fit for a Parson as a Soldier.*

I am going to night to see Mrs. Siddons who performs the part of Mrs. Beverley in the Gamester. I do not wish you were with me on this occasion for I am sure that your eyes would suffer so severely that not all the Leeches and all the Kentish assistance that could be procured would restore their brilliancy in less than a month. I dined yesterday in Company with Mr. Hampson & Mrs. Stevenson – This latter looks most wretchedly, for She is thinner than I ever saw any other human being, and as yellow as Saffron, but independent of these circumstances She must have looked ill for She dresses in the most unbecoming manner which She can possibly devise, She is going to Brighton (dear Brighton) in June with Mrs. Gwyn, her Aunt. Adieu dearest Phillida, give My Love to your good Parents & believe me ever your faithful & affectionate Friend & Relation, E. de F.

Eliza as usual gives Phylly a mixed budget of London and family news: the Princess Royal, Charlotte-Augusta-Matilda (1766–1828), was now engaged to the exceedingly fat widower Duke (later King) of Württemberg, and the marriage took place on 18th May 1797. Napoleon is reported in later years as saying that God had created the Duke to demonstrate the utmost extent to which the human skin could be stretched without bursting. The estranged wife of the ugly little 12th Earl of Derby had died on 14th March 1797, and on 1st May he had married the celebrated actress Eliza Farren, who had been performing on the London stage since 1777; she is said to have declined to become the Earl's mistress in his wife's lifetime. Sir Thomas Lawrence painted her portrait, and she is described as being tall, genteel, with a face not regularly beautiful, but animated, prepossessing, and full of sensibility, eyes blue and penetrating, a fascinating smile, and a voice clear but rather sharp, and as possessing ease, vivacity, spirit, and humour.

Cassandra Austen had become engaged to the Revd Tom Fowle, one of her father's old pupils, late in 1792, but as they could not afford to marry immediately he had gone to the West Indies in January 1796 as chaplain to his cousin and patron, Lord Craven, whose regiment was part of the military force sent out to defend Britain's interest in the colonies; and tragically Tom had died of yellow fever just as he commenced his return journey.

Eliza now wished to strengthen her status as an independent young widow, by taking control of her own funds, and wrote to Mr. Woodman accordingly:

Manchester Street, 12th June 1797 – Dear Sir, I am under the necessity of troubling You with a few Lines in order to request your concurrence with my Uncle Austen in transferring the Stock which stands in your Name as Trustees for myself, to my own. I had long been of opinion that the Decease of my Father, Mother, & Husband annulled the Trust, but aware how little my own Judgment was to be relied on in a matter of this nature, I consulted Mr. Cruise, a very able Member of the Law, and I now send you an extract from the Letter which he has returned in Answer.

My Uncle has consented to join with You in whatever measures are necessary for establishing the cessation of the Trust and making over the Sum to which it relates, entirely to myself. I conclude that a power of Attorney on each of your parts will be sufficient. With my best Regards & Compts. to Mrs. Woodman and your Son & Daughter, I remain Dear Sir your obliged & affectionate Humble servant, E. de Feuillide.

Mr. Woodman did not answer, and Eliza reminded him sharply a fortnight later: 'I must now request You would no longer delay your Reply, as I am desirous of concluding this business.' On the same day she wrote again to Phylly:

Manchester Street, 3rd July 1797 – As my dear Cousin knows me to be 'the worst Correspondent in the World' She will not be surprized that my Answer to her last kind Letter should have been delayed some weeks, tho' I meant to have dispatched it within the same number of Days. Alas My dear Phillida your Wishes for my departure from the Metropolis have not yet prevailed, and I really cannot guess when they will, for I have a variety of rural Plans and cannot determine which to adopt. I believe however that I shall neither climb the Welsh Mountains, retire into the embowering shades of the Rectory, or quarter myself near a Camp, but rather hearken to the dashing Billows on the

Sussex Coast. I certainly do feel a very strong Propensity towards revisiting that retired quiet Spot usually called Brighton and perhaps in this case as in many others the only effectual means of getting rid of the temptation, will be to give way to it.

If I should be guilty of such a weakness, may I hope that You will again favor me with your Company, and pay me that share of it which my illness obliged me to relinquish, but what am I saying, no such shabby business will content me, and you must positively tell me whether You can, and will stay a Month with me – I think I hear You exclaim what an unreasonable request, and how impossible for me to comply with, but indeed my dear Friend it is too tantalizing to have your Company a few days, and plan twenty pleasant schemes for the ensuing ones in the midst of all which the Horse & Chaise come to convey you home; not however but what I am well aware how much your presence is wanted there, and how chearfully you give up all you are so well calculated to enjoy. I know that your happy Temper together with the consciousness of fulfilling the most sacred of all Duties support You under every sacrifice and enable You to submit to Confinement, & Seclusion with a degree of Philosophy which few of your Age (I won't say Sex for I think that we beat the other at Self Denial) could arrive at. I am sorry to find that your good Father suffered from the small portion of Heat which we have had this Summer, and I fear that the succeeding Damp Weather has not been more favorable to his weak nerves – I know not what sort of a Sky You experience but we have been deluged with Rain, which, my stock of Philosophy being much inferior to yours, has teized me not inconsiderably by deranging various parties to Kensington Gardens &cc.

In answer to your kind enquiries concerning Hastings I have the pleasure of informing you that he is quite well and has had no return of his Faintings which were I fancy entirely owing to the degree of Relaxation occasioned by the Heat which then prevailed – I wish much to give him some Sea bathing and if I should not be able to reach Brighton, I will certainly send him thither, or to some other place of the same kind.

I had the pleasure of seeing our Uncle Austen some little time since when himself & his youngest Son Charles dined with me; This latter is really a fine youth and I think his Father looks as young & as well as he did ten years since. Have you heard that Cassandra's Intended has left her a thousand Pounds – I was extremely glad to learn it and thought you would be equally so, but as it is perhaps a secret do not mention it when You write to Steventon. I do not hear that Mrs. James Austen is breeding, but I conclude it is so, for a Parson cannot fail of having a numerous Progeny. Henry is at Norwich. Whilst I think of it

I must ask you whether you know any thing of a Mr. Courthope, He is a tall young Man with light hair, and I understand his Family reside near Sevenoaks – He is extremely well acquainted with all the Motley Austens and is related to Mr. Campion whom their eldest Daughter has married – Do not forget to answer this enquiry as I have reasons for making it.

As to your enquiry concerning another youth, I have to say that I believe his Match with a certain Friend of ours, which I know You looked upon as fixed, will never take place – For my own part I think the young Man ill used but the Lady is so well pleased with her present situation that She cannot find in her Heart to change it, and says in her giddy way that independance and the homage of half a dozen are preferable to subjection and the attachment of a single individual; [?you may prea]ch to her and rehearse all the wise things which I have [read] or heard, concerning the dangers of flirtation and emptiness of [?occupa]tion, but She will have her own way, and I am more & more convinced that She is not at all calculated for sober Matrimony.

The Town still continues much fuller than it usually is at this time of year; Mrs. Barton is not yet gone to Frant; Mr. Hampson called on me yesterday – Is it since I have written to You that his Sister is gone to Brighton? – Little George Hampson is also gone, not to Brighton but to Eaton [sic], *from whence he writes his Father most lamentable letters by every Post, as he by no means relishes his new situation.*

What do you think in regard to Peace? The Public seem to be less sanguine about it than they were, and I who certainly know nothing of the matter, am also very far from expecting it, and wish that Lord St. Helens had been employed instead of Lord Malmesbury, as this latter has already been unsuccessful, and I know Lord St. Helens to be a very clever Man, and much liked on the Continent. Lady Aylesbury is returned from accompanying the Princess of Wirtemberg [sic] *whom She left in good Health, and declaring that if She could chuse from all the Princes in the World She would take her own – Lady A. has received most magnificent presents of jewels from the royal Family.*

Have you heard any thing more of that provoking inconsistent creature DBB. How I wish you may one day have it in your Power to plague him most heartily. What becomes of the Kentish Beau? in short tell me all your goings on, and whether you have been to see Lady Delawarr in her pleasant retreat. I conclude you have long since received the promised Visit from your Friends the Cookes.

With regard to what I have said concerning Brighton, I must once more repeat that I have by no means determined on going there or indeed any where else, but I only wish to know whether I may hope for your Company in case I should be able to effect a scheme of this kind; in the mean while do not mention the project in your letters to some of our relatives – I will give You my reasons for this (tho' perhaps you may be aware of them) whenever we meet. Adieu My dear Friend, I am a little apprehensive that even your patience will fail before You get thro' this scrawl, but if that should be the case cast your eyes to the bottom of it, and once more receive the assurance of my being faithfully & affectionately yours, E. de F.

The Mr. Courthope concerning whom I have enquired, studies the Law & his Christian name is George, I want to know something about his fortune.

Mr. George Courthope (born 1767), was the son and heir of Mr. George Courthope senior, of Whileigh, Sussex; he was called to the Bar in 1796 and married Amelia Campion on 20th January 1808. It would seem that, notwithstanding Henry Austen's renewed courtship, Eliza was hedging her bets and considering whether she should try to acquire a richer husband. Jane Motley Austen (1776–1857), was the eldest daughter of Mr. Motley Austen of Lamberhurst (and therefore a second cousin and almost exact contemporary of Jane Austen the novelist), and had married on 10th January 1797 Mr. William John Campion of Danny in Sussex. Lord Malmesbury went to Lille in July 1797 to enter into negotiations for peace with France; but the coup d'état of Fructidor, on 3rd September, followed by increased territorial demands on the part of the French, meant that the negotiations broke down later in 1797. Lady Delawarr, recently widowed, was the daughter of Mr. Henry Lyell of Bourn in Cambridgeshire, and as such seems to have kept up a friendship with the family of her father's employee, now inviting Phylly to visit her at East Grinstead in Sussex.

Mr. Woodman passed on Eliza's two letters to his brother-in-law Warren Hastings for his opinion as to the winding-up of her trust, and the latter wrote tersely:

Daylesford, 6th July 1797 – Dear Brother, You have set a case to me, which I am not qualified to solve; nor can I with propriety take the opinion of Counsel upon it, or take any other steps regarding it. As Mme. de Feuillide is desirous of taking the money, which is now in trust with you and Mr. Austen, into her own hands, you certainly ought to comply with her desire, if you have the power to part with the trust. If you have doubts respecting this, it is your business, not hers, to satisfy them by applying to some able counsel for advice upon it; and this, I think, you ought to do.

Mr. Woodman left rough notes of his reply to Eliza, dated 15th July 1797: it would be necessary for Eliza to produce confirmation of her husband's death, as otherwise, if the Comte were to re-appear, he would have an interest in her property, and Mr. Austen and Mr. Woodman might become liable to pay out the trust funds a second time.

After all, Eliza did not go to Brighton again, but to an inland spa instead:

Cheltenham 4th August 1797 – The date of this letter will probably surprize You My dear Cousin and perhaps it will also surprize You to learn that I left London too soon after the receipt of your last to allow myself the pleasure of answering it, but when I found there were no hopes of your company which I trust You are convinced I most sincerely regretted, I determined to try my luck with another Cousin that is to say the eldest Miss Payne who was kind enough to accompany me hither the 21st of last Month, for I found London so hot and so empty that I hastened my departure from it as much as possible.

I cannot say that I had the pleasantest journey I ever made, for I was persuaded to make but one day of it, altho' Cheltenham is near one hundred miles from Town, and as we were rather late in quitting this latter, the consequence was that we travelled by star light for the two or three last stages, which was not altogether so pleasant as we had a drunken Post Boy, and some very steep hills to ascend & descend – At length we reached this place and found the People of the Inn very cross at being forced to get up for us and our Pug Dogs, for You must know that Miss Payne has as great a partiality as myself for these lovely animals, and consequently a Pug of hers as well as my own is of the travelling party – You would laugh if you were to see the fuss that Manon makes with these black faced beauties, and the notice that is taken of them on the Walks – You will laugh too when I tell you that they drink the Waters, being of a bilious Habit.

The place is very full, and I have met with many of my acquaintance amongst the rest some relations of my Aunt Austen, that is to say Mr. & Mrs. Leigh, and Lord & Lady Say & Sele, I don't know whether you are acquainted with them – There are Plays three times a week which are exceedingly well attended, and Balls twice – At the last I danced every dance, which was taking a tolerable degree of exercise considering there were above thirty

Couple – On Monday is the Master of the Ceremony's Ball, and most sincerely do I wish that you could join my party thither.

I believe You have never visited this place, and therefore I think I am in Duty bound to inform You that it consists of one very long and handsome Street, and that the Country about it is exceedingly pretty and affords a great variety of delightful Walks – One of my principal inducements for coming here was the neighbourhood of my old Friends the Hastings's whom I am just returned from visiting; They have got a place called Daylesford, which is one of the most beautiful I ever saw I will not wrong it by endeavoring to give a description of it and it shall therefore suffice to say that the Park and Grounds are really a little Paradise, and that the House is fitted up with a degree of Taste & Magnificence seldom to be met with – At Daylesford I heard the confirmation of our old friend Mr. Thomas Woodman's having taken orders, which surprizes every one, as his Father can give him a very handsome fortune, and it is rather late in Life to enter on a Profession – It is reported too that he means to make a still further change in his situation by marrying a Widow with six Children.

Your account of your poor Father gives me much concern, for I know he was one of the best tempered men in the world, and this very circumstance must render his present frame of mind so much the more grievous to yourself & your good Mother – I perfectly agree with you that it is very unfortunate that he no longer sleeps as he used to do, for the time must appear insupportably tedious to him, and his restlessness & impatience must greatly distress you; but indeed My dear Friend, it seems to be decreed for wise purposes no doubt, and perhaps to increase and shew your virtues, it seems to be decreed I say that your trials of temper & fortitude should be greater than are usually sustained. Do not however let your sense of Duty carry You too far and induce you to give up that little portion of relaxation and change of scene which You can enjoy – I shall rejoice to hear that You have spent a little more time with Lady Delawarr, as I think the Tunbridge Wells air always agreed with you, and that your spirits require the benefit of the society which you would probably meet with.

After having spoken so favorably of this place, You will perhaps be surprized to hear that I mean to quit it so soon as [Wedn]esday next ye 9th when I shall return to London for a [short] while, and proceed from thence to Lowestoffe in [Suffo]lk which I am anxious to reach on Hastings' account [who] was much disordered by the last hot weather, and Sr. Walter Farquhar has declared that Sea bathing & Sea air are more likely to be of service to him than any thing else. I should proceed from hence to Lowestoffe but Business obliges me to spend some days in London; on my return thither I shall lose Miss P's Society, which I shall regret as her good humour and Ease render her a very pleasant Companion – How does the Kentish Beau, and all your other Beaux? there is a pretty plentiful crop of them here, and you may conclude if you please that Miss P. & myself gather hearts by dozens, seriously however I have made one conquest, who has between thirty & forty thousand pr. Annum, but unfortunately he has also a Wife, so that I cannot even indulge myself in a little flirtation. Direct your next to me in Manchester Street for I shall certainly be there before it – Adieu My dear Phillida continue to love me and believe me ever most faithfully and affectionately yours, E.

I am afraid all the Postmen between this & Seale will read my letter for my paper is very thin and my Ink very thick – If I had but had a new pen, but that is a luxury I have not known for ages, the writing would not have been quite so tell tale as I fear it now will prove.

The Cheltenham waters were held to be 'singularly efficacious in all bilious complaints, obstructions of the liver and spleen, indigestion, loss of appetite, in habitual costiveness, and obstinate obstructions, which lay the foundation of so many chronic disorders'. The little town itself was much admired by visitors, set as it was in a rich well-wooded plain bounded by the blue Malvern hills in the distance, with its long winding High Street off which led the charming Well Walk, 'a magnificent gravelled promenade, twenty feet wide, shaded by venerable elms at twelve feet distance, whose embowering tops exclude the fierce rays of the sun. A quickset hedge bounds this Elysian walk on each side, and here and there a bench or garden chair is placed ...' Eliza's childhood playmate, Thomas Woodman (1760–1825) had become a lawyer like his father before him; but as she was now surprised to learn, had abandoned this profession in favour of becoming a clergyman. The rumour of his marriage to a widow was incorrect, however, for some years later he married Louisa Chapuset, niece by marriage of Warren Hastings.

Eliza returned to London early in August, and had another brisk exchange of notes with Mr. Woodman regarding the winding-up of her trust, before travelling to the East Anglian sea-coast for a holiday at Lowestoft in Suffolk. Henry's regiment, the Oxfordshire Militia, were now in that district, to defend the vulnerable flat coastline against invasion from Holland – hence

Phylly's hints to Eliza that this is the reason she has decided to go to Lowestoft. Eliza points out virtuously that the regiment was based at Norwich, in Norfolk – but omits to say that a detachment was also quartered at Great Yarmouth.

Lowestoffe [sic], *22nd September 1797 – I received yours My dear Cousin soon after my return to London, and should not have delayed answering it so long but from want of health and some other perverse circumstances which have concurred to render writing, to which I must confess I am never very prone, a more difficult Task than usual.*

My stay in London was protracted to three weeks, instead of one which I had intended to spend there, and when I had at last ordered my Post Horses, I was taken ill with a Feverish Complaint which obliged me once more to defer my departure, and at length to make two days of my Journey hither, which however I the less regretted from the beauty of the Country I passed through and which had moreover the great merit of Novelty, as I had never visited this part of England. You are however mistaken in the motives which You have so cunningly found out for my visiting it now – Hastings whose pale looks I am sure you must have remarked when you last saw him, and whose faintings I mentioned to You, had gradually sunk into a state of such extreme debility that I sent for Sr. Walter Farquhar who declared that the only chance of reestablishing his Health was sending him immediately from London & to the Sea, and that as clear dry Air was equally necessary for him with bathing he particularly recommended his going to Lowestoffe on account of its very elevated situation; I was at that time under the necessity of visiting Cheltenham (whither Business & not pleasure conducted me), and consequently could not accompany Hastings, but Made. Bigeon I consider as more than myself in every thing that relates to him and I immediately sent her, and another servant, off with him to this place, from whence I very soon had the satisfaction of receiving the most favorable accounts – Indeed it is wonderful how the Child's Health improved in the course of a very few days after his arrival – My wish for occular demonstration on this interesting subject abridged my stay at Cheltenham, but I was detained in London as I have already mentioned, and instead of joining my Invalid in three weeks, seven elapsed before I could get to him – thus My dear Friend, You see that the contiguity of Suffolk & Norfolk was not my motive for visiting this place, and indeed had You known that Lowestoffe is no less than 28 Miles from Norwich, You would probably have dismissed all your wicked surmises for You must allow that a Person who cannot absent himself from his Corps for more than a few hours at a time, cannot very conveniently travel 56 Miles to pay a Visit.

This place still contains a good many families but as there are no Rooms there is no opportunity of getting acquainted with them (there is a Play House but I have not yet been there) however I am not in total Solitude for there are three families here with whom I am acquainted, and what with walking, occasionally driving over to Yarmouth, with which I am delighted, and plenty of Books, to say nothing of dipping in the Sea [which] I detest, I contrive to fill up my time [quite] tolerably, & for Hastings sake and that of my own bathing from which I mean to reap great benefit I shall remain here till ye 12th of next Month, when I shall once more repair to the great City.

Having thus given You a very circumstantial account of myself of which I was vain enough to think You might be desirous, let me no longer defer assuring You how sincerely I sympathize in the too real subjects of affliction with which it has pleased Heaven to try your fortitude and virtue – Alas my dear Friend, it must indeed be exquisitely painful to see a Parent in such a situation as You have described, and to experience unkindness so opposite to what the natural sweetness of his temper would suggest towards his bitterest foe much less to the best of Daughters who has sacrificed every thing to her filial Duties; however I cannot help thinking that so strange and violent a state of mind cannot be lasting, but in the mean time I fear for your Health of which I intreat You to be careful, and not to be so squeamish as to miss an opportunity of taking air & exercise because You will not ride Tete a tete with a Beau – I think the plan of sticking up an agreement against the Church Door a very good one, and honor the Kentish Squire for so bright a thought – not however that it has routed some wicked surmises on my part of a certain sneaking kindness which will perhaps get both parties a little further than the Church Door one day or other.

I hope the frail & penitent Fair is returned to You by this time, for I am well aware of the extreme inconvenience which the deprivation of so good a servant must have occasioned You – I highly approve the lenity of your conduct on this occasion, and think that Mercy would have reclaimed many an offender which its opposite has confirmed in Vice. I am vexed to make You pay postage for so stupid a letter, but I am totally deserted by all my franking Friends. You do not tell me whether You have heard any thing more of D.B.B. and what becomes of your other Innamorato whose name I believe begins with a W. and whom you have allowed there is some likelihood of your accepting one day or other –Adieu My dear Phillida believe me with sincere & unalterable regard very affectionately yours, E.

If you should be disposed to write before my return to Town direct to me at the Post Office Lowestoffe Suffolk.

Despite Eliza's protestations that Lowestoft was too far away from Norwich for Henry to be able to visit her, they evidently met half-way, at Great Yarmouth. In this letter there is the first mention of Mr. George Whitaker (1769–1846), whom Phylly Walter eventually married some years later; he was one of the sons of the Revd John Whitaker, vicar of Pembury, near Tonbridge, in Kent.

Eliza returned to London on 20th October, and was finally able to settle her business affairs with Mr. Woodman, with the intention of then going to see her friends the Egertons again; but her next letter to Phylly shows that these plans had to be changed.

Manchester Street 11th December 1797 – You will be surprized My dear Friend, to see my letter dated from London, but the day before I was to have commenced my Northern Journey, Hastings was taken so very ill that I thought I must have lost him – His seizure was of the convulsive kind and for many days after it he had a very high fever – He is now thank God much better but continues so weak and I think in so uncertain a state that I cannot bring myself to go three hundred miles from him, for it was my intention to have left him here with Madame Bigeon on whose care You know I can thoroughly depend – thus is my intended Journey put a stop to for the present and probably till the Spring, for the Season must necessarily become more & more unfavorable for travelling.

I fear You will think that I have neglected your Commission but I do assure You that has not been the case – I have called four times at Butlers and sent as often, and been vexed beyond measure at the constant reply of the wool not being yet come in; Twenty other persons, they said, were waiting for it, and they could not say when they should have it tho' they expected it every day. Finding the matter stand thus I determined to try elsewhere and accordingly applied at Osbaldiston's in Bond St. and Fishers & Wells, but they were destitute of the desired Commodity and referred me to Butlers as the only place where it was to be got – At length this morning came the long wished for parcel, but when I examined it I found two pair of Black Needles, and white Patent Net, instead of a pair of Black and a pair of white Needles and black patent Net, but this piece of stupidity was presently rectified by my sending back to the Shop and exchanging what was amiss, and I shall now proceed to pack up the whole and forward it to Saville Row where it will certainly be this evening, and from whence I hope it will safely reach You and afford You sufficient amusement to compensate for the vexation of such a delay, I am sure even your patience must have been worn out as to mine it was thread bare a fortnight since and I was the more chagrined, as I feared you would think me inattentive or dilatory. I beg your pardon for having been so stupid concerning the patent Net, and must also beg you will do me the favor of accepting the article which I have procured instead of what you wished for – I shall really be hurt if You make any difficulty of this, for you know I am a Hat in your Debt (recollect that You would not let me take one either at Tunbridge or Brighton) which would have cost much more than a little dab of netting. The other articles come to £0.s.8.d.9 which I can wait for, tho' almost ruined by the hard times. These new Taxes will drive me out of London, and make me give up my Carriage for I cannot afford an increase of House Rent which my Landlord already talks of, Thirty two pounds a Year in addition to the present expence of a vehicle, and four Guineas more on my Man Servants Account.

I have heard very lately from our Cousin Jane who is still at Bath with her Mother & Sister, Mr. Hampson whom I saw yesterday and who enquired after yourself and Family, told me he had heard Cassandra was going to be married but Jane says not a word of it – James Austen has been very near losing his second Wife.

I hope your Balls proved pleasant, and that the recreant Kentish Knight has made all due Apologies, but I believe I shall not however insist on your overlooking W for the sake of K – You speak so highly of the former that I am quite impatient to direct to you by his name, and am delighted to think You will have no trouble in changing the Initials on your Linen or your Seal. It grieves me to leave so much Paper [unem]ployed, but the Post is going out and I fear [miss]ing it – Adieu then My dear Cousin and believe me [sincerely] with every good wish for the Health & Happiness ..... [the end of the paper is missing].

This rumour of Cassandra Austen's possible marriage was incorrect, for she never found anyone to replace Tom Fowle in her affections and remained a spinster for the rest of her life; James's wife Mary Lloyd had probably had a miscarriage.

At last Eliza admitted to the world what Phylly Walter had guessed – that she had decided to marry her cousin Henry Austen – and told Warren Hastings of her decision:

No. 33 Manchester Street, Manchester Square, 26th December 1797 – Dear Sir,

As I flatter myself You still take an interest in my welfare, I think it incumbent on me to acquaint You with a circumstance by which it must be materially influenced. I have consented to an Union with my Cousin Captn. Austen who has the honor of being known to You. – He has been for some time in Possession of a comfortable Income, and the excellence of his Heart, Temper, & Understanding, together with his steady attachment to me, his Affection for my little Boy, and disinterested concurrence in the disposal of my Property, in favor of this latter, have at length induced me to an acquiescence which I have withheld for more than two years. – Need I say, My dear Sir, that I most earnestly wish for your approbation on this occasion, and that it is with the sincerest attachment I shall ever remain, Your much obliged and affectionate God-daughter, Elizabeth de Feuillide.

I beg leave to present my affectionate Compts. to Mrs. Hastings.

Henry and Eliza were married by special licence at St. Marylebone parish church, London, on 31st December 1797, one of their witnesses being a Mrs. Marriott, no doubt a relation of the Randall Marriott of Eliza's Calcutta childhood. The Revd George Austen gave Henry £40 to pay for wedding celebrations with his brother officers of the Oxfordshire Militia.

CHAPTER V

Quite in style

1798–1813

✡

ELIZA WROTE TO PHYLLY with the news of her marriage, but for some reason the letter was unfortunately not preserved. The next we hear from her she is back in East Anglia, and thoroughly enjoying herself as the wife of a British officer, her previous life as a French officer's wife apparently quite forgotten:

Ipswich 16th February 1798 – Matrimony is generally accused of spoiling Correspondents, but I was so bad a one before I entered the holy state, that it could not well make me worse, and therefore I trust my dear Friend that you do not put down my late silence to its account – Indeed the fact is that in addition to my accustomed dislike to writing, my time has been constantly taken up, for on my arrival here most of the families in the place were civil enough to visit me, and my Brother Officers and Brother Officers Wives of course did likewise. To all these visitations succeeded invitations to Parties which are as thick in this Country as Hops in yours, and besides these parties there is at least one Ball every Week – so that what with my morning avocations and walks or drives for I am sometimes so gracious or so imprudent as to trust my neck to Henry's Coachmanship, I find it difficult to make a leisure hour –

And now having accounted for, if not justified my late omission let me return You my sincere acknowledgments for your good wishes and kind congratulations on an event by which I have hitherto had every reason to hope that my Happiness will be greatly forwarded – Unmixed Felicity is certainly not the Produce of this World, and like other People I shall probably meet with many unpleasant and untoward circumstances but all the Comfort which can result from the tender Affection & Society of a Being who is possessed of an excellent Heart, Understanding, & Temper I have at least ensured – to say nothing of the pleasure of having my own way in every thing, for Henry well knows that I have not been much accustomed to controul and should probably behave rather awkwardly under it, and therefore like a wise Man he has no will but mine, which to be sure some people would call spoiling me, but [I] know it is the best way of managing me.

I am sure You will not doubt the pleasure which I experienced from your intelligence concerning your good Mother's Will – Too much cannot indeed be done for such a Daughter, and I am happy to find that another of your Relatives is of this opinion, but as justice is not always rendered to merit I cannot but greatly applaud the liberality of Sentiment which your Brother James has shewn on this occasion – I am sorry I cannot bestow equal Approbation on your other Brother, but as you say, Old Batchelorship is very apt to generate selfishness, and certainly the habit of attending only to our own wants & interests, is but too likely to make us insensible to those of others. I was grieved to find that you had spent so dull a Christmas, and had been deprived of all those Amusements which I know you so thoroughly enjoy. It was very provoking too that the smart Gown & Bugles could not be sported, but I hope your excellent Temper which enables you to bear these and many more perversenesses of fate without repining will not always be thus tried, and that a time will come when You may bestow your Society upon those friends wh[o are] at present deprived of it, in which List you may be sure that I include myself, and look forward with much pleasure to the visit which has so long been promised me. Perhaps I may never be Mistress of a Rectory but as soon as I have done Campaigning I shall look out for some settled Residence where you will ever be a most welcome Guest.

I have some thoughts of going to London for a few days in the course of next month, and proceeding from thence into Hampshire. It will be a comical sort of an expedition, for I mean to send my servants &cc by the Stage and let Henry drive me because it will save Post Horses, for you must know that I am become excessively stingy and am scraping up all I can against the arrival of the French who will of course deprive me of every thing but the few Guineas which I may have contrived to hoard. I suppose you have seen a print of the Rafts on which they mean to reach us – It seems these Rafts are to be worked with Wheels which have the effect of oars, that they are to be bordered with Cannon and support a Tower filled with Soldiers – I can hardly believe that they seriously mean to trust to such a Contrivance, which I should suppose a rough Sea would soon render ineffectual – however I do believe that they will make an attempt on this Country, and Government appears to be convinced of it, for we have received orders to add one hundred & fifty Men to our Regiment, and hold ourselves in readiness to march at the shortest notice, so that I am going to be drilled and to bespeak my Regimentals without further delay.

I have not yet given you any account of my Brother Officers of whom I wish You could judge in Person for there are some with whom I think You would not dislike a flirtation – I have of course entirely left off trade but I can however discover that Captn. Tilson is remarkably handsome, and that Messrs. Perrott & Edwardes may be chatted with very satisfactorily, but as to my Colonel Lord Charles Spencer if I was married to my third husband instead of my second I should still be in love with him – He is a most charming creature so mild, so well bred, so good, but Alas he is married as well as myself and what is worse he is absent and will not return to us in less than a Month. The inhabitants of this place are much more fashionable People than I expected, and are exceedingly [kind] to us strangers – As every thing is known in such small circles they [are] acquainted with my having been a Comtesse and politely give [me the pr]ecedence which Courtesy grants to that title in England. [I think] we shall not remove from hence till May and to what [place we] shall then remove is yet undetermined.

I had a letter from [Jane] the other Day in which She says that her Mother has had [a slig]ht return of her Complaint – She had benefited very much by the Bath Waters.

Talking of Bath reminds me of one of our Officers Wives who was a Bath Beauty of the name of Bedingfield – About eight months since She married Lord Shrewsbury's Brother Captn. Talbot who went out of his senses in a very few days after his Nuptials, He continued in this melancholy state for some months and now to the great astonishment of every one is perfectly recovered. His Wife is very young & very beautiful and what made me mention her to you is her style of Dress of which I think it will entertain you to have a description. She wears only one thick muslin Petticoat and a thin muslin Robe over that, of which the sleeves come only three inches below her shoulders. Her Ears throat & bosom are entirely bare for She never wears either Earrings, necklace, tucker, Handkerchief or Stays, and on her Head She generally has no other ornament or covering than a little curled black wig which I suppose you know to be the height of the present fashion – Such a mode of Dress or rather undress would be remarked even in London, so that you may guess what an uproar it makes in a Country Town.

I much regret my inability of getting a Frank for I am sure this scrawl is not worth paying for, but I will endeavor to manage better when I write again. You will continue to direct to me at this place for my going to London is very uncertain, and should it take place will not keep me from hence more than a fortnight. I think you will be glad to hear that Hastings has already benefited very materially by change of Air – There is a garden to the house which I now occupy in which he spends great part of the day, and by this means takes constant air and exercise which I have ever found of much more service to him than medicine. Adieu My dear Phillida I don't teize you with soft things from my Cousin (I have an aversion to the word Husband & never make use of it) because they are all implied, for I trust you do not doubt the very sincere regard which I assure you he often expresses for you and yours – once more Adieu say every thing that is kind for me to your good Mother & poor Father when ever he shews any recollection of me and believe me your truly affectionate Friend & Relation, Eliza.

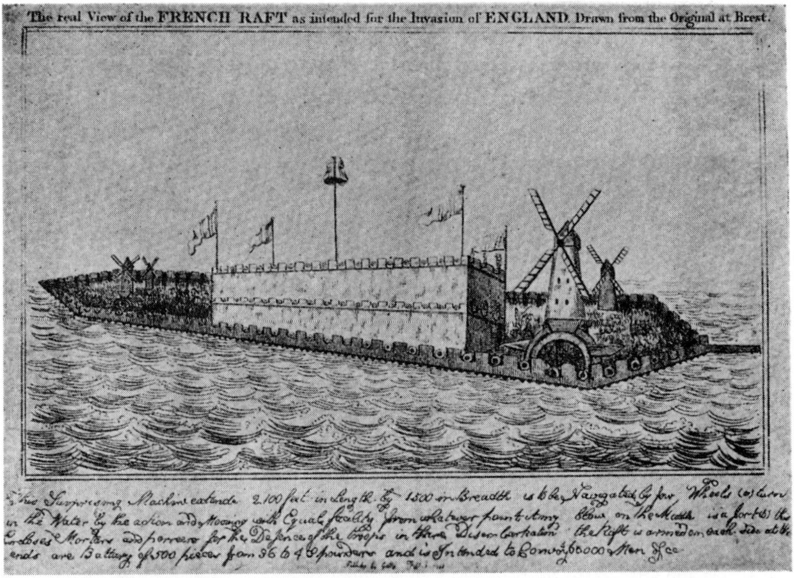

'The real View of the French Raft as intended for the Invasion of England. Drawn from the Original at Brest,' 1797-1801.
British Library 2394 f.3

The French were issuing propaganda pictures of the 'war machines' which they claimed would be used for the invasion of England: these were, as Eliza says, giant rafts, with paddles powered by windmills. The biggest of these, supposedly being built at Brest, had four windmills and supported a battlemented wooden fortress, with batteries of 48-pounder guns at each corner. A raft at St. Malo was of much the same design, except that its fort was provided with a dome, and it carried two tents; smaller rafts, to be built at Calais, were to be three hundred feet square and capable of carrying sixty guns and four thousand men. The officers in the Oxford Militia were Col. Lord Charles Spencer, brother of the 3rd Duke of Marlborough; Captain John-Henry Tilson, elder brother of the James Tilson who later became one of Henry Austen's business partners; Lieuts. Thomas Perrott and John Edwardes; Captain John-Joseph Talbot, already a widower with two small children, married Harriet-Anne Bedingfield on 4th May 1797 and in due course had several more children by her.

Phylly's father, William Hampson Walter, died on 6th April 1798, after being senile for some years, and Phylly was now left alone with her old mother. No doubt Eliza wrote a formal letter of condolence; but there is another long interval of eighteen months for which no record survives. During this period Henry spent some months in Oxfordshire on regimental duties, and may well have taken Eliza with him to visit Steventon, as this last letter of hers suggests. In the spring of 1799 the Oxfordshires were sent to Ireland, but Eliza did not accompany them, as her next letter shows:

Dorking 29th October 1799 – My dear Cousin, I had so little expectation of hearing from You after a silence of near twelve months that when your letter was brought me, I could hardly believe it was your hand writing which met my eyes – I am sincerely concerned to find that You have undergone such a series of affliction, and that the future still presents so gloomy an aspect, and I also much regret the effect which these severe trials have had on your health, but I cannot wonder that it should be materially affected since sad experience has taught me on more than one occasion that mental and bodily sufferings are ever closely connected. I do not remember ever to have heard of a being so totally void not only of parental but even the common feelings of humanity as Mr. W. Senior, but such are the effects of selfishness which hardens the heart and renders it callous to every thing but personal interests – It is however wonderful that this unnatural Father is not softened by the sight of his son's broken spirits & health, and that he can let him sink under the pressure of disappointment rather than make the smallest exertion to facilitate his union with one whom he professes to approve & esteem – I hope however that Mr.

G.W. for your sake as well as his own will endeavor to shake off despondence and look forward to better times which I trust still await You both.

I am very sorry that it is utterly out of my power to comply with your Brother's wishes concerning Mr. Hastings, but having the most insuperable aversion to asking favors, and moreover knowing how much Mr. H. was teized with requests & solicitations, I long since mentally bound myself never to add to their number, and I have been further confirmed in this resolution by hearing Mr. Hastings declare that some unpleasant consequences of his interference had determined him never again to use his interest in favor of any one – I therefore believe that your Brother's application would be useless, but if he is resolved to make it, I must entreat that no mention may be made of myself – Mr. H's address is, Warren Hastings Esqr. Daylesford House near Chipping Norton Oxon – I cannot drop this subject without expressing my regret at having been thus obliged to put a negative on any request of your brother's, for tho' he is in fact a stranger to me (for we have not met since we were children, and I have not the slightest idea of his person) yet such is my esteem for his Character, and regard for all your connexions, that I should have been happy to have obliged him.

Cassandra very rightly informed You of my residence in this place where I have now been six months, and a recluse the greatest part of that time; but Lady Burrell, Lady Talbot and one or two more neighbours having politely sought me and shewn me such civilities as an utter stranger had no right to expect, I have not found it possible to persevere in my plan of shunning all society, to which I must honestly confess that I greatly prefer my Books, my Harp & my Pianoforte. Austen who has now been absent near seven months gives me hopes of his return some time in December; He is now at Dublin but is kind enough to say that he would prefer my hermitage, altho' the Irish Metropolis is rendered particularly pleasant to him by the attentions which he experiences from the Lord Lieutenant in consequence of having been introduced to him by his very good friend Lord Charles Spencer; he (I mean Austen) has been so fortunate as to enjoy uninterrupted health but I cannot say as much for myself, having been far from well for these last two years. I had hoped much from Country air, early hours, and a very quiet life, but I have been disappointed. Hastings too suffers much from frequent & very violent returns of fits which I believe to be epileptic and which have hitherto baffled all the aid of medicine – their effects on his mental powers, if his life should not be destroyed by them, must be of the most melancholy nature, and are a constant source of grief to me.

I am truly sorry to find that You are denied the benefits of change of scene, and equally surprized that any motive can outweigh the desire which I think so natural of making every sacrifice to restore the health & spirits of those who are dear to us. The pecuniary loss which You mention having met with was indeed a sad addition to other vexatious circumstances, but it has often been said, and I begin to believe, justly, that there is a tide in the affairs of this life – I hope that yours will soon turn and make you amends for all the ills which have so abundantly flowed in upon you. Adieu My dear Cousin, believe me ever your affectionate & sincere Friend, E.A.

It may perhaps be news to you that Mrs. S. Freeman was married about three months since to Admiral Allen, a Widower.

Phylly's woes were the result of the fact that the Revd John Whitaker, father of her admirer George Whitaker, was most distressingly at odds with his sons, quarrels which lasted for years. In the summer of 1802 the extended Woodgate family, neighbours of the Whitakers, were still writing to each other on the subject:

Tomorrow Mrs. Whitaker, Charlotte, George and Augustus dine with us; and I am sorry to tell you yesterday week they had a terrible rumpus, what about I do not know, but the old man turned Augustus out of doors and said he never wished to see him alive again. The poor fellow went to George and has been there ever since; what they will do I cannot think. I suppose I shall hear the whole of it tomorrow from her, as she sent me word she wished much to see me.

.... What a terrible time the Whitakers have. I really have no patience with that old Fellow; I suppose you have heard he has turned Augustus out of doors, for what Cause I know not.

Lady Burrell's husband, Sir William, had died on 20th January 1796, and in May 1797 she married the Revd William Clay, Bishop of Kildare, but still kept her previous title of Lady Burrell. Lady Talbot was the widow of Sir Charles-Henry Talbot and lived nearby at Mickleham in Surrey. Miss Stella-Frances Freeman, an elderly cousin of both Eliza and Phylly ('Mrs.' by courtesy of her age), of Devonshire Place, London, had married an equally elderly widower, Adml. John-Carter Allen, on 29th June 1799.

Later in 1799 the successful young Corsican general, Napoleon Bonaparte, seized power in France, granting himself the title of First Consul, and for a time it seemed that the threat of an invasion of England by France had receded. The Oxfordshires were brought back from Ireland, and over the next few months Henry decided to resign his commission and set himself up in London as a banker and army agent, in partnership with Henry Maunde, one of his military friends; and by the summer of 1800 he and Eliza had moved there and were living at No. 24 Upper Berkeley Street, a recently-built terrace off Portman Square, with a French chef, M. Halavant, added to their domestic staff. (This house still survives, now used as a small private hotel.) Henry finally left the Oxfordshires in January 1801, and opened his business premises in Cleveland Court, close to St. James's Palace, where he could be sure of attracting the attention of rich young officers. He also later became the Deputy Receiver General of Taxes for Oxfordshire, another lucrative occupation.

During this same period the Revd George Austen decided to retire to Bath, and his eldest son James moved into Steventon parsonage to act as his father's curate. There is another gap in Eliza's correspondence, but Phylly tells her brother of a visit to London:

Seal, 4th June 1801 – I spent one day with our cousins the Henry Austens. She is much the same, but talks of retiring into Wales & resigning the world, in which he seems perfectly ready to agree. He has given up the Army. They live quite in style in Upper Berkeley Street, Portman Square.

The pathetic invalid boy Hastings finally died in the autumn of 1801, and was buried in Mrs. Hancock's grave in Hampstead: 'Also in Memory of her Grandson Hastings Only Child of Jean Capot Comte de Feuillide and Elizabeth his Wife Born 25th June 1786 Died 9th October 1801'. Eliza wrote in acknowledgement of Phylly's letter of condolence:

Upper Berkeley St. 29th October 1801 – My dear Philadelphia, I will not lose the opportunity which You afford me of thanking You for your kind letter although I am so much straightened for time that I shall perhaps not be able to send You more than a few lines. I am much obliged by your kind participation in an event which though, as You justly consider it, a desirable release has greatly affected my spirits. So awful a dissolution of a near & tender tie must ever be a severe shock, and my mind was already weakened by witnessing the sad variety and long series of pain which the dear sufferer underwent – but deeply impressed as I am with the heart rending scenes

I have beheld I am most thankful for their termination, and the exchange which I humbly hope my dear Child has made of a most painful existence for a blissful immortality.

In addition to my affliction on poor Hastings account, I have undergone much anxiety concerning Henry, who for five months never enjoyed an hour's health – His complaints were a Cough, Hectic pain in the side and in short every thing which denotes a galloping consumption in which I believe all his acquaintance thought him. At length a prescription of Dr. Baillie's (who had already tried a variety of medicines to no purpose) removed some of the above symptoms, and from that time he has mended so fast that he is now nearly as well as I had always known him to be previous to this attack.

I conclude that you know of our Uncle & Aunt Austen and their daughters having spent the summer in Devonshire – They are now returned to Bath where they are superintending the fitting up of their new house – Their eldest Son James is in possession of Steventon where he has made such alterations & embellishments that it is almost a pretty place – not however that I have seen it, for You know that I am not given to visiting and have taken near four years to accomplish a journey to Godmersham Park, for which place I purpose setting out to-morrow morning. Mrs. E.A. produced her seventh child about six or seven weeks since, and I think bids fair to rival your Sister – I was really astonished to hear of your having 15 Nephews & Nieces – If I were in spirits, I should make some observations on the premium to which your brother is entitled for such an addition to the number of his Majesty's liege subjects. I sincerely rejoice in your brother Weaver's acquisition – Perhaps he may prevail on your Mother and yourself to keep his house for him, in which case You will see one of the finest Counties in England.

I do remember the Miss Eyles you mention (for I conclude it is not the eldest but the second Sister who was rather pretty) and I also recollect the name of Delves which is a very common one at Tunbridge Wells, indeed to say the truth it was the appellation of my Butcher. I have not heard any thing of Mr. or Mrs. Eyles for a great while – The last account I had of his health was very unfavorable for he was thought to be in a confirmed decline. I do not know whether You have heard of the death of my poor friend Mrs. Egerton who was settled in the neighbourhood of Durham. I am extremely glad to find You are likely to have an agreable companion with you during the ensuing winter for I am sure that the hours will glide away more smoothly and that your spirits and of course your health will be greatly benefited, in which comfortable hope I bid You Adieu, entreating You to believe me ever affectionately yours, E.A.

Henry is not at home or would desire to be kindly remembered to you. Many thanks for the recipe. I believe I have not told you that my stay at Godmersham will not exceed a fortnight.

Dr. Matthew Baillie, of Lower Grosvenor Street, was one of the fashionable physicians of the period, and in later years became one of the Prince Regent's medical advisers. The Revd George Austen had now taken a lease of No. 4 Sydney Place, Bath, where he and his family stayed until 1804. Eliza's friend Mrs. Egerton had died on 11th July 1801.

Phylly's elder brother, the Revd Weaver Walter, had acquired the Norfolk livings of Brisley and Gateley; her sister-in-law Frances-Maria Walter was in her sixteenth pregnancy, and Edward Walter was born on 13th November 1801; but as several of the elder Walter children had already died, Phylly did not in fact have fifteen nephews and nieces alive. The family of Edward Austen (Knight) at Godmersham were much healthier, and all their eleven children survived; Eliza refers here to the birth of Marianne, on 15th September 1801.

This is the last letter which Phylly Walter preserved, and from now on the remainder of Eliza's biography has to be pieced together mainly from other people's letters and diaries, as she leaves behind the restless travelling and hectic social whirl of her younger days and moves gently into an elegant, leisured, and rather frail middle-age. The following year Warren Hastings paid his usual Spring visit to London, and noted in his diary that he called on the Austens on Monday 1st March 1802, but apparently did not find them at home. Eliza wrote to him thereafter:

Saturday Evening [? 6th March 1802] – My dear Sir, Lady Burrell has a house in Chesterfield Street, but in consequence of Sr. Lucas Pepys directions has been for many months past at Richmond – I grieve to say that her health is in a deplorable state, and that the nature of her complaint which appears to be a confirmed decline, leaves but little hope of her restoration to the many friends who love and esteem her.

I the more regret having missed the pleasure of seeing You the other day, as the time, Alas! is fast approaching when I must entirely renounce the blessing of your society – I am always at home till twelve, and whenever You can make it convenient to call on me before that hour, You will confer an additional favor on your affectionate and much obliged God daughter, Elizabeth Austen.

Lady Burrell's present address is merely Richmond Surry – The number of her house in Chesterfield Street (near Curzon Street) is, I believe, 9.

Sir Lucas Pepys was another fashionable physician of the day; Lady Burrell later moved to the Isle of Wight, no doubt for her health's sake, but died there on 20th June 1802.

There is a curiously valedictory tone in Eliza's letter to Warren Hastings, and it may perhaps be that she and Henry were now contemplating leaving England and settling in France. The preliminaries of peace between Britain and France had been signed on 1st October 1801, and even before this cessation of hostilities was officially ratified by the Peace of Amiens on 27th March 1802, many English immediately crossed the Channel to enjoy Continental travel once again, flocking especially to Paris for a close-up view of the formidable General Bonaparte. Though little Hastings de Feuillide was now dead, Eliza, as the Comte's widow, could still lay claim to a share in the property at Le Marais, and it would certainly have been worth her while to make an attempt to do so. In July or August 1802, therefore, she and Henry, accompanied by their friend Mrs. Marriott, set off for France, but whether they actually got any further than Paris is uncertain.

Many years later Henry's younger brother Frank told his family that Eliza managed to bring the case of her dispossession to the notice of Napoleon, who granted her an allowance as some measure of compensation for the loss of her husband's estate; but in view of the fact that Napoleon did not promote himself from First Consul to Consul-for-life until August 1802, it hardly seems likely that Eliza could have had much opportunity to contact his government, or to receive any compensation, before he broke the Peace of Amiens and resumed war with Great Britain on 16th May 1803. Henry had already returned to England earlier in the year to attend to his financial duties, and so escaped the sudden order issued on 22nd May, that all English travellers should be detained. According to Austen family tradition, Eliza gave all the necessary instructions herself when her carriage stopped at the post-houses en route to the coast, and her French was so perfect that she passed everywhere for a native, so that Mrs. Marriott, who could speak nothing except English, escaped with her under this protection. Those unfortunates who were caught by this decree were interned in France for eleven years, until Napoleon's abdication in 1814. So far as compensation from Napoleon is concerned, it seems more likely that Eliza may have made some wishful-thinking joke about her financial problems, which the practical-minded Frank Austen took rather too literally.

In the spring of 1804 Henry and Eliza moved from Upper Berkeley Street to a small house in Brompton, which was at that time a semi-rural village on the south-western outskirts of London, and Henry also moved his office to No. 1 The Courtyard, Albany, Piccadilly. Their home was at No. 16 Michael's Place – named after its architect Michael Novosielski – which had been planned as a terrace of 44 small houses on the south side of Brompton Road, at the corner of Yeoman's Row; but the speculation was unsuccessful, perhaps because the site was low-lying and damp, and when the terrace was eventually rebuilt as blocks of mansion flats in 1886, many of the houses were still unfinished shells. They then joined the other Austens for a family-party summer holiday touring the seaside resorts along the South Devon/Dorset coastline. In September the party divided, and while Jane and her parents remained in Lyme Regis, Henry and Eliza took Cassandra on with them to Weymouth. The latter was rather disappointed with the town, and Jane agreed: 'I am really very glad that we did not go there, & that Henry & Eliza saw nothing in it to make them feel differently.'

In April 1805 Jane sent Henry and Eliza a screen and a brooch, both apparently made or purchased by Cassandra and herself, and passed on the couple's united thanks to her sister: '[Henry] expresses himself as greatly pleased with the Screen, & says that he does not know whether he is "most delighted with the idea or the Execution", – Eliza of course goes halves in all this, and there is also just such a message of warm acknowledgement from her respecting the Broche [*sic*] as you would expect.' As the Revd George Austen had died at Bath in January 1805, it may be that the brooch was an item of mourning jewellery in his memory.

Later in 1805 another source of information regarding Eliza appears – the diaries kept by Fanny Knight, eldest daughter of Edward, the third of the Austen sons, who changed his name to Knight when he inherited the Godmersham estate. Fanny was born on 23rd January 1793, and even at the age of 12 was accompanying her parents on social occasions, including trips to London with them. On 10th September 1805 they '... went to Brompton to dine', and the next day: 'Dined at Albany with Lord C. Spencer, & Aunt Eliza, not forgetting Uncle H. Austen. We afterwards went to the Lyceum Theatre.'

Now that Henry had his bank and other business affairs to manage, presumably he and Eliza spent more of their time at home in Brompton, for the only news of them in 1806 consists of some brief entries in Warren Hastings's diary, when he made his annual visit to London and called on them in March and May of that year.

After the death of the Revd George Austen, Mrs. Austen and her daughters moved in 1806 from Bath to a rented house in Southampton, and moved again in the summer of 1809 to Chawton, when, following the sudden death of his wife Elizabeth in the autumn of 1808, Edward Knight established his mother and sisters in a cottage there on his Hampshire estate. During these years of bereavement and insecurity there are not many mentions of Eliza in Jane's surviving letters – Cassandra expressed thanks to her for some unspecified reason in June 1808, which Jane in turn passed on to Henry; and in October of that year Jane suffered from earache and Eliza sent her advice as to a remedy for this minor ailment.

In 1807 Fanny was again in London in the summer with her parents, and recorded in her diary: 'Tuesday 25th August – We took a Coach & horses for the day & drove to Brompton, saw Aunt Eliza.' A further visit occurred in the autumn:

Wednesday 30th September – We all dined at Brompton & met Mr. & Mrs. Tilson ... Thursday 1st October – Aunt Eliza dined with us & Uncle H. & afterwards we went to the play at Drury Lane, & saw Mrs. Jordan, Mr. Elliston & Mrs. Bannister, in 'The School for Scandal' & 'A House to be sold!!'

The last known letter from Eliza herself was sent to her godfather, and as it was addressed to him at Portugal Street in London, must have been written in either 1807 or 1809, when his diaries show he was staying at this address:

Brompton 18th March – My dear Sir, I have taken the liberty of sending you a breakfast cup & Saucer, which I have had much pleasure in painting and gilding for you. They are not worthy your acceptance, but as the work of my hands I trust you will kindly receive them, and also grant my earnest request that you will make daily use of my imperfect performance; by which means I shall have the pleasure of knowing that once in every twenty four hours you probably bestow a thought on, your much obliged and truly affectionate God daughter, Eliza: Austen.

Like the Painter who was forced to write under his works what they were designed to represent, I think it necessary to say that the subject on the cup is meant for Zephyr and the Rose.

I beg to present my best regards to Mrs. Hastings.

Decorating plain porcelain ware was then a elegant hobby for ladies – the former Princess Royal, now the Duchess of Württemberg, had her own little kiln constructed in the palace grounds so that she could fire her hand-painted vases and table-ware. Unfortunately Warren Hastings does not mention in his diary when he received this present, but it can be identified in two inventories made of the contents of Daylesford House in later years (1834 and 1837): '1 china cup & saucer, richly gilt within, with black antique figures painted round', that was kept in Mrs. Hastings's bedroom.

In August 1808 Eliza and Henry called on Warren Hastings at Daylesford, and this is the last time her name is mentioned in his diaries. At the end of 1808 Jane was hoping to have some news of Eliza from Cassandra, who was going to meet Henry at Godmersham over the New Year – '... it is a long while since I have heard of her'; and a few days later Jane wrote again to Cassandra: 'Your report of Eliza's health gives me great pleasure, and the progress of the bank is a constant source of satisfaction.'

By 1809 Fanny Knight, still aged only sixteen, had had thrust upon her all the responsibilities of acting as surrogate mother to her ten younger brothers and sisters, as well as being her father's hostess and managing the Godmersham household. Eliza and Henry came to stay at Godmersham in the summer of 1809 while in the process of moving from Brompton to a larger house, No. 64 Sloane Street, Chelsea, this visit being the first Eliza had paid since the one she mentioned in 1801. On this occasion Fanny was impressed by her aunt's Parisian culture: 'Thursday 22nd June 1809 – Aunt Eliza came in the evening from Town .... Tuesday 11th July

1809 – Aunt E. and I took a long walk ... Saturday 15th July 1809 – Uncle & Aunt H.A. went away early ce matin. Quel horreur!!'

In the autumn of 1809 Fanny visited Sloane Street twice, while passing through London on a round trip to Steventon and Chawton and so back to Kent, but seems to have felt bored amongst Eliza's middle-aged London friends: 'Thursday 19th October – Aunt Eliza & I drove about the Town, shopping & visitting ... Mr. & Mrs. Tilson & Mr. Hampson dined here'; and on 'Tuesday 21st November – Aunt Eliza, Anna & I drove about shopping all the morning & we all dined at Mr. Hampsons; met a Sir John & Lady Head & Miss Cuthbert & a Mr. Saunders & spent a very stupid evening.'

There are no letters of Jane's surviving from 1810, nor did Fanny visit the Henry Austens that year; the next news of Eliza is in the spring of 1811, when Jane went to stay in Sloane Street to correct the proof sheets of *Sense and Sensibility* as they were delivered from the publisher Thomas Egerton of Whitehall, and in between whiles wrote to Cassandra at Godmersham with details of the party Eliza was busy planning:

Sloane St. Thursday April 18, 1811 – ... To night I might have been at the Play, Henry had kindly planned our going together to the Lyceum, but I have a cold which I shd. not like to make worse before Saturday; – so I stay within, all this day. – Eliza is walking out by herself. She has plenty of business on her hands just now – for the day of the party is settled, & drawing near: – above 80 people are invited for next tuesday Eveng. & there is to be some very good Music, 5 professionals, 3 of them Glee singers, besides Amateurs. – Fanny will listen to this. One of the Hirelings, is a Capital on the Harp, from which I expect great pleasure. – The foundation of the party was a dinner to Henry Egerton & Henry Walter – but the latter leaves Town the day before. I am sorry – as I wished her prejudice to be done away – but shd. have been more sorry if there had been no invitation. – Saturday 20th April. If the weather permits, Eliza & I walk into London this morng. She is in want of chimney lights for Tuesday; – & I, of an ounce of darning cotton. – She has resolved not to venture to the Play tonight. The D'Entraigues & Comte Julien cannot come to the Party – which was at first a greif, but she has since supplied herself so well with Performers that it is of no consequence; – their not coming has produced our going to them tomorrow Eveng. – which I like the idea of. It will be amusing to see the ways of a French circle.

Henry Egerton may have been a son of Eliza's old friends the Egertons of Washington, co. Durham; Henry Walter is presumably her young cousin, the eldest son of the Revd James Walter, now aged 26 – though why Eliza should be prejudiced against him is not known.

Jane Austen's next letter to Cassandra gives a pen-picture of Eliza's elegant entertainment:

Sloane St., Thursday April 25, 1811 – ... Our party went off extremely well. There were many solicitudes, alarms & vexations beforehand of course, but at last everything was quite right. The rooms were dressed up with flowers &c, & looked very pretty. – A glass for the Mantlepiece was lent, by the Man who is making their own. – Mr. Egerton & Mr. Walter came at ½ past 5, & the festivities began with a pr. of very fine Soals. ... At ½ past 7 arrived the Musicians in two Hackney coaches, & by 8 the lordly company began to appear. Among the earliest were George & Mary Cooke, & I spent the greatest part of the eveng. very pleasantly with them. – The Drawg. room being soon hotter than we liked, we placed ourselves in the connecting Passage, which was comparatively cool, & gave us all the advantage of the Music at a pleasant distance, as well as that of the first veiw of every new comer. – I was quite surrounded by acquaintance, especially Gentlemen ... Including everybody we were 66 – which was considerably more than Eliza had expected, & quite enough to fill the Back Drawg. room, & leave a few to be scattered about in the other, & in the passage. The Music was extremely good. ... Between the Songs were Lessons on the Harp, or Harp & Piano Forte together – & the Harp Player was Wiepart, whose name seems famous, tho' new to me. – There was one female singer, a short Miss Davis all in blue, bringing up for the Public Line, whose voice was said to be very fine indeed; & all the Performers gave great satisfaction by doing what they were paid for, & giving themselves no airs. – No amateur could be persuaded to do anything. – The House was not clear till after 12. ...

Henry has been to the Watercolour Exhibition, which open'd on Monday, & is to meet us there again some morng. – If Eliza cannot go – (& she has a cold at present) Miss Beaty will be invited to be my companion. ... Eliza caught her cold on Sunday in our way to the

D'Entraigues; – the Horses actually gibbed on this side of Hyde Park Gate – a load of fresh gravel made it a formidable Hill to them, and they refused the collar; – I believe there was a sore shoulder to irritate. – Eliza was frightened, & we got out – & were detained in the Eveng. air several minutes. – The cold is in her chest – but she takes care of herself, & I hope it may not last long. ... Eliza enjoyed her eveng. very much & means to cultivate the acquaintance – & I see nothing to dislike in them, but their taking quantities of snuff. – Monsieur the old Count, is a very fine looking man, with quiet manners, good enough for an Englishman – & I believe is a Man of great Information & Taste. He has some fine Paintings, which delighted Henry as much as the Son's music gratified Eliza – Have you ever mentioned the leaving off Tea to Mrs. K.? – Eliza has just spoken of it again. – The Benefit she has found from it in sleeping, has been very great. – ... We have no engagements but for Sunday. Eliza's cold makes quiet adviseable. Her party is mentioned in this morning's paper.

Morning Post, 25th April 1811 'On Tuesday, Mrs. H. AUSTIN [*sic*] had a musical party at her house in Sloane-street.'

No. 64 still survives, and though enlarged and re-fronted at the end of the nineteenth century the reception rooms on the first floor – the front drawing room overlooking the street, and the octagonal drawing room at the back – where the party was held, together with the connecting passage or staircase landing where Jane sat and kept several gentlemen amused with her witty conversation, can still be identified. A later inventory of Henry's property shows that the 'chimney lights' which Eliza purchased were 'a pair of female figures in imitation of bronze supporting lustres for two lights, each with paste icicle drops', and that the overmantel mirror which was being made for them was 'a brilliant chimney glass in a neat gilt frame, plate 48″ x 34″.' The fitted or 'planned' carpet (still quite a furnishing novelty) was probably a handsome Brussels design, and nearly all the furniture was mahogany.

The Comte d'Antraigues (1756–1812), with his wife and son Comte Julien, were living at No. 27 The Terrace, Barnes – then a separate Thames-side village several miles upstream from London – and their river-facing house is still known as 'D'Antraigues'. Although Jane Austen makes no further comment about them,

Eliza must surely have known that the Comte's wife was the one-time operatic prima donna Mme. St. Huberti, whom she had heard perform in Paris in 1784. The artist Mme. Vigée-Le Brun remembered: 'Mme. St. Huberti was not at all beautiful, but her features were entrancing and glowed with expression. The Count d'Antraigues, a fine-looking man noted for his sharp mind, became so infatuated with her that he married her.' A little over a year after this visit by Jane and the Henry Austens, the Comte and his wife were both stabbed to death in their Barnes house by an Italian servant. The man then committed suicide, and was later said to have been deranged, but there were also rumours that the murders could have had a political motive.

In her next letter from Sloane Street, that of 30th April 1811, Jane ended up: 'Eliza has not yet quite resolved on inviting Anna – but I think she will.' This invitation was to the teenage Anna, daughter of the Revd James Austen, to come and stay in Sloane Street; but many years later one of Anna's daughters remembered:

The invitation was sent, but my mother was not permitted to go. The reason of the hesitation on Mrs. H. Austen's part was that she was not on terms with her sister-in-law, who would neither go to her house nor receive her at Steventon – I believe the *ci-devant* Countess, who was an extremely pretty woman, was a great flirt, and during her brief widowhood flirted with all her Steventon cousins, our Grandfather inclusive, which was more than his after wife could stand or could ever forgive – and I think it is very probable that *he* hesitated between the fair Eliza and Miss Mary Lloyd. I can testify that to the last days of her life my Grandmother continued to dislike and speak ill of her. It must have cost Mrs. H. Austen a great effort to send the invitation, and certainly shows her to have been the more amiable woman of the two.

The last news of Phylly Walter, the cousin with whom Eliza's correspondence had started thirty years before, is in 1811. Since her father's death in 1798, Phylly had been obliged to remain at home with her aged mother, and in consequence seems rather to have dropped out of touch with Eliza and her fashionable life in London. It was only following Mrs. Walter's death at the age of 95 that Phylly was eventually able to marry her faithful and long-suffering admirer, Mr. George Whitaker. Cassandra Austen wrote with congratulations:

Chawton, 18th August 1811 – My dear Cousin, Your friends at Chawton have been anxiously searching the Papers ever since the beginning of this month for intelligence of you & they have at length had the pleasure of seeing your Marriage announced. I hope you do not need to be assured of our good wishes, I cannot however let the occasion pass without telling you how much we feel interested by an event so important to you nor how sincerely we rejoice in every prospect of good that attends it. I think I cannot give you a better wish, than that you may be as happy as you deserve & that as a Wife you may meet the reward you so well earned as a Daughter. Mr. Whitaker will of course feel himself included in every good we desire for you; pray assure him it will give us great pleasure to have an opportunity of being introduced to our new relation, and make our best compts. to his Mother & Sister. I shall hope soon to receive from you a very particular account of your new home. From what you have already said I am sure it must be comfortable & tho' there may be some things you would wish otherwise for where is the situation on earth exempt from evils? you are too wise & too good to dwell on the wrong side of the Picture. Use will reconcile you to some things which appear evils at first & others you will bear as the necessary attendants of humanity, so you see I am determined you shall be happy whether you will or no.

Mrs. H. Austen has been spending a fortnight with us lately & I think I never saw her in such good health before. We frequently talked over your plans & prospects, but we did not get the newspaper which contained your Marriage till an hour after she had left us or I am sure she would have united with my Mother, Jane & me in our good wishes on the occasion.

We all unite in kind regards to you & Mr. W. & I am my dear Cousin, Yrs. affectly., Cass. Elizth. Austen.

In the following month Henry and Eliza paid another visit to Godmersham, but by now Fanny's admiration for her aunt seems to have changed into disapproval verging on dislike, and between 4th and 10th September 1811 she entered in her diary: 'Uncle & Aunt H.A. came to dinner ... Mrs. H.A. & I walked to the Hop Ground. ... Mrs. H.A. & I got on a little, but we never shall be intimate ...: Mrs. H.A. & I had a tete-a-tete, how agreeable!' – and there is this time no word of regret when Eliza leaves on 23rd

September. Fanny was a prosaic, unadventurous girl, conscientiously devoted to her large family and to her peaceful Kentish home, and not surprisingly had little in common with her cosmopolitan, sophisticated aunt.

At some time between the autumn of 1811 and the spring of 1812 Eliza fell ill, but unfortunately there is no information in either Jane's letters or Fanny's diaries as to what her ailment was, or when precisely it manifested itself. It may perhaps have been cancer of the breast, like her mother, because it seems to have been obvious to the family that the outcome could only be fatal; and the Austens, with their usual practicality, accepted this fact without any sentimental moralising or useless repining. In May of 1812 Fanny and her father stayed for a few days in London, and there is the significant entry in her diary for Wednesday 13th May: 'Papa & I dined quietly in Sloane Street' – presumably Eliza was now too ill to go out or to receive any guests other than members of her immediate family. In early November 1812 Fanny was again in London, and on this occasion Henry came to join the Godmersham family party at their hotel for dinners and a theatre trip, but Eliza did not accompany him and Fanny makes no reference to her.

By early 1813 the Austens were awaiting the inevitable, and Jane wrote to her friend Martha Lloyd in February of that year: 'We have no late account from Sloane St. & therefore conclude that everything is going on in one regular progress, without any striking change.' In April 1813 Edward Knight brought his family from Godmersham to Chawton for a summer visit, and even as Fanny – now aged twenty and very much in control – was bustling round settling everyone in to their new quarters in the rambling old Great House, Henry sent word that Jane's presence was needed to comfort Eliza's last days. Fanny's eldest brother, Edward junior, was called upon to escort his aunt to London, and she recorded in her diary. 'Thursday 22nd April 1813 – Edward went to Town with Aunt Jane as we had a very bad account of poor Mrs. H.A. .... Monday 26th April 1813 – We heard that poor Mrs. H.A. died on Saturday night.'

Although she had been living in the parish of Chelsea, Eliza was buried at Hampstead, in the same grave with her mother and son, and Henry added her epitaph to the ledger-stone:

Also in memory of Elizabeth wife of H. T. Austen Esq. formerly widow of the Comt. Feuillide a woman of brilliant generous and cultivated mind just disinterested and charitable she died after long and severe suffering on the 25th April 1813 aged 50 much regretted by the wise and good and deeply lamented by the poor.

Later in the year Jane Austen wrote to their brother Frank:

Chawton 3rd July 1813 – My dearest Frank ... Upon the whole [Henry's] Spirits are very much recovered. – If I may so express myself, his Mind is not a Mind for affliction. He is too Busy, too active, too sanguine. – Sincerely as he was attached to poor Eliza moreover, & excellently as he behaved to her, he was always so used to be away from her at times, that her Loss is not felt as that of many a beloved wife might be, especially when all the circumstances of her long and dreadful Illness are taken into the account. – He very long knew that she must die, & it was indeed a release at last.

Epilogue

✡

THERE ARE TWO MORE slight mentions of Eliza in Jane's letter of 15th September 1813. By that time Henry had given up the large house in Sloane Street and moved to live over his banking premises at No. 10 Henrietta Street, Covent Garden; as both Fanny Knight and Jane were staying with him in September, Jane hastened to tell Cassandra that even in this much smaller house there was adequate room for visitors: 'The little adjoining dressing-room to our apartment makes Fanny and myself very well off indeed, and as we have poor Eliza's bed our space is ample every way.' During August Henry had visited Warren Hastings at Daylesford, but the latter had not noted the news of Eliza's death in his diary and after the lapse of these three or four months had already quite forgotten about it, hence he made none of the proper consolatory remarks to Henry regarding his bereavement. Jane therefore added, sounding slightly shocked at this unusual omission: 'Mr. Hastings never <u>hinted</u> at Eliza in the smallest degree.'

In accordance with his resilient nature, Henry was soon thinking of marrying again, and Jane's letters mention a Miss Burdett, a Miss Moore and a widowed Mrs. Crutchley as being possible candidates in this respect. However, in 1814 the ending of the long war with France caused economic upheavals, and Henry's bank failed in the spring of 1816, reducing him to near-poverty and causing all plans for matrimony to be indefinitely postponed. He went to France in the summer of 1816 and set in motion a lawsuit against the remaining members of the de Feuillide family in the hope of claiming some money from the estate as Eliza's heir; but proceedings dragged on for years, complicated by the fact that small parts of the lands of Le Marais had already been sold off separately, and it was not until 1825 that Henry's claim was finally dismissed by the French courts.

In the meantime, with his chameleon-like ability to adapt to changing circumstances, Henry had returned to his boyhood idea of entering the Church; he was ordained late in 1816, and became rector of Steventon in 1819 following the death of his brother James. With the income from this living, he was able to marry in 1820 Miss Eleanor Jackson, whom he had probably met as a neighbour in Chelsea; the union was childless and in later life Eleanor did not enjoy good health, but nevertheless Henry was devoted to her and they lived happily together for thirty years. Henry had to relinquish the Steventon living to his nephew William Knight in 1822, and thereafter moved between Farnham, Bentley and Colchester before his death and burial in Tunbridge Wells in 1850. His niece Anna recalled that he had become 'a zealous Preacher of the Gospel, according to the religious views of the Calvinistic portion of the Evangelical Clergy, and so consistently remained to his life's end.'

Notes and References

✡

Provenance of Eliza's letters

In all, forty-six of Eliza's letters survive – thirty-six to her cousin Phylly Walter, six to her trustee Mr. Woodman, and four to her godfather Warren Hastings. These latter ten are amongst the Hastings Papers, which were acquired by the British Museum in 1872 and now form part of the British Library's collections.

When Phylly Walter received Eliza's letters from France, she usually endorsed each one with a number, the date of receipt, and the date when she answered it. This methodical recording of her correspondence not only confirms the dates of the letters, but also shows up gaps where some letters are missing from the sequence. As Phylly's belated marriage left her childless, it seems her personal effects were inherited by her niece Anna Maria Philadelphia Walter, daughter of the Revd James Walter. This Miss Walter never married, and the two collections of letters, those from Eliza to Phylly, and Phylly's letters to her brother James, passed on down to one of James's great-grandsons, John Charles Guy Nicholson (1861–1925) who lived in Lincolnshire.

In 1869 the Revd James-Edward Austen-Leigh wrote his *Memoir of Jane Austen* (published 1870), and mentioned Eliza by name as one of the novelist's cousins; at that date, however, the existence of Eliza's letters was not known to the Austen-Leigh family, who had lost touch with their distant Walter connections.

At the turn of the twentieth century Sydney C. Grier (a *nom de plume* for the novelist Hilda Caroline Gregg) was researching amongst the Hastings Papers in the British Museum and found Mr. Hancock's letterbook, which she used as the basis for her article 'A Friend of Warren Hastings' in *Blackwood's Edinburgh Magazine* in 1904. Mr. Nicholson saw this article and subsequently lent Eliza's letters to Miss Gregg/Grier, allowing her to use them for a sequel, 'A Goddaughter of Warren Hastings', which appeared in 1905 in *Temple Bar*.

A few years later, William and Richard Arthur Austen-Leigh were planning to write a more complete biography of Jane Austen and, having read Miss Grier's articles, contacted Mr. Nicholson; he apparently provided them with some copies or quotations from several of the letters in his hands, including those of Phylly Walter to James, and this information was used by the Austen-Leighs in their *Life and Letters of Jane Austen*, published in 1913. Eventually, in November 1919,

Mr. Nicholson gave nearly all the Eliza letters to Mr. R. A. Austen-Leigh – 'just as I had them from Sydney Grier' – and they were then part-published by the latter in *Austen Papers 1794–1856*, (1942), together with a part-publication of Mr. Hancock's letterbook. These letters remain in the possession of the Austen-Leigh descendants, but microfilm copies are now in the Hampshire Record Office.

At the time of his gift of the letters, Mr. Nicholson noted that some of them were missing, but did not know where or when the losses had occurred; it may be, of course, that Phylly Walter simply did not keep all the letters which she received from Eliza, but only a choice or chance selection. R.A. Austen-Leigh included in *Austen Papers* one letter, that of 27th March 1782, which was not then in his possession; unfortunately he did not make any reference to its ownership – though presumably it was held by some member of the Walter family other than Mr. Nicholson – and it has consequently proved impossible to discover its present location, if indeed it still survives. Another letter, that of 25th July 1785, also escaped from the main group – apparently before Miss Grier saw the collection, as she makes no reference to it in her article – and surfaced many years later in the salerooms, when it was purchased by Mr. T. Edward Carpenter, who bequeathed it to the Jane Austen Memorial Trust in 1969. This letter was first published in 'Three Austen Family Letters', in *Notes and Queries*, 1985.

Some of Eliza's letters written from England to her husband in France survived in Guienne until about 1870, when a local historian, Chanoine Ducroc, salvaged the archives of families in the Nérac district; he referred to the Capot de Feuillide family in an article in the *Revue de Gascogne*, vol. XXVI, pp. 328–30 (1885), and it is believed that their papers were then deposited in the presbytery of Cazaubon, Dept. Gers. Chanoine Ducroc's researches were pursued by another local historian, M. l'Abbé Devert, in the late twentieth century; but attempts by the latter to find out if Eliza's letters still survived at Casaubon, or possibly in the archives of the town of Agen, met with no success.

Provenance of Phylly Walter's letters

The extracts given here are as published by R.A. Austen-Leigh in *Austen Papers*, and may have been made in 1910 either by himself or by their owner, Mr. Nicholson. The latter died unmarried in Lincolnshire in 1925, and it seems likely that the letters were destroyed during the hasty auction of his personal effects, as all efforts to trace their present location have proved fruitless.

Description of Eliza's letters

[Watermarks are as classified in Edward Heawood: *Watermarks, mainly of the 17th and 18th centuries*; The Paper Publications Society, Hilversum, Holland, 1950.]

[The first eight of Eliza's letters written from Europe have not been preserved.]

1. Eliza to Phylly, 16th May 1780.
   Addressed: A Mademoiselle/Mademoiselle Walter/At the Parsonage/Ightham near/Sevenoaks/Kent/Angleterre/Par Ostende; postmark: 26 MA; endorsed: 10 [*sic, recte* 9] / Dress of the Queen of France. Watermark: device of coronet over escutcheon containing a post-horn [Heawood no. 2752–62], over A VANDERLEY.
2. Eliza to Phylly, 27th June 1780.
   Addressed: A Mademoiselle/Mademoiselle Walter/Parsonage, Ightham/near Sevenoaks/Kent/Angleterre/Par Ostende; postmark: IY 10; endorsed: 9 [*sic, recte* 10] /cloaths/In all/LSD.0.1.2. Watermark: Heawood no. 2752–62, over D & C BLAUW
3. Eliza to Phylly, 27th March 1782.
   Address damaged: Mademoiselle P. Walter ... /Green near ... am Kent. Not owned by the Austen-Leigh family, and present location unknown. It must have been either 11, 12, 13, or 14 of Phylly's numeration, and the other three out of these four letters are also missing. The text here is as published in *Austen Papers* and may be incomplete.
4. Eliza to Phylly, 1st May 1783.
   Addressed: Miss Walter/at William Hampson Walter's Esqr/Stone Street/near Wrotham/Kent; no postmark; endorsed: 15/recd. th. 11 May 1783/Ansd th. 18 Do.Do. No watermark.
   [No. 16 is missing.]
5. Eliza to Phylly, 7th May 1784.
   Addressed: Miss P. Walter/at Wm. Hampson Walter's Esqr/Stone Street near Wrotham/Kent; postmark: 19 MA; endorsed: 17/recd. 23 May 84/and. July th.15 1784. Watermark; Heawood no. 2752–62, above monogram GR.
   [Nos. 18 and 19 are missing.]
6. Eliza to Phylly, 25th(?) July 1785.
   Addressed: A Mademoiselle/Mademoiselle Walter/at Wm. Hampson Walter's Esqr/ Cottage Seal/near Sevenoaks/Kent/Angleterre; postmark: ...VE PARIS and

.../AU; endorsed: 20/recd. th. 27 August 1785/ansd. th. 15 Septr. Do. Watermark: D & C BLAUW.

7. Eliza to Phylly, 17th January 1786.
   Addressed: A Mademoiselle/Mademoiselle Walter/at Wm. Hampson Walter's Esqr/ Cottage Seal near Sevenoaks/ Kent/Angleterre; postmark: 4 FE; endorsed: 21/Recd. th. 9 Feby. 1786/And. th. 28 Do. Watermark indecipherable.
8. Eliza to Phylly, 23rd May 1786.
   Addressed: A Mademoiselle/Mademoiselle Walter/at Wm. Hampson Walter's Esqr/ Cottage Seal near Sevenoaks/Kent; postmark: 8 IU; endorsed: Par Calais/franc/LSD 0.1.2./22/Recd. th. 9 June 1786. Watermark: device of triangles above an urn(?), above J. BASSUE.
   [Nos. 23 and 24 are missing.]
9. Eliza to Phylly, 9th April 1787.
   Address damaged: ... Walter/ ...-son Walter's Esqr/ ... Seal near Sevenoaks/Kent; no postmark; endorsed: 25 [with some very faint pencil notes of domestic purchases]. Watermark: Heawood no. 2752–62 above GR.
10. Eliza to Phylly, 16th November 1787.
   Addressed: Miss Walter/Seale near Sevenoaks/Kent; postmark: 16 NO 87; endorsed: 26/Recd. th. 18 Novr. 1787/And. th. 21 Do. Watermark: Heawood no. 2752–62 above GR.
11. Eliza to Phylly, 23rd November 1787.
   Addressed: Miss Walter/Seale near Sevenoaks/Kent; postmark: 23 NO 87; endorsed: 27/Recd. 25 Novr. 87/Ansd. 9 Decr. Do. Watermark: I PORTAL.
12. Eliza to Phylly, 22nd August 1788.
   Addressed: Miss Walter/Seale near Sevenoaks/Kent; postmark: AU ...; endorsed: Recd. th. 24 Augt. 88/28. Watermark: Heawood no. 2752–62 above GR.
13. Eliza to Phylly, 31st August 1788.
   Addressed: Miss Walter/Seale near Sevenoaks/Kent; postmark: TUNB. WELLS; endorsed: Sepr. 88/29/1788. Watermark: Heawood no. 2752–62, above O & S.
14. Eliza to Phylly, 11th February 1789.
   Addressed: Miss Walter/Seale near Sevenoaks/Kent/Angleterre; postmark: F... 2... ... 20 89; endorsed: Recd. Feby. th. 22 89/And. March 3 Do./30/1789. Watermark: FIN DE M with device of fleur-de-lys, and IOHANNOT DANNONAY 1783 with device of crown above chalice(?) – see Heawood, p. 25.
   [No. 31 is missing.]

15. Eliza to Phylly, 7th January 1791.
Addressed: Miss Walter/Seale near Sevenoaks/Kent; postmark: JA 8 91 MARGATE; endorsed: 32/1791/Recd. Jany. th. 10 – 91/And. th. 18 Do. Watermark: Heawood no. 2752–62 above GR, and another device of a bell with FJBB across it.
16. Eliza to Phylly, 23rd June 1791.
Addressed; Miss Walter/Seale near/Sevenoaks/Kent; postmark: JU 23 91; endorsed: 33. Watermark: PORTAL & CO.
17. Eliza to Phylly, 1st August 1791.
Addressed: Miss Walter/Seale near Sevenoaks/Kent; postmark: AU 1 91; endorsed: 34/1791 [and in a later hand]: From Ctsse de Feuilide [*sic*] nee Eliza Hancock subsequently Mrs Henry Austen. Watermark: Heawood no. 2752–62 above GR.
[Nos. 35 and 36 are missing.]
18. Eliza to Phylly, 13th October 1791.
Addressed: Miss Walter/Seale near Sevenoaks/Kent; postmark: OC 13 91; endorsed: Recd. Octr. 14 91/And. 27 ditto/37 1791. Watermark: W & CO.
19. Eliza to Phylly, 14th November 1791.
Addressed; Miss Walter/Seale near Sevenoaks/Kent; postmark: NO 14 91; endorsed: 38/1791. Watermark: PORTAL & CO.
20. Eliza to Phylly, 23rd December 1791.
Addressed: Miss Walter/Seale near Sevenoaks/Kent; postmark: DE 23 91; endorsed: 39. Watermark: PORTAL & CO.
[Nos. 40 and 41 are missing.]
21. Eliza to Phylly, 7th June 1792.
Addressed: Miss Walter/Seale near Sevenoaks/Kent; postmark: JU A7 92; endorsed: 42. Watermark: Heawood no. 2752–62 above GR.
22. Eliza to Phylly, 16th July 1792.
Addressed: Miss Walter/Seale near Sevenoaks/Kent; postmark: IY B16 92; endorsed: 43. Watermark: J. TAYLOR.
23. Eliza to Phylly, 26th October 1792.
Addressed: Miss Walter/Seale near Sevenoaks/Kent; postmark: OC 27 92 BASING STOKE; endorsed: Recd. Octr. 92/44. Watermark: PORTAL & CO.
[After this date Phylly ceased to number Eliza's letters, presumably because there was less risk of correspondence going astray in the domestic postal service.]
24. Eliza to Warren Hastings, 19th September 1794.
BL AddMS 29,173, f. 257.
25. Eliza to Phylly, 22nd September 1796.
Addressed: Miss Walter/Seale near Sevenoaks/Kent; postmark:

TUNBRIDGE WELLS; endorsed: 1796. Watermark: WE ...AR 1796.

26. Eliza to Phylly, 17th October 1796.
Addressed: Miss Walter/Seale near Sevenoaks/Kent; postmark: OC 17 96; endorsed: 1796 [with list of small sums of money added up below the address]. Watermark: FLOYD & CO 1794.
27. Eliza to Phylly, 7th November 1796.
Addressed: Miss Walter/Seale near Sevenoaks/Kent; postmark: NO ...; endorsed: 1796, 7th. Novr. Watermark: Heawood no. 2752–62 above GR.
28. Eliza to Phylly, 13th December 1796.
Addressed; Miss Walter/Seale near Sevenoaks/Kent; postmark: DE E 13 96; endorsed: Manchester St./1796. Watermark; FLOYD & CO.
29. Eliza to Phylly, 30th December 1796.
Addressed; Miss Walter/Seale near Sevenoaks/Kent; postmark: DE F 30 96; endorsed: 1796 [and some scribbled letters and words, as if Phylly were trying out ink and pen before replying]. Watermark: FLOYD & CO 17 ....
30. Eliza to Phylly, 3rd May 1797.
Addressed: Miss Walter/Seale near Sevenoaks/Kent; postmark: MA F 4 97; endorsed: 1797. Watermark: CURTEIS SONS 179...
31. Eliza to Mr. Woodman, 12th June 1797.
BL AddMS 29,175, ff. 162–63.
32. Eliza to Mr. Woodman, 3rd July 1797.
BL AddMS 29,175, ff. 182–83.
33. Eliza to Phylly, 3rd July 1797.
Addressed: Miss Walter/Seale near Sevenoaks/Kent; postmark: JY F 3 97; endorsed: 1797/Recd. July 4 97. Watermark: W EDGAR.
34. Eliza to Phylly, 4th August 1797.
Addressed: Miss Walter/Seale near Sevenoaks/Kent; postmark: CHELTENHAM A.. B 7 9...; endorsed: 1797. Watermark; Heawood no. 2752–62, above date 1796.
35. Eliza to Mr. Woodman, 14th August 1797.
BL Add.MS 29,175, f. 204.
36. Eliza to Mr. Woodman, 19th August 1797.
BL Add.MS 29,175, f. 212. This letter was cut up, presumably to use the spare paper, and the signature is missing, but the handwriting is unmistakably Eliza's.
37. Eliza to Mr. Woodman, 29th August 1797.
BL Add.MS 29,175, ff. 218–19.

38. Eliza to Phylly, 22nd September 1797.
Addressed: Miss Walter/Seale near Sevenoaks/Kent; postmark: SE C 23 97 LOWESTOFFE; endorsed; 1797. Watermark: Heawood no. 2752–62 above GR.
39. Eliza to Mr. Woodman, 21st October 1797.
BL Add.MS 29,175, ff. 250–51.
40. Eliza to Phylly, 11th December 1797.
Address damaged, as end of paper cut away: ... Walter/ ... near Sevenoaks/Kent; postmark: DE 11 97; endorsed: 1797. No watermark.
41. Eliza to Warren Hastings, 26th December 1797.
BL Add.MS 29,175, f. 296.
42. Eliza to Phylly, 16th February 1798.
Addressed: Miss Walter/Seale near Sevenoaks/Kent; postmark: IPSWICH G FE 17 98; endorsed: 1798. Watermark: Heawood no. 2752–62 above CS.
43. Eliza to Phylly, 29th October 1799.
Addressed: Miss Walter/Seale near Sevenoaks/Kent; postmark: F OCT 30 99; endorsed: 1799. Watermark: Heawood no. 2752–62 above AT.
44. Eliza to Phylly, 29th October 1801.
Addressed: Miss Walter/Seale near Sevenoaks/Kent; no postmark; endorsed: 1801/Letters of Eliza Cmtesse de Feuillide nee Hancock subsequently Mrs. Henry Austen. Watermark: Heawood no. 2752–62 above GP.
45. Eliza to Warren Hastings, ?6th March 1802.
BL AddMS 29,192, f.34.
This letter is one leaf only, with no address, direction, postmark or date, and the second leaf is missing. Watermark: G PIKE
46. Eliza to Warren Hastings, 18th March 1807 or 1809.
BL Add.Ms 29,192, f. 32.
Addressed: Warren Hastings Esq/Portugal Street; no postmark. Watermark: J WHATMAN 1806.

Bibliography and Further Reading

☆

Unpublished sources

de Feuillide, Eliza. Letters to Phylly Walter; in Austen-Leigh family archive, with microfilm copies in Hampshire Record Office; part-published in *Austen Papers*. One letter owned by the Jane Austen Memorial Trust, Chawton.

Hancock, Tysoe Saul. Letterbook, preserved amongst the Hastings Papers, British Library Add MS 29,236. Part-published in *Austen Papers*.

Hastings, Warren. Hastings Papers, British Library: letters, accounts, diaries – volumes consulted fall within the range Add MS 29,125–41,608.

Hoare's Bank, London. Ledgers 1765 onwards, containing accounts of several members of the Austen family.

Knatchbull, Lady (Fanny Knight). Diaries, 1804–72. Centre for Kentish Studies, Maidstone.

Lefroy, Mrs. Anna. Lefroy MS – volume of notes on family history, compiled ca. 1855–72: great-grandsons of Adml. Sir Francis Austen.

Lefroy, Fanny-Caroline. Family History (written ca. 1880–85). Austen-Leigh archive, Hampshire Record Office.

Milward, Richard. The Tombstone Inscriptions at Hampstead to 21.11.1881. London Borough of Camden Central Library.

Walter, Mrs. James (Frances-Maria Walter). Reminiscences, 1809. Original MS now untraceable, as also a typescript copy made early in the twentieth century; MS copy of typescript made by Dr. F. Henthorn.

Published sources

Asquith, Annunziata. *Marie-Antoinette*. London, 1974.

Austen-Leigh, Richard Arthur. *Austen Papers, 1704–1856*. Privately published, London, 1942.

Blanc, Olivier (trans. Alan Sheridan). *Last Letters*. London, 1987.

Booker, John. *Travellers' Money*. Stroud, 1994.

Burrell, Lady. *Poems*. London, 1793, 2 vols.

Caplan, Clive, and Breihan, John. 'Jane Austen and the Militia', in *Persuasions* (Journal of the Jane Austen Society of North America), 1992, No. 14, 16–26.
Caplan, Clive. 'Jane Austen's Soldier Brother – the Military Career of Captain Henry Thomas Austen of the Oxfordshire Regiment of Militia, 1793–1801', in *Persuasions*, 1996, No.18, 122–143.
— 'Jane Austen's Banker Brother, Henry Thomas Austen of Austen & Co., 1801–1816', in *Persuasions*, 1998, No. 20, 69–90.
Cole, Revd William. *A Journal of my Journey to Paris in the Year 1765*. Ed. Francis Griffin Stokes, London, 1931.
Collyer, Graham. *The Surrey Village Book*. Newbury, 1990.

Devert, Abbé Michel. 'Le Marais de Gabarret et de Barbotan', in *Bull. de la Société de Borda*, Aire-sur-l'Adour, 1970.
Drewett, J. *Surrey*. (Shire County Guide) Aylesbury, 1985.
Duffy, Michael. *The Englishman and the Foreigner, the English Satirical Print 1600–1832*. Cambridge, 1986.

Elmes, James. *Topographical Dictionary of London*. London, 1831.
Evans, Sian, trans. & ed. *The Memoirs of Elisabeth Vigée-Le Brun*. London, 1989.

Feiling, Keith. *Warren Hastings*. London, 1954.
Fitzgerald, Brian Vesey. *The Domestic Dog*. London, 1957.

Gleig, G. R. *Memoirs of the Life of Warren Hastings*. London, 1841.
Greater London Council. *John Joseph Merlin, The Ingenious Mechanick*. (Catalogue of exhibition at Kenwood, London). London, 1985.
Grier, Sydney C. 'A Friend of Warren Hastings', in *Blackwood's Edinburgh Magazine*, No. 175, April 1904, 497–514.
— 'A God-Daughter of Warren Hastings', in *Temple Bar*, No. 131, 562–571. London, 1905.
— *The Letters of Warren Hastings to his Wife*. London, 1905.
A Guide to all the Watering and Sea Bathing Places. London, n.d., post 1817.

Henthorn, Frank. *The History of Brigg Grammar School*. Brigg, 1959.
Hibbert, Christopher. *The French Revolution*. Harmondsworth, 1988.
Hoare, H.P.R. *Hoare's Bank*. London, 1932.
Hubback, J.H. and Edith C. *Jane Austen's Sailor Brothers*. London, 1906.

Jane Austen Society, Chawton: *Collected Reports*, Vol. I, 1949–65; Vol. II, 1966–75; Vol. III, 1976–85; Vol. IV, 1986–95; and individual *Reports* for 1996, 1997, 1998, 1999, 2000.

Kincaid, Dennis. *British Social Life in India, 1608–1937*. Newton Abbot, 1974.

Kindersley, Mrs. *Letters from the Island of Teneriffe, Brazil, the Cape of Good Hope, and the East Indies*. London, 1777.

Knipe, H.R. ed. *Tunbridge Wells and Neighbourhood*. Tunbridge Wells, 1916.

Le Faye, Deirdre. *Jane Austen, a Family Record*. London, 1989.

— 'Jane Austen and her Hancock Relatives', in *The Review of English Studies*, NS Vol. XXX, No. 117, February 1979, 12–27.

— 'Three Austen Family Letters', in *Notes and Queries*, Vol. 32, No. 3, September 1985, 329–335.

— *Fanny Knight's Diaries: Jane Austen through her Niece's Eyes*. The Jane Austen Society, Chawton, 2000.

— (ed.). *Jane Austen's Letters*. Oxford, 1995.

Little, B. *Cheltenham*. London, 1952.

Losty, J. P. *Calcutta, City of Palaces*. London, 1990.

Mackenzie, E., and Ross, M. *View of the County of Durham*. 1834.

Melville, Lewis. *Society at Royal Tunbridge Wells*. London, 1912.

Mercer, Doris, and Jackson, Alan A. *The Deepdene, Dorking*. Dorking, 1996.

Oman, Carola. *Britain against Napoleon*. London, 1943.

Parker, Eric. *Highways and Byways in Surrey*. London, 1925.

Pearson, Alicia, ed. *A Journey through France and Belgium 1784–1785, the Letters and Journals of Catherine Knatchbull, Mrs. Thomas Knight*. Privately printed, ?1964.

Phillips, Sir Richard. *A Morning's Walk from London to Kew*. London, 1817.

Pressnell, L.S. *Country Banking in the Industrial Revolution*. Oxford, 1956.

Ribeiro, Aileen. *Dress in Eighteenth Century Europe*. London, 1984.

Rolt, L.T.C. *The Aeronauts: A History of Ballooning 1783–1903*. Gloucester, 1985.

Sprange, John. *Tunbridge Wells Guide*. Tunbridge Wells, 1797.

Sprott, Duncan. *1784*. London, 1984.

Standen, Hugh W. *Kippington in Kent*. Sevenoaks, 1958.

Syrett, David, and DiNardo, R.L., eds: *The Commissioned Sea Officers of the Royal Navy, 1660–1815*. London, 1994.

Tomalin, Claire. *Jane Austen, a life*. London, 1997.

Tucker, G.H. *A History of Jane Austen's Family*. Stroud, 1998.

Van der Kiste, John. *George III's Children*. Gloucester, 1992.

Vansittart, Col. Eden. *The History of the Vansittart Family*. Privately printed, Bournemouth, 1910.

Wade, Christopher, ed. *Buried in Hampstead.* Camden History Society, London, 1986.
Watson, James. *The Dog Book.* London, 1902.
Watson, Winifred. *Jane Austen in London.* Jane Austen Society, Chawton, 1960.
Weiner, Margery. *The French Exiles 1789–1815.* London, 1960.
Wild, Antony. *The East India Company, trade and conquest from 1600.* London, 1999.
Woodgate, Revd Gordon, and Woodgate, G.M.G. *A History of the Woodgates of Stonewall Park and of Summerhill in Kent.* Wisbech, 1910.

Austen Family Pedigree (simplified)

- John AUSTEN d. 1704
  - John AUSTEN (1696-1728)
    - Elizabeth m. John FERMOR
  - Francis AUSTEN (1698-1791) m. (1) Anne MOTLEY
    - F. Motley AUSTEN m. Elizabeth WILSON
  - m. (2) Jane LENNARD
    - Sackville AUSTEN
    - John AUSTEN
  - William AUSTEN (1701-37) m. Rebecca WALTER née HAMPSON
    - George AUSTEN (1731-1805) m. Cassandra LEIGH
    - Philadelphia AUSTEN (1730-92) m. T. S. HANCOCK
- Rebecca HAMPSON m. (1) William WALTER
  - W. Hampson WALTER (1721-98) m. Susanna WEAVER

- F. Lucius AUSTEN
  - Thomas
  - Jane
  - John
  - Henry
  - Elizabeth
  - Marianne
  - George
  - Frances
  - Edward
  - William

- John Thomas AUSTEN

- James AUSTEN — Anna AUSTEN
  - George
  - Edward — Fanny KNIGHT
  - Henry
  - Cassandra
  - Francis
  - Jane
  - Charles

- Eliza HANCOCK
  m.(1) 1781 J.C.DE FEUILLIDE — Hastings DE FEUILLIDE
  m.(2) 1797 Henry AUSTEN

- Weaver WALTER
  - William
  - George
  - James — Henry WALTER
  - Phylly
    m. George WHITAKER

Hampson Family Pedigree (simplified)

- Sir George HAMPSON 4th Bart, d. 1724
  - Sir George HAMPSON 5th Bart, d. 1754
    - Sir George HAMPSON 6th Bart, (1738-74)
  - Rebecca HAMPSON m. (1) William WALTER
    - W. Hampson WALTER (1721-98) m. Susanna WEAVER
  - m. (2) William AUSTEN
    - George AUSTEN (1731-1805) m. Cassandra LEIGH
    - Philadelphia AUSTEN (1730-92) m. T.S. HANCOCK
  - Jane HAMPSON m. Capel PAYNE
    - George PAYNE
  - Margaret HAMPSON m. Cope FREEMAN
    - John Cope FREEMAN
    - Stella F. m. Adml. ALLEN
    - Catherine M. m. C. STANHOPE

Sir Thomas HAMPSON — Sir George HAMPSON
7th Bart, (1765-1820) — 8th Bart, (1789-1833)

Mary
m. Samuel STEVENSON

Weaver WALTER
William
George
James — Henry WALTER
Phylly
m. George WHITAKER

James AUSTEN — Anna AUSTEN
George
Edward — Fanny KNIGHT
Henry
Cassandra
Francis
Jane
Charles

Eliza HANCOCK
m.(1) J.F.CAPOT DE FEUILLIDE — Hastings DE FEUILLIDE
m.(2) Henry AUSTEN

Maria PAYNE
Louisa
Harriet
Amelia
George

H.T.Cope FREEMAN

Philip STANHOPE

Index

✡